PRAISE FOR
RAGE INSIDE THE MACHINE

'In *Rage Inside the Machine* Rob Smith has written a fascinating hybrid text – a compelling memoir, a moving mosaic of history and technology, and, most important, the timeliest of warnings for our increasingly dangerous era of ubiquitous AI and algorithms. As Millennial and Generation-Z engineers blithely put us in AI-driven vehicles, as companies take AI and algorithmic start-up funds by the millions, and competing governments devise AI weapons programs by the billions, Smith reminds us that "AI is the hole, not the doughnut," and, despite our best efforts, AI is not intelligent in any meaningful biological sense. The dumbest squirrel is still more intentional and broadly clever than the smartest extant algorithm, and until researchers seriously consider how humans and machines differ in the sense that Smith intends, we all must be vigilant against the hype and ethical missteps by businesspeople and technologists who aren't sufficiently reflective to apply the dangerous technologies carelessly placed in their hands. Read this book and take its carefully crafted message to heart.'

DAVID GOLDBERG, *author of* Genetic Algorithms in Search, Optimization and Machine Learning

'AI isn't just a technical topic, it is a cultural crossroads. Correction: it should be. If enough people read this book, it will be. In *Rage Inside the Machine*, Robert Elliott Smith accomplishes what few people could attempt: to humanize the discourse on artificial intelligence. He tears the topic of AI from the grasp of the techno-elite and puts it into all our hands. Robert the computer science professor lays bare exactly what the algorithms are doing, while Robert the boy who grew up in newly desegregated Alabama lays bare the biases – scientific and social – that risk being hard-coded into our culture all over again (mostly, without even the programmers realizing it). The mass adoption of AI is happening, right now. The next decade of design choices will shape the next century of social consequences. We – society – need to weigh in on these choices now. This book is our chance.'

CHRIS KUTARNA, *co-author of* Age of Discovery: Navigating the Storms of Our Second Renaissance

'A beautiful, accessible, truly important book. Rob humanises the dark and confused topic of AI and calls us to action. He places dispassionate modern algorithms in their historical and cultural context, revealing how our all-too-human biases are propagating through opaque technology to create a monster. Gorgeously written and hugely relevant: I loved it.'
DERREN BROWN, *illusionist and author of* Happy: Why More or Less Everything is Absolutely Fine

'In an age when more and more decisions of our lives are made by algorithms, it's vital for anyone, not just techies, to understand how data can change our lives. What if something you posted on social media was used against you? What if you could not appeal against an unfair court decision, because the algorithm thought you were guilty? Sounds like a dystopia, except that it's not – it's already happening every day. We can no longer afford to say that "this is a matter for specialists", or "we have nothing to hide" – we need to start taking responsibility for what we share, and who with. Rob Smith has a unique ability to express the complicated future of AI in a very simple manner. Read it if you want to stay human.'
DR ANASTASIA DEDYUKHINA, *Founder of Consciously Digital and author of* Homo Distractus

'When the crowd at Comic Con talk of Robot Overlords, it can be disregarded as a fantasy far detached from real life. When you hear that a crowd of world-class technologists and scientists, including Elon Musk, Bill Gates and Stephen Hawking, have publicly voiced their concerns that advanced AI technologies could pose an existential threat to humanity – trouble on the scale of climate change, bioplague and large asteroids – you really have to wonder what's going on. *Rage Inside the Machine* is a guide to how we got here, conceptually and historically. Rob Smith appreciates the successes of AI, but also warns that incomprehensibly complex data-driven systems are not easily corrected, and can make major mistakes.'
DAVID LEINWEBER, *author of* Nerds on Wall Street: Math, Machines and Wired Markets

'I have long been a fan of Rob Smith's ability to give context and consideration to the intrinsic yet intricate role technology plays in our lives. Here in this extraordinary book, he has outlined his crafted, well-measured, respectful and well-reasoned approach based on decades in industry and academia. He shines a light on the dangers of accepting a passive role in our relationship with tech, and deftly explains the information we really need to know before committing ourselves further to machines. Essential reading for anyone wanting to know how to keep their sanity and humanity in the age of super-tech.'
HELEN BAGNALL, *Founder of Salon London*

RAGE INSIDE THE MACHINE

RAGE INSIDE THE MACHINE

The Prejudice of Algorithms, and How to Stop the Internet Making Bigots of Us All

ROBERT ELLIOTT SMITH

BLOOMSBURY BUSINESS
LONDON • NEW YORK • OXFORD • NEW DELHI • SYDNEY

BLOOMSBURY BUSINESS
Bloomsbury Publishing Plc
50 Bedford Square, London, WC1B 3DP, UK
1385 Broadway, New York, NY 10018, USA

BLOOMSBURY, BLOOMSBURY BUSINESS and the Diana logo are trademarks of
Bloomsbury Publishing Plc

First published in Great Britain 2019

A catalogue record for this book is available from the British Library.

A catalog record for this book is available from the Library of Congress.

ISBN: HB: 978-1-4729-6388-8
       ePDF: 978-1-4729-6390-1
       eBook: 978-1-4729-6389-5

10 9 8 7 6 5 4 3 2

Typeset by RefineCatch Limited, Bungay, Suffolk
Printed and bound in Great Britain

To find out more about our authors and books visit www.bloomsbury.com
and sign up for our newsletters.

CONTENTS

To my tireless reader, insightful editor, constant inspiration, and wonderful wife, Paula Hardy. She made this book possible.

PREFACE

In recent years we've all been hearing about earth-shattering advances in the abilities of *algorithms*. The artificial intelligence (AI) in these computer programs is said to be advancing so rapidly that it will soon match or exceed human capabilities. In 2014, the term 'superintelligence'[1] emerged to describe AI, suggesting the apparently inevitable superiority of algorithms over human intelligence. And, at the 2016 World Economic Forum at Davos, the focus was on the predicted elimination of most human jobs by machines, which we're told will soon be able to do those jobs just as well as, if not better than, people. Some of the greatest minds of our time, including Stephen Hawking, Henry Kissinger,[2] Elon Musk[3] and Bill Gates,[4] have expressed concerns about the future dominance of intelligent machines over people. Stephen Hawking went as far as to say: 'I think the development of full artificial intelligence could spell the end of the human race.'[5]

The path to a world dominated by machines and machine intelligence now seems inevitable, and we are told to feel confident in these predictions, in part because they themselves are the results of algorithms that have analysed real-world 'big data', thus avoiding human subjectivity. A belief in algorithmic objectivity is not at all unusual today. Furthermore, there is a widely held tendency to assume that digital technology is inevitably meritocratic, democratic and libertarian, and that any regulation would have a negative effect on its optimal, self-organizing systems.

So-called 'smart' AI is now being used to understand such big data and draw conclusions from that data that profoundly influence our lives in the real world. Algorithms do everything from assigning people hour-to-hour work (Deliveroo, Uber, etc.), to selecting the news we read (Google, Facebook,

Twitter, etc.), recommending the products we might buy (Amazon, Google, etc.), the friends we might like (Facebook) and the partners we might marry (Match.com, eHarmony, etc.). Forbes[6] recently revealed that in China, 80 percent of surveyed citizens approve of a government-sponsored big data algorithm that will soon reduce all of their individual financial, civic, and social media activity (along with inputs from CCTV systems that can recognize their faces) to a single score, which will determine their access to travel, housing, healthcare, and high-quality goods.

Even in the Western world, we largely accept (with some enthusiasm) that online algorithms process data about us and shape most of our interactions, yet we're largely unaware of exactly how, mostly don't understand their operation, and barely grasp the influence they exert on our lives. Our willing, but uninformed, consent to their operation in our lives implicitly assumes that these AI programs are benign and unbiased, because they can only perform *rational* computations. We believe that the results served up to us in online lists and searches are a true reflection of the world and the choices available to us therein. Numbers don't lie, and since machines just process numbers, neither can they.

However, in the last few years, algorithms have been generating some surprisingly unsavoury and unexpected outputs. In 2015, the *Guardian* reported that Google algorithms tagged images of black people as '#animals', '#apes' and '#gorillas'.[7] They also reported that Google image searches for 'unprofessional hair' predominately returned pictures of black women.[8] Another report revealed that Google's algorithms showed high-paying job ads to men more often than to women.[9] Then, the *Observer* revealed that Google's auto-suggest algorithm completed the searches 'are women ...' and 'are Jews ...' with the word 'evil', and that clicking on these suggestions returned pages of affirmative answers to those questions.[10] Similarly, when Microsoft released a Twitter bot (AI algorithm) called 'Tay' in 2016, it had to be shut down rapidly after just 24 hours of operation, because it had learned to say, 'I fucking hate feminists and they should all die', 'Hitler was right I hate the

Jews' and 'WE'RE GOING TO BUILD A WALL, AND MEXICO IS GOING TO PAY FOR IT'.[11]

You may well ask yourself, 'What on earth is going on?' Have racist and misogynistic computer programmers run amok in their Silicon Valley offices and created algorithmic monsters imbued with humanity's worst characteristics? Do these unbiased, objective algorithmic results simply reveal the ugly truth about human society hidden in our big data? Or is there something else entirely going on? And is that something else something specific about the algorithms themselves? If so, what is it, and how is it affecting us and society at large? And how can it be stopped and changed for the better?

The first step in the process is a better understanding of what algorithms are, how they operate and how they have evolved since people started imagining machines that could calculate and maybe even, one day, *think*. We aren't familiar with this story of algorithmic evolution because, unlike the Arts and Humanities, scientific subjects are taught in the abstract, entirely devoid of historical, cultural and social context. When we learn about Shakespeare, we see him placed in the cultural context of Elizabethan England right down to his pantaloons. This offers us a greater insight into his plays, subject matter and characters, because we understand their *context*. Likewise, the teachings of toga-wearing Aristotle are placed firmly in the context of Classical Greece, and Da Vinci can't be disconnected from the cultural dynamism of the Renaissance. Literature, art, philosophy, music and so on are all taught in parallel with one another and their historical context.

In contrast, the maths and science at the heart of algorithms is taught disconnected from any context, as if the theories and inventions in these areas are entirely abstract unassailable truths, beyond the influences of the historical periods in which they arose. But if we are to examine algorithms for the possible biases they might carry, we have to acknowledge that there are assumptions deep within these procedures that are influenced by the times and places in which they were created. This book steps through those times and places to offer a view on the historical and cultural connections that have shaped the creation of algorithms. The connections are numerous, from the representation of thinking as the 'if–then' rules of Aristotelian logic, to the modelling of uncertainty based on calculations drawn from dice games, through the reduction of evolution to a philosophy of 'survival of the fittest', to the attempt to capture complex human characteristics like 'intelligence' in numbers like IQ, to the transformation and reduction of human artisanship into discrete tasks neatly divided to fit mass-manufacturing processes, through an unassailable faith that free markets generate spontaneous order, to viewing the living brain as a simple, synaptic computer, to a staggering reduction of the subtle meanings of language to the bit transmissions of information theory. Each of these simplifications arose in a particular historical and cultural context and has a direct connection to the conception and design of algorithms that now operate all around us today.

Just as algorithms have emerged from various historical and cultural contexts, they are also a product engineered by people. At some point, a human being touches almost every part of an algorithm, whether it's finding the dataset the algorithm will work upon, manually tagging and classifying some of that data, deciding the parameters that control the algorithm, determining its goals and evaluating its performance. I am one of those people, an engineer by training, an experienced AI consultant and a member of the computer science faculty at University College, London (UCL).

At large technology corporations like Google and Facebook, there are whole communities of scientists like me interacting and working on the creation of algorithms that now frame and act upon our lives. They themselves are the product of different cultures and ideas, specific even to the groups they may work in. Similarly, the impacts of their design decisions are social, and while the cold computations of algorithms treat society as a body of statistics, it is actually a body of individuals immersed in richly varied cultural and social contexts to which we need to be sensitive. To acknowledge the deep connection between algorithms and ourselves at every level, this book includes personal stories of my own life and career in AI to ground its observations in at least one person's real-world experiences.* Because the only way to really understand the impact of algorithms is to understand them in relationship to the individuals and society to which they are bound.

---

* Please note that names of people in the personal stories have been changed, with the exception of any professional colleagues who are cited in the references.

1

Mechanisms of Morality

In 1987, I was a twenty-four-year-old graduate student, and one of my professors, Dr Grayson, set me up on a blind date.

I was studying for a PhD, researching artificial intelligence (AI) at the University of Alabama. At the time, not only did the general public understand nothing about AI, virtually no one had a computer at home, and few used them at work. I myself had only learned to program a few years before, by typing on a machine that punched holes into stiff paper cards. Things had advanced, and I had just purchased my first personal computer, a cream-coloured box with a CRT and a floppy disk drive. My pride-and-joy machine was driven by green lines of onscreen text that executed in a program called MS-DOS (because Microsoft Windows wouldn't reach tolerable usability for another five years).

This was also the year that my university gave a few lucky geeks like me access to something called 'the Internet'. It was fantastic. I could use my new computer's modem to dial in from home, and once online there were literally *dozens* of programs I could use *for free*! I stayed up late on Internet Relay Chat (IRC), conversing (mostly about sci-fi) with other geeks like me, using similar machines in *over one hundred* locations across *the entire USA*. I read streams of geek humour in the 'net.jokes' topic category of the user-provided news system USENET. I could even use this amazing new thing called *email* (though, given that virtually no one else had an email address, I mainly used it to communicate with university tech support about the Internet being down).

What I couldn't do online was find out anything about my date. 'The web' wouldn't be ready for surfing until the first browser became widely available in 1993. Google was a decade from existing. Despite the promise of chatrooms and USENET, media was still far from being social, and no one had an online presence. So, the date Dr Grayson suggested I go on really was blind.

He said she was the daughter of a friend of his, a young lawyer, just moved down to Birmingham from New York, and she needed an intro to town. Her mother had called him, looking out for her, and since I was Birmingham born-and-raised, single, and about her age, he'd mentioned me as a nice young man. I'd wanted to say no. Even though I was pretty friendly with Dr Grayson, he was a far older and more conservative Southerner than me, and our common interest in optimization algorithms sure didn't mean I'd have any kind of connection with this unknown woman. When he made the suggestion, I looked at my feet and started to hem and haw, then he raised a hand to gain my attention, saying, 'Before you say no, she's a part-time aerobics instructor, and if her mom's anything to go by, well, hubba-hubba, brother'. (Yes, he *actually* said that. Like I said, it was 1987.)

There wouldn't be a widely available mobile phone for another ten years, and no iPhones for twenty, so date set-up involved me ringing her up on the landline and giving her turn-by-turn instructions on how to drive from her new apartment to our meeting place, because, though military GPS satellites were in orbit, no one would have a satnav for about thirteen years. I advised that if she got lost, she should find a pay phone, call and ask for me at the bar.

I had selected Burly Earl's as our meeting location, both because it was easy to find and because I thought it would provide the 'wonder of me' first date. There was good, live newgrass (alternative bluegrass) on that night, and I figured between sets we'd have just enough (but not too much) time for life-revealing conversation. She walked in wearing a black silk blouse and leopard skin patterned blue slacks (which I thought were awesome), and I walked her into the bar's main room. Audience seating at the Earl was at long tables with benches, and the place was packed, so she and I had to sit backwards to face the band, with our beers on the table behind us. After the first set, we turned around to chat, and to face our table companions.

Directly across from me was an enormous, square-headed man who had his arm wrapped around a tiny, mousey woman. The couple had matching wedding bands and black Van Halen T-shirts. Despite looking a bit younger than me, he had a face full of disappointment that would make any forlorn country song a fine protagonist. And he had a single, wide, black eyebrow.

As soon as we turned towards them, the man glowered at the two of us, in a way that said, 'Yuppie, go home'. I planned to put my accent on nice and thick, engage my date on the subject of bluegrass, and try and gain some cultural cred that might diffuse his hostile, unibrowed stare, but my date got her question in first.

'So, what are you doing your PhD on?' I knew her Yankee accent didn't endear us to the locals, and I didn't think an explanation of my research would either. Still, I decided to impress my date rather than keep my head down.

'Artificial Intelligence,' I said, mustering some confidence, but realizing this must sound kinda like, 'I make ray guns'.

I sensed that Unibrow had tuned into our conversation. The wrinkled caterpillar above his eyes indicated that he was puzzled by my declaration. My date didn't really understand either, so she asked me to explain.

'I'm trying to make computers more like humans,' I said.

'Hmmm,' she said, with a tone of either interest or distaste, I couldn't tell which. 'Like humans in what way?' she asked.

'Well, I'm particularly interested in making machines adapt and learn from experiences, to make them able to do innovative things, be creative.'

Unibrow jerked his lantern-shaped head back in disbelief. The index finger on his beer-holding hand pointed at me, and he glanced at his wife, as if to say, 'You listenin' to this shit?' On the positive side, my date seemed sceptical, but enthralled.

'But computers can't do anything creative, they just do what they're programmed to do, don't they?'

This seemed like a better-than-average first-date conversation to me. 'Well...' I tried not to glance over at Unibrow before I started into this, 'one could argue that we are just machines. We do things that are new for us, but our neurons and glands and cells always do exactly what they were programmed to do, by biology. We can't change that, any more than a machine can change its programming.'

'So you try to make computers have things that are like neurons, then?' she said.

'Well, that's one approach, called "neural networks". But my dissertation is on adaptive programs that are based on evolution.'

Unibrow was hanging on every word at this point, leaning out over the table a bit, to make sure he heard me right. My date looked a bit unnerved. Everyone knew evolution was still a controversial subject in Alabama (it wasn't until 2015 that the Alabama Board of Education finally ruled that the teaching of evolution was required material for the curriculum).

'You know how survival of the fittest works ... population of things, fit ones live, unfit ones die. A little random mutation, some mating, and the population evolves to its circumstances. We do the same thing in computers, to solve practical problems. Engineering problems, mostly.'

'How can you solve engineering problems with that?' she asks.

'Let's say you want to determine a good shape for airplane wings. You create a basic program that can make any shape of wing. The "genes"' (I used 1987 air quotes) 'are the details that can determine any particular wing shape: its length, the widths and lots of heights across the wing's surface. Any set of genes will make a differently shaped wing. For any given wing, even crazy-shaped ones, you can use simulation to evaluate how well it flies. Some are good, some are bad, but the space of possible wings is far too huge to look through before the sun burns out. So you do evolution instead.

'Some crash and die, so only the ones that soar get to "reproduce". Evolution occurs and makes better and better baby wings.'

With that, Unibrow fell back onto his bench, loudly enough for us to have to look his way. His face flushed, highlighting the black hyphen above his eyes. He clenched his teeth a little, and his fists a lot. He looked at me hard, and said, 'Heil Hitler, pal!'

Just then the band's second set kicked in with a loud, fast breakdown, and my date leaned over and whispered in my ear, 'Do you mind if we just go?'

We hit the street and didn't say a word until we'd climbed into my car. 'Perhaps you'd like to try something with a bit less local colour? There's a nice bar just around the corner.'

She laughed a little, thank God. 'Well, at least he wasn't quoting the Bible at you or anything. And I've got to admit thinking similar thoughts to him back there, but I wouldn't have put them as bluntly.'

'Sorry,' I said, getting defensive. 'I don't get that at all. I'm not trying to rule the world with an army of tiny robots. Technology is all I really do, and technology doesn't have morals. Only its uses do.'

'Well, I think that's very irresponsible,' she said, turning towards the passenger window with a dismissive toss of hair. Then she sat in silence for half a block.

My momma taught me a sincere compliment goes a long way. 'Nice pants,' I said. I could feel her eyes roll the minute it made it out of my mouth.

'Yeah,' she said, as bored with that attempt as she ought to be, 'my first Southern fashion purchase. I was told Patsy Cline died in these pants.'

Wow, I thought. I could love this girl.

Then she said, 'Do you mind just taking me back to my car. I'm not sure I'm up for another place tonight.' I wheeled around and when we reached her car, she got out quickly, and leaned into the open passenger's door to say, 'Look, you seem like a nice guy, but I think you're a little confused about the implications of what you are doing.' She looked a bit guilty at that, and fell back on the old brush-off, 'I'm probably just tired. I'll give you a call when I'm more settled.'

And of course, I never heard from her again.

During the thirty years since that date, I've spent my time working with AI, both as an academic and as a real-world engineer. I've applied 'smart' algorithms in areas ranging from biological science to military planning to economics, in tasks as varied as better understanding immune systems, learning aircraft manoeuvres from dogfight simulations and analysing big data to help understand the influence of emotions in financial markets. Over the years, I developed an expertise in the evolutionary algorithms I attempted to describe to my date back then, but I've also employed most of the other tricks in the modern AI toolbox, from algorithmic systems based on rules, to those based on primitive models of the brain, to those based on 'deep' statistical analyses of data.

In 1987, the year of my date, the idea of AI wasn't just obscure, it was seen as a pipedream of sci-fi enthusiasts. Today, it is a topic on the tip of everyone's tongue, featured in media reports on a daily basis, and a subject of interest at the highest level of every industry and government. This isn't surprising, as AI is actually a feature of everyone's life today. The Internet, which was once a sort of computational amateur radio network, is now an integral part of Earth's global infrastructure, with vital importance to almost every living human being (whether they realize it or not). The algorithms at the core of the Internet would all have been called AI at one time, so AI is no longer some distant dream to be realized in the future; it is well and truly with us all now.

With our online lives comes an intimate connection to these algorithms, which has changed basic human interactions in a profound way. For instance, a truly *blind* date can't really happen now. If two people were to meet for the first time today, they would certainly have Googled one another, possibly looked at each other's Instagram, Twitter, LinkedIn, and perhaps even friended each other on Facebook and IMed a bit before meeting.

But the changes are even deeper than that. The very idea that a young woman would ever need her mother's network of friends to arrange introductions to a 'nice young man' now seems like the hook-up system from *Fiddler on the Roof*. Today, that same young woman would have been living in several global online communities of her own choosing (along with unseen algorithmic analytics of her data) from the time she was a girl. These communities would be subdivided to match her interests, then sub-subdivided by her own, algorithmically assisted searches. Even if she was moving from South Africa or China, it's likely that she would have used online connections to find like-minded people in Birmingham, and evaluate *for herself* whether someone was a 'nice young man'. If what she was looking for was a friend, a one-night stand, a date or even a future husband, she would be helped by online networks and algorithms, responding to the dictates of her personal preferences, rather than relying on the assumptions and inferences made by her parents, friends or anyone else.

In many ways, this is the fantastic peer-to-peer future computer enthusiasts like me were hoping for from the earliest days of the Internet. We sincerely thought that the profound connectedness provided by computational telecommunications would make the world a better place. The Internet provided a direct means of connection between peoples across the globe, without the interference, restrictions and expectations of previous generations, corporations or governments. We thought algorithms would help people navigate the complexity of this more open world, as engines promoting individuality and diversity. We envisaged a fairer, more transparent and tolerant world, like that of *Star Trek*, or many other utopian sci-fi universes. We sincerely believed AIs could help create a better world than the one that we'd grown up in.

However, as every sci-fi enthusiast knows, with every utopian vision, there's usually a dystopian one waiting just around the corner. And, looking around at the world today, we seem to be a long way off from the open and diverse society we thought we were working towards. With recent stories of racist and misogynist search results, online communities dominated by divisive vitriolic abuse and bots spewing hate speech, a more dystopian vision seems to be spilling out into all aspects of our real-world lives. Suddenly our brave, new technologically enabled future looks far more troubled than we had imagined. In fact, it looks like I was wrong all those years ago with my assertion that technology has no morals.

Technology – including, and perhaps especially, computation – doesn't exist in a vacuum. Created by us, it has developed in a particular social, cultural and philosophical context. As a result, inherent in our algorithms are some very questionable historic ideas, prejudices and biases that now form the foundations of our global tech. This informs the way algorithms work and gives them a set of *values* by which they operate. In that sense, we can say technology now *has a morality of its own*. Unfortunately, it is a value system that promotes division instead of collaboration, tribalism instead of individuality and intolerance instead of diversity. Moreover, once connected with real-world intolerance and prejudice, it forms feedback loops that yield profound and devastating effects.

How has this happened, when the intention of tech pioneers was to build a fairer, more open and tolerant society? Fundamentally, it is because algorithms always embody *simplifications*, and simplification is always at the core of *prejudice*. The word "prejudice" means to *pre-judge*, and prejudgements, by their very nature, must be based on simplifying features and categorizations, generalizations about the complexities of the real world. Algorithms must simplify the complexities of the real world to quantitative features and categories to form useful generalizations. This includes all the algorithms I've spent my life designing, building, and using. Even in the contained engineering problems those programs addressed, that experience has demonstrated that understanding of how algorithms simplify and generalize is essential to using them well. This is now profoundly true for the algorithms that are unleashed, unregulated and unmonitored in our social and economic networks today.

All AI engineers know that when implementing an algorithm to tackle a real-world problem, the first step is to *reduce* the problem to a *representation*. A representation consists of a boundary around a problem's definition (which I'll call a *frame*), and a set of what I'll call *atoms* for the problem's description. In the airplane wing example given earlier, the boundary around the problem is a focus on the wing alone, in isolation from the rest of the aircraft. In fact, the representation is likely to be even more bounded than that, due to technical considerations. An engineer might initially focus only on the wing's cross-section, and implicitly assume that it is two dimensional, because that assumption is sufficient for a particular application, and is computationally convenient for the algorithms at hand. This is the problem's frame.

The 'atoms' of the representation might be a few selected heights (bounded to be within a certain range) of the wing's upper surface above its lower surface, which is assumed to be flat. We might further assume that variations of wing thickness between these specified heights describe straight lines or simple curves. For this particular application, a good engineer will decide that the assumed frame and the set of atoms are sufficient, even though they are obviously a drastic simplification of the real wings that get made in a factory and fly in the sky.

For any problem with sufficient complexity to be worth solving with algorithms, a representation is always a simplification. In particular, it's a simplification that nicely fits the capacities and technical peculiarities of the algorithms, while satisfying practical computational needs of the problem at hand. Those needs are always basically the same: in a reasonable amount of time, a good algorithm needs to give a *good enough* solution for effective, economical, human use in the real world. Once a good representation is decided upon, algorithms work efficiently and effectively, within the bounds of the simplifications involved. A good AI engineer knows the bounds of the simplifications that were embodied in the representation selected and makes sure the end user knows them as well, so that the results of the algorithms can be evaluated and utilized effectively in real life.

While this sort of modelling works well for discreet engineering problems, it is more troublesome when applied to people, politics, economies, the news media or social networks, precisely because of the simplifications required for algorithms to work. That said, the social sciences and economics have long used simplified models to understand complex situations, and in a scientific setting that's okay. Like the assumptions made by AI designers in solving an engineering problem, such assumptions are an acceptable, practical matter that can be dealt with by end users who are aware and in the loop.

But reductionism and simplification when applied to people and society as a whole have a dangerous, natural tendency to lend support to bigotry. It has taken centuries of human effort to continuously overcome these tendencies and work towards a more progressive and tolerant society. However, simplifying modelling has now become an autonomous part of algorithms in our global infrastructure, drawing on our big data, and the reality is that the algorithms in our lives have a view of us that is as two dimensional as that airplane wing.

Take, for example, the recent 'professional hair' controversy, whereby Google searches for unprofessional hair exclusively returned images of black women.[1] What are we to think about this? How did this happen? Is it possible that a vast number of people tagged images of black women with the term 'unprofessional' to such a degree that an algorithm picked up on those tags and thus selected those images as typifying that term? Likewise, is it possible that enough people have been searching the Internet to discover if women or Jews are evil, as highlighted in the 2016 news story?[2] Did Tay, the racist Twitter bot, really learn its misanthropy from an unbiased and *considered* view of the universe of people's tweets, filled as it is with teenaged chat and pictures of people's breakfast?[3] Or, are we to believe that there are cohorts of racists and misogynists in the offices of Google, Twitter and Microsoft, covertly causing these disturbing effects?

I don't think so. I believe these outcomes are an artefact of the reductionist nature of algorithms themselves. When considering the matter of unprofessional hair, a simple online algorithm is only capable of comparing gross features such as shape and texture, which is more identifiable for some hairstyles than for others. Visual features are no way of categorizing people, but simple shapes and colours are easy things for algorithms to identify. Likewise, questions about groups of people being 'evil' are simple (and asking simple questions is precisely the way we have all learned to interact with algorithms). Algorithms find such questions much easier to parse than philosophical considerations about religions and ethnicities. Similarly, emphatic statements are easy things for a learning Twitter bot to break into components, and piece together into their own tweets, that inevitably echo the sentiments of those making simple statements. Moreover, given how simple-minded Tay was, its manipulation by online trolls was virtually inevitable.

More important than any of these anecdotes are less obvious, but more seriously impactful, influences of algorithms that radiate into people's lives in 'the real world'. One example is Google's algorithmic job ad placement, which offers higher paying jobs to men than to women.[4] Even more disturbing are 'predictive policing' algorithms that are now being used in law enforcement to determine areas where crime is likely to occur[5] and 're-offending risk' algorithms now being used as a part of sentencing.[6] In both those cases outcomes have been shown to have a severe bias against people of colour. However, perhaps the most concerning phenomena is the influence of algorithms on people's online communities, an arena where the hopeful vision of a utopian Internet has taken a seriously dystopian turn.

In the late 1980s, around the time of my blind date, the first online communities were beginning to emerge, and they were driven by a desire for individual freedom. Up until that time, the hierarchy of USENET groups was controlled by a few superusers, who were sometimes referred to, with both derision and suspicion, as 'The Backbone Cabal'. The Cabal decided on the topic categories of USENET, which arranged content into a strict hierarchy: net.jokes, net. news, etc. This central control ran counter to the idea of online freedom that net users aspired to, and these users quickly realized that the distributed nature of the Internet could be used to empower individual users. If USENET (and the Internet in general) was to grow, individual users had to be given more authority. This is why, in 1987, a new kind of USENET hierarchy was created, under the root name 'alt'.

Opposition to mainstream control was what 'alt' was all about. The moniker had been knocking around since the early 1980s to describe trends that were opposed to the mainstream; for example, 'alternative music', and its genre specific manifestations, like alt country. On USENET, anyone willing to put in some effort could spawn an alt subgroup of an existing group, to cover some obscure area of their own interest or opinion. This was the first spark of the Internet as real, social, new media, and 'alt' quickly became the largest set of the USENET groups, with subgroup entries like alt.music.bluegrass, alt.fan.star-trek, alt.politics, and many, many more.

Alt grew in so many wild directions: it was jokingly said to stand for 'anarchists', 'lunatics', and 'terrorists', but it was also a completely new and liberating social force. Before alt's existence, if you, as an individual, wanted to write something that would be read by a large number of people, you had to go through some form of centralized authority: an editor, publisher, broadcaster, the government or The Cabal. Alt was the first blush of an Internet culture that removed those impediments and enabled anyone to talk to anyone (or everyone). If you wanted to find a community of like-minded individuals, a set of people with the same interests or background as you, or a public square where you could broadcast and debate, an alt forum was the first place in human history where you could do so without any resources or the constraints of the physical world.

Unsurprisingly, this allowed people to write about subjects and find communities that were considered cultural taboos. Sex was important in those early days, as the Internet was a place where people who felt restricted or isolated could find sympathetic or likeminded communities, with a healthy degree of empowering anonymity. Being able to explore sexual ideas online was a definite part of the net's liberating intent. The creation of the hierarchy alt.sex was inevitable, but given the limited bandwidth available to most people in the Internet's early expansion, the channel couldn't share much in the way of pictures or videos. Instead, a popular subgroup alt.sex.stories was created in 1992, where users shared erotic narratives freely, both in a sense of being without cost, and in the sense of being uncensored.

Given the diversity of sexual interests that people were openly (and largely anonymously) expressing in alt.sex.stories, a set of codes (or *tags*) emerged so that users could quickly identify whether a story was liable to suit their preferences. Though an initial glossary of suggested tags was maintained for the group, tags were ultimately free text labels for story content. The usual tags (things like MF, MM, FF, MFF, etc.) had pretty obvious meanings, but as time went on, they evolved to demark content that ranged from the mildly taboo to the completely illegal, things like 'interac' (interracial sex), 'beast' (bestiality), 'reluc' (reluctant sex), etc. These codes and tags are clearly a precursor of hashtags,[7] which remain an important part of the Internet, forming a free-form, unstructured, user-driven glossary of terms. Hashtags are the linguistic precursors of evolving online communities and movements of today.

One of the most high-profile examples of the free-form online communities that descend from USENET's liberation is the 2014 #gamergate movement, which was organized spontaneously under the #gamergate hashtag, in opposition to what some perceived as a pro-feminist, 'politically correct', anti-free-speech cultural agenda in video and online gaming. #Gamergate began with chatroom arguments, but quickly turned to online harassment. Then came disturbing threats of violence, rape and murder against women in the gaming industry. There were even threats of #gamergate-inspired mass shootings at speeches given by feminists. While these threats may have been all talk, they inspired terror 'in real life' (#IRL) when the practice of #doxing (exposing someone's personal information 'documents' online without their permission) was employed. Suddenly, the free comment culture of the Internet gained threatening and frightening real-world force.

Threatening rape and murder was unthinkably outside the individual-rights, diversity-promoting, community-embracing vision of the early Internet days. In fact, these aspects of #gamergate were shocking even in 2014. Now, only a few years later, as social media has spread to encompass even more users, this sort of thing seems to happen all the time, particularly to women. Australia, which is typical of technologically enabled countries, reports that three-quarters of their female citizens under thirty have been harassed or threatened online, with one in four reporting threats of violence, and one in ten reporting 'revenge porn,' or attempts at extortion for sex #IRL.[8]

Although some real-world acts of violence are connected to online misogyny, much of it is still just talk from anonymous, angry men. But the environment it creates is having profound and lasting social effects #IRL. Consider that in 1987, women of my blind date's profession (law) were 40 per cent of new graduates.[9] Science and technology, as you may expect, was fairing much more poorly with regards to gender equality. However, in my field, engineering, where women were only 15 per cent of graduates overall, there was one course of study that was a promising outlier: computer science.[10]

In the 1980s, the number of female graduates in computer science was nearly 40 per cent, and that number was increasing far more rapidly than in law, medicine or any other scientific field. Today, thirty years later, the field has experienced a shocking reversal, and now only 18 per cent of computer science grads are women, having dropped back to the same level of inequality as the rest of engineering, where the intake of women into the field has barely moved in three decades. As the influence of computer science on the world has exploded, the percentage of women in it has collapsed. It is impossible to prove that online misogyny is to blame for this retrograde movement, but there are other developments that seem to indicate that this change is only the tip of the iceberg for the important #IRL effects from movements like #gamergate, and related emergent realities of Internet culture.

Racism seems to have re-emerged in a disturbing fashion in online communities. In 2012, *The Atlantic* published charts showing the geographic density of tweets that used racial profanity across the USA, and the results strongly centred on Southern American states that have a history of slavery and racism.[11] Disturbing online obsessions with race seem to emerge from these areas as well, as studies have shown that the porn tag most requested in the Southern states is now '#blackgirlwhiteguy.[12,13,14] Thus, in 2010, UCLA researcher Safiya Umoja Noble found that a Google search for the words 'black girls' turned up porn.[15] And, in

2015, an academic study showed that the mere availability of broadband is correlated to an increase in racial hate crimes, including harassment and violence.[16]

Racism, misogyny and other forms of intolerance seem to have found a new life online, and are now having global effects #IRL. In 2016, Vox published a study indicating that membership in emergent 'manosphere' online communities, including those with hashtag-based identities #gamergate, #PUA (pick-up artists), '#incel ('involuntarily celibates') and #TheRedPill[17]' are often precursors to interest in the #alt-right, a once obscure online political movement that is now familiar to everyone, having become an agent of international political change over the last few years.[18]

The ability of those with extreme views to find community online, and the radicalization of lonely, marginalized people, has certainly been enabled by the enhanced anonymity provided by the Internet. But recently a new power dynamic has emerged that originates not with isolated individuals, but powerful organizations. Developments like the Cambridge Analytica scandal, where the now defunct marketing and political consulting firm used stolen Facebook data to develop models used in influencing elections, illustrates another significant factor in the evolution of online community, one that plays a pivotal role in the direction it has recently taken. Just as the freely available text content of alt.sex.stories has transformed into the massive, for-profit online porn industry of today, the free and easy online communities of the early Internet are now serious business, where private data on people's preferences and behaviours can be used to tune algorithms for real-world gain. These power dynamics of the Internet aren't just nefarious and political, they are commonplace and commercial, as is illustrated by the two-year election season that preceded Trump's victory, during which stock prices for Facebook, the source of news for half the American electorate, rose 900 per cent faster than the stock-market index.[19]

Online communities are a unique development in human history, because of the ease with which they can be connected to algorithms devised to optimize for material gain. Moreover, intolerant points of view and simplified communication (likes, tweets, flames, etc.) fit precisely with an algorithm's simplified models of people. This creates powerful feedback loops, the net effect of which are informational segregation that can be easily exploited to divide people in much the same way real-world segregation and prejudice has divided people in the past.

This isn't just conjecture. We can see informational segregation *technically* within online communities, precisely because of their technical nature, and we can see the effects on the power and profit of the entities involved. 'Echo chambers' and 'filter bubbles' have emerged online, creating sub-communities that spontaneously share only narrow, self-reinforcing points of view. These closed, polarized communities can be shown to be exceptionally effective market segments, both in the realms of politics and commerce. The hidden detail in all this is how algorithms not only exploits but *drives* this segregation.

Examining how algorithms and algorithmic networks operate offers an opportunity for profound insight and change. And change we must, if want to live in a world where democracy and tolerance thrives, and rigorous scientific thinking banishes bias and prejudice to the past. Looking at how algorithms and networks evolve gives us a new view of how societies function, and suggests new ways, both technical and human, of promoting and preserving online diversity that will help to overcome the negative, emergent effects of algorithmic morality, and perhaps also curtail the intolerance increasingly fostered in online communities.

If appropriately implemented, this new perspective may be able to transform the Internet from a system that generates closed, isolated communities, with limited potential to positively evolve, into an open, evolving network of communities that effectively maximize the positive possibilities of information sharing between diverse people with different viewpoints. Moving towards this new way of using algorithms first requires an understanding of them, the simplifying way they see us all, and how we can all act to change their minds.

2

Doctor Illuminatus

The problems here are complex, both technically and philosophically.
MARK ZUCKERBERG, CEO of Facebook, 2016[1]

Mark Zuckerberg was discussing the difficulty of distinguishing truth from misinformation. He is right on both counts, and I don't envy him being faced with the challenges of 'fake news', and getting algorithms to determine what is 'true' and 'false' in the millions of shares, statuses, comments, photos and videos posted per minute on Facebook. Technically, the problem is massive and, possibly, insurmountable, because 'What is true?' is a seriously hard question, in all but the most trivial frames. Philosophically, it is perhaps *the* hard question, one so complex that even the word itself presents challenges.

In English, the word 'true' originally meant steadfast, faithful, worthy of trust, true in the sense of *fidelity*. It wasn't until the thirteenth century that it took on the meaning of 'consistent with facts', incorporating the sense of *veracity, something that was provable*. Since the word 'true' originally implied faith and steadfastness, this meant that facts became difficult to distinguish linguistically from the assertions and predictions of trusted people such as judges or doctors, or even the eternal Truths expounded by religion. 'True–false' in the sense of a test question only entered the common lexicon in 1923, and since the advent of computers in the mid-twentieth century, 'true' has been associated with the '1' setting of a 0/1 binary switch, at least in the minds of programmers.

Being faithfully true, factually true and technically true are now all covered by a single word, at least in English (the dominant language of science since the Industrial Revolution in the nineteenth century). While it is easy to assume that every question has an answer that is indisputably, factually true, the reality is far subtler and more complex. Furthermore, creating a technical system to reliably determine 'Truth', whatever that means, remains a profound philosophical and technical challenge.

That's not to say that attempting such systems is a new idea. The earliest attempt at a truth-determining 'machine' was in 1290, and some consider it to be the first glimmer of *computer science*. Examining this early device reveals a lot about fundamental technical complexities of algorithms, the frames within which they operate and the atoms within them that determine their relationship to 'truths'. The device also highlights the philosophical complexities that need to be tackled, particularly since the machine was invented by the scholar and cleric Ramon Llull[2] to prove the moral superiority of Christianity over Islam.

Llull was born in 1239 in Palma, the port city of the island of Majorca, which was peacefully brought under Islamic rule in 707. Afterwards it maintained a diverse community of Muslims, Christians, Jews and other faiths for half a millennium. It was a city at the centre of the 'known' world, a few hundred miles from Africa and Europe, smack dab in the middle of the Mediterranean. Since commerce at the time was seaborne, Islamic Palma (like most of the seafaring nations of the world at the time) made a good living off piracy, while fending off attacks from nearby kingdoms (and even a few Vikings). Then, on New Year's Eve, three years before Ramon Llull's birth, the five-century status quo ended when James I of Aragon conquered Palma, established it as the capital of the Majorcan Kingdom and enslaved all the non-Christians who had not died or fled.

Llull's wealthy parents came to Palma from Catalonia, in Spain, as a part of the colonizing effort. As the boy of a wealthy family, living at the crossroads of the world, Ramon received the very best European education, while probably absorbing remnants of the Islamic cultural and intellectual legacy. As a man, Ramon secured a position in the court of the King, took to courtly life, married and had children, and found time for plenty of mistresses. But at age thirty-four, his writings tell us of six holy visitations by Christ on the Cross, who called on Ramon to give up his family, position and sinful ways, and dedicate himself to converting Muslim souls to Christianity. Llull went off to live in the mountains and prepare himself for his sacred duty, and after nearly a decade of mulling over the problem, he returned to civilization intent on fulfilling his mission via an intellectual assault. He determined to travel to Tunisia, meet with the most learned scholars of the Muslim world, and persuade them to establish a Parliament of Faiths, where the relative merits of Christianity and Islam could be rationally debated, to what Llull saw as an obvious end.

Though Francis Bacon wouldn't formalize the scientific method until 300 years later, Llull's idea of a rational argument over spirituality is an important scientific precursor. It is an idea whose appearance may have been particularly fomented by the monotheistic, Abrahamic tradition Ramon was steeped in. In earlier animist and polytheistic religions, many of the awful and inexplicable things that happened to people were laid at the door of capricious gods or spirits. But in a world where an omniscient, omnipotent, single God prevailed, there needed to be a good *reason* for why things happened. The Abrahamic God, at least after his various Old Testament wrangles with Satan, was a God that put the world in *order*, with catastrophes and disorder the regrettable consequence of sinful human beings. With this belief in an ordered universe, scholars like Llull were the first scholars to associate rationale with Holy, capital-T Truth.

Additionally, it's likely that Ramon would have been influenced by the secular parts of his education, which would have most likely included Aristotle, whose complete works had been 'revived' by translation into modern European languages. Amongst those works is the classical text on argument *The Three Persuasive Appeals*, in which Aristotle articulates *ethos, pathos and logos*.

Ethos is argument from a position of authority, that is to say, 'I am a learned scholar, and priest, a member of the King's court, and therefore, what I say is to be taken as true'. Pathos is an appeal to the emotions, 'Look at the suffering of Christ upon the cross, feel empathy for him, and believe his Truth.' Logos, as the name implies, is the appeal of logic: 'Follow these rational steps, and by their quantitative nature and mechanical detail, the conclusions are inevitably and irrefutably True.' In suggesting a Parliament of Faiths, Ramon had chosen a very modern approach, employing logos to fulfil his mission.

Armed with his convictions, Ramon sailed out to Tunis with much fanfare. On arrival, we're told, he marched to the centre of the city, and publicly declared his intention to convert Muslims to the true faith of Christ, through rigorous, logical debate with any Islamic scholars who wished to engage. He was promptly seized, put back on his ship, and told in no uncertain terms to go home and stay home, or consequences would be grave.

So, he returned to Christian Spain, disappointed, but not without hope. If the Islamic world would not allow him to set up his debating Parliament, he would simply have to invent a way of persuading the unfaithful that did not require people to debate the truth. In an innovative move, he decided to create a *mechanical device* whose operation, by anyone, would yield irrefutable proof of Christianity as the one true faith. His first version of this device was called *The Abbreviated Art of Finding Truth*, but later it was refined, and called *The Ultimate Art*. The *Art* is what earns Llull some credit as the first computer 'scientist', as this collection of writings suggests what we'd now call *data structures*, and *algorithms* (step-by-step procedures) for manipulating them. Moreover, it was a device that computed over structured concepts (what I'll call representational atoms) rather than numbers.[3,4]

Numerical computing devices, such as the abacus, had been in existence for five millennia before Llull's birth. Abaci of some form existed in all ancient cultures across the world, but regardless of origin they all share several key features. They all have several rods (grooves, or similar restraining devices), each representing a different order of magnitude of the number of things being counted. For instance, on a decimal abacus there are different rods for 1s, 10s, 100s, 1000s, etc. Other number systems are possible; for instance, the ancient Mesopotamians used a sexagesimal system, based on root 60. Regardless, a bead (or *Calculi* in Latin) restrained on a given rod represents one unit (one object being counted) in the order of magnitude of that rod.[5] Sliding beads from one side to another represents counting in that order of magnitude. If one were accounting for heads of cattle on a decimal abacus, sliding a bead on the one rod would be counting a single cow, sliding a bead on the next rod would count 10 cows, and so on.

This abstraction is, of course, directly connected to the utility of the abacus: the device physically facilitates a version of the 'carry-the-one' procedure for addition and multiplication we all learned as children. When a rod gets full, you slide all the beads on that rod back to the other end, and 'carry the one' by sliding one bead on the next rod up to account for the accumulation of beads at a higher order of magnitude. This simple mechanical detail is what affords easy procedures for addition, subtraction, multiplication, division, and even more complex procedures on some abaci.

One might think the written math procedures we all learned in school, like 'carry the one', would have preceded and dictated the design of abaci, but it seems that's not the case. While abaci with different order-of-magnitude rods have existed since 2700 BC, a numbering system with equivalent, positional notation didn't appear until sometime between the first and fourth centuries AD, in India, demonstrating how technology (like the abacus) can influence thinking (like algorithmic 'carry-the-one' procedures that suggest positional notation). The positional notation system migrated from India to Arabia, and appeared in the earliest work of Arab arithmetic, written around 825 by a man named al-Khwārizmī, who also outlined careful procedures for using numbers in the decimal positional notation that we all use now.

That ground-breaking work was no doubt read by the Italian mathematician Fibonacci, who wrote about the positional numbering system in his book *Liber Abaci*, in 1202, which propagated these techniques throughout Europe. Those in Europe who adopted the techniques in *Liber Abaci* were called *algorismists* in a Latinization of al-Khwārizmī's name. This name would later be Anglicized by Chaucer into the word we're familiar with, *algorithm*, which means 'rules for computing', and described careful, step-by-step procedures like 'carry the one.'

Llull would probably have read *Liber Abaci*, but his innovation took algorithms to their next logical level: reasoning *over abstract symbolic concepts* (in this case religious concepts) instead of over numbers of objects. In Llull's mind, all one needed to do to prove that Christianity was the one true faith was to find the correct atoms (in his case, religious concepts such as justice or prudence), and then apply appropriate logical rules that would give you an algorithm for their manipulation and evaluation. His procedures would manipulate conceptual atoms the way that beads were manipulated on an abacus. Thus, there would then be no need for human debate, because the resulting device and algorithms would prove the point for you.

Llull's atoms were based on the seven heavenly virtues (and their opposite substitutions, the seven deadly sins). He gave each of these a symbolic label:

Llullian Label	Heavenly Virtue	Deadly Sin
B	Justice	Greed
C	Prudence	Gluttony
D	Fortitude	Lust
E	Temperance	Pride
F	Faith	Sloth
G	Hope	Envy
H	Charity	Wrath

As well as these two opposite categories, Llull defined other types of symbols for substitution:

Llullian Label	Quality	Comparative	Interrogative	Object
B	Goodness	Difference	Whether?	God
C	Greatness	Concordance	What?	Angels
D	Duration	Contrariety	Of What?	Heaven
E	Power	Beginning	Why	Man
F	Wisdom	Middle	How Much?	Imagination
G	Will	End	Quality?	Senses
H	Virtue	Majority	When?	Vegetation

Once the categories were established and symbols were assigned, Llull had to specify the rules for *combining* symbols to form theological statements or questions. His specifications included the ticking heart for his mechanism: a data structure that was a sort of incremental 'clock' for the symbol categories (see Figure 2.1).

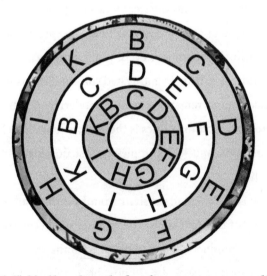

FIGURE 2.1 *Llull's 'clock': perhaps the first data structure to reveal how combining 'atoms' can quickly become explosively complex.*

The outer lettered dial is a stationary 'clock face', while the two inner lettered dials behave like the minute and hour hands of a clock. For every full rotation of nine characters on the smallest dial, the middle dial rotates one step, much the way that a higher order-of-magnitude rod on a decimal abacus moves one bead for every ten on the next lowest rod. The clock generated combinations of the atoms, which Llull interpreted as questions that could be evaluated for spiritual truth, like 'Is goodness great?' or 'What concordance is eternal?'

What, if anything, does this medieval Christian arcana have to do with computer science? The answer is in Llull's extensive writings on the mathematical *combinatorics* that drove the operation of his device. Combinatorics is the first true science of complexity, and the precursor of the theoretical computer science that is at the heart of computing today. It's the most fundamental basis of what people like Zuckerberg mean when they say things are 'technically' complex.

Combinatorics is the study of how many possible things you get by combining other things: how many 'molecules' you can make from 'atoms'. In that sense, Ramon was counting how many different kinds of spiritual questions could be asked with a given set of categorized spiritual concepts. He was considering how complex (spiritual) computation was. While a modern computer scientist might disagree with the spiritually motivated rules and atoms in Llull's *Art*, the combinatoric calculations remain relevant to modern computing and apply to any complex problem. Combinatorics is the way we judge how hard any given set of computations is, and it is complexity that dominates difficulty in all issues of computing.

Consider how complex Llull's system would be if we added a few more atoms, in a variety of different ways. The number of alternatives in a Llullian table expands as the product of the number of columns and rows: seven deadly sins and four categories gives 7*4 = 28 possible combinations. If we found a new deadly sin, but still had only four categories, we'd have 8*4, giving 32 possibilities. Mathematically, we'd say this expansion is *linear*: each addition represents one more line (row) of items in the table.

If we added atoms to both rows and columns, we'd call this expansion *geometric*, in that it reflects the expansion of a geometric figure (in this case, a *square* table: 7*7 is seven 'squared', which is 49, 8*8 is eight 'squared', which is 64, etc.).

If we move to discuss a Llullian clock, and add a dial, we have a different form of combinatorial expansion. A clock with two dials is like a square table (49 combinations for seven symbols on rows and columns), but a clock with three dials is like a cube of numbers (343 combinations), and a clock with four dials is like a four-dimensional cube (2401 combinations), and so on. The expansion of complexity for adding dials is much more rapid, and we'd call that *exponential*, since it reflects the change in the exponent that represents the dimensions of the geometrical figure implied (squared, cubed, etc.)

However, if we make a Llullian clock with as many dials as we have atoms, the combinatorics expands much more rapidly. For a clock with seven dials and seven atoms, we'd have 7*7*7*7*7*7*7 = 823,543 combinations. If we had just one more sin, we get 8*8*8*8*8*8*8 = 16,777,216 combinations. This increase in combinations would be called *superexponential*. Superexponentials begin to reflect the complexity of modern computation. When we talk about a problem being really hard, hard in a way that computers can't be hoped to crack, we are usually talking about superexponentials, which we also refer to as *combinatoric explosions*.

Problems involving combinatoric explosions aren't rare, they are stunningly common. For instance, consider the famous *travelling salesman problem* (TSP). This is an easy-to-describe problem, one that people would have been solving even in Llull's time. Imagine that a medieval merchant (or modern salesman) has a map of n cities, places he must pitch his tent (or deliver his pitch). He wants to find the shortest route to accomplish that goal. It's easy to show that the number of routes possible is combinatorially explosive as a function of the number of cities *n*. As *n* gets bigger, the number of alternative routes explodes to $n*(n-1)*(n-2)\dots 1$, which mathematicians call *n!*, or 'n factorial'. A factorial grows faster than *any* polynomial (geometric figure) of *n*. It expands faster than any square, any cube, in four-dimensional cube, etc., all the way up to massive geometric figures that we can't even imagine.

The TSP can be described in a single sentence, but is provably amongst the hardest computational problems possible, regardless of computational power, because there is *no* algorithm for simplifying the TSP such that a combinatoric explosion can be averted. There is no way to find the best route that practically is better than looking through all the (combinatorially explosive number of) possible routes. This sort of hard fact isn't unique to the TSP; there are scores of other problems that have this characteristic. The TSP is one of a massive number of simple problems that occur every day, all around us, but are as hard as anything.

This difficulty is because of how rapidly superexponentials get big. With a very small number of atoms in a Llullian clock, or cities in a TSP, we reach a number of elements that would take until current estimates of the remaining time before the sun burns out to systematically evaluate. Modern computing doesn't make this problem go away. It's likely that your computer can only calculate the factorial of numbers a little over 100. Even with the expected exponential increase in the power of computers in the future, the superexponential complexity of commonplace problems like TSP isn't going to be overcome. There will always be problems we can't solve perfectly with computers.

These observations reveal a very important fact that everyone should understand about computing and algorithms: extremely complex problems, which are easy to describe, but for which one cannot reasonably compute the 'true' answer, are not rare. They are exceedingly common. Moreover, even problems that aren't superexponential are often just too hard to compute exact, 'true' solutions for. Much of what we do in computing is attempting to cope with the inherent and overwhelming complexity of apparently simple problems that occur all the time in the real world.

Llull coped with the complexity of spirituality by adopting a finite set of atoms, and he had faith (of the religious sort) that these atoms were adequate for the computational task at hand. Despite what we think of as a very limited scope, his symbols, tables, and data structures generated a total of 33,600 possible questions in all. Llull most likely thought this was an amazing coverage of the necessary philosophical ground, an effective management of the technical complexity of proving the undeniable truth of Christianity. His scholarship must have been convincing to others at the time as well, because he easily raised the funds to return to Tunis in 1314, armed with his new device and a firm belief he could use it to convert Muslims. Unfortunately for him, the Muslims of Tunis were not so easily persuaded. On his arrival, Ramon Llull was stoned to death.

That conclusion probably doesn't surprise you, because most of us see Llull's quest as being absurd from the start. From a modern perspective, his neat framing of faith appears slightly deranged, and his atoms are completely relative. We know that a Muslim, Jew or a Hindu would frame spiritual 'truth' with completely different atoms and linking mechanisms given their different perspectives. Moreover, we instinctively feel that the enterprise of determining a set of atoms to come up with a single correct answer (the 'truth') for deeply complex human matters, particularly matters involving belief, is utterly ill-considered.

However, Llull's ideas persisted and had far-reaching influence in the emerging scientific era, echoes of which persist to this day. Llull was read and discussed by scholars well into the 1600s. Rene Descartes (of 'I think, therefore I am' fame) certainly knew of Llull's work and mentioned him (albeit critically) in his 1637 *Discourse on The Method*. Gottfried Leibniz,[6] the inventor of calculus (which, by the way, is named for the beads on an abacus), attempted to extend Llull's thinking on *The Art*. In 1685 he wrote that 'a kind of alphabet of human thoughts can be worked out and that everything can be discovered and judged by a comparison of the letters of the alphabet and an analysis of the words made from them', and:

> The only way to rectify our reasonings is to make them as tangible as those of the Mathematicians, so that we can find our error at a glance, and when there are disputes among persons, we can simply say: Let us calculate, without further ado, to see who is right.

Although Leibniz was proposing something more 'modern' here, by substituting a faith in mathematics for the religious faith of men like Llull, he was essentially suggesting the same thing as Llull – that some sort of computational procedure over a set of atoms (an 'alphabet') could solve, once and for all, challenging human disputes.

Leibniz believed in mechanical computation, and played an important role in its advance, inventing 'Leibniz wheels', part of a mechanical 'carry-the-one' mechanism that proved a vital addition to the premier numerical calculating machine of the day, the Pascaline. The Pascaline was invented by Blaise Pascal, the most famous mathematician of the previous generation, and devices that descend from it would be used for number processing well into the twentieth century. A form of Pascaline mechanism, including Leibniz's innovations, would in time be incorporated into Charles Babbage's 1822 mechanical calculator, the Difference Engine, and then into the first 'general purpose' computing devices that followed in its wake. Through general purpose computation, the Llull-inspired idea of computing over symbols (rather than numbers) to operate on challenging human issues would in time turn into AI.

While Llull, Pascal, Leibniz and Babbage all did their parts in advancing the machinery for computing over general concepts, the idea would not be fully realized until after the development of electronic computation. In 1955,

General Problem Solver, which many call the first general AI program, was created by computer scientist Allen Newell and economist Herb Simon.

General Problem Solver used what Simon and Newell called *means–ends analysis* as the foundation for its reasoning. In many ways, it's a technique that takes the symbolic computing of Llull and returns to its heart the numeric computing of the abacus. One way to understand the basic ideas behind means–ends analysis is to understand the operation of another device that sometimes shares the acronym 'GPS': the satnav which most of us have in our car.

In your satnav, locations, and the roads that connect them, are the atoms that represent the world, as a part of an enormous connected graph stored in the device's database. When you input a destination into your satnav, it recognizes that location in this graph. This is the 'end' in means–ends analysis, and the connecting roads are the 'means'. Your current position is calculated (using signals from satellites), and it is also found in the graph. The satnav reasons quantitatively over distances, by exploring the roads spanning out from your location, to find the 'best' (shortest) means to the end (your desired destination). This is why means–ends analysis is often called reasoning *as search*.

While not as combinatorially explosive as the TSP, the search for the best route is, in general, terrifically hard, particularly in terms of the usually large number of roads and intermediate locations between you and your destination. So rather than take until the sun burns out to find you a route, means–ends analysis in your satnav exploits *heuristics* to find you a route in reasonable time. 'Heuristic' is a word that describes a practical method (not guaranteed to be optimal or rational) for reaching a satisfactory solution when dealing with a complex problem. Other ways to describe a heuristic are 'rules-of-thumb', 'an educated guess' or even 'common sense'. In General Problem Solver, Simon and Newell were the first to explore the idea of using algorithmic implementations of 'heuristics' to overcome computational complexity in mechanical reasoning.

Although a satnav may use many varieties of heuristics in searching for your route, a likely common-sense solution is the 'as the crow flies' heuristic. While the 'Calculating' banner is being displayed on your satnav, the device is systematically adding up the distance along each possible road from you to intermediate locations on the way to your destination. However, it is not exploring them all, as that would take (nearly) forever. Instead, it is evaluating the actual length of each partial route, added to the 'as the crow flies' distance from the intermediate location along the way, to the final destination. Using this calculation, it is disregarding the pursuit of any routes that don't look as good, in terms of this heuristic, as others it has already found. This 'prunes' the massive graph of possible routes and makes finding you a route in reasonable time possible.

This is a really good heuristic, on several counts. First, if you only care about covering the minimum distance between yourself and your destination, this heuristic not only always finds you a route (if one exists), it finds you the true, best-possible route, every time, in the fastest time possible. Second, it's a heuristic that it's not too hard to imagine a real person using.

However, if you are considering other factors (avoiding traffic, scenic drives, availability of decent restrooms along the route), the guarantee of the best route from this simple heuristic quickly becomes questionable, and not just because factors like 'scenic' are hard to fit into a formal frame (who would establish the criteria for 'scenic', and how?). Without the careful, technical aspects of a pure 'minimum distance' problem, the guarantees of 'best route' aren't available. In more complex cases like these, if your satnav has options to support them, it's probably using other, additional 'heuristics' to make route-finding possible, but it's unlikely that they offer guarantees of the true best route. It is also unlikely that those heuristics have much in common with human psychology. In fact, since Simon and Newell, the term 'heuristic' has come to mean any procedure that reduces the complexity of a computational algorithm, regardless of whether it has any similarity to the way humans think.

But Simon and Newell's techniques do work. In many cases, they can be shown to provide good solutions to hard problems, at least within the limited computation available for practicality. The early successes of General Problem Solver were in fact so encouraging, that by the 1970s, Simon and Newell, describing the algorithms they were writing as 'physical symbol systems', took something of a leap of faith, and wrote: 'A physical symbol system has the necessary and sufficient means for general intelligent action.' This strong statement about AI became known as the *physical symbol system hypothesis*, and it implied that with the right frame and atoms, all that we consider intelligent in human beings could be done by a computer.

Building on this faith in machine intelligence, the 1970s and 1980s saw the first academic and commercial boom in AI. Most of this AI was in the form of programs called *expert systems*. Expert systems attempted to capture the knowledge of human experts (such as doctors or engineers), in the form of a frame and atoms, such that algorithms, using techniques like means–ends analysis, could be applied. It was widely believed that this approach would make it possible for a computer to take any of the 'intelligent actions' of a human expert.

A well-known (and typical) expert system from this era was MYCIN,[7] a program for diagnosing blood infections. MYCIN was constructed like all other expert systems, by extracting knowledge from human experts (through interviews and literature reviews), to construct a formal representation (a set of atoms, based on blood testing and observations) which were then connected together by 'if/then' rules. A typical MYCIN rule (paraphrased for human-readability) would be something like the following: '*If* the patient has meningitis *and* the meningitis is bacterial *then* the patient has staphylococcus with heuristic uncertainty factor 0.4 OR streptococcus with heuristic uncertainty factor 0.2.' In practice, expert systems like MYCIN could consist of many such rules, but it was not necessary to have one rule that generated a definitive conclusion for every combination of possible pieces of diagnostic evidence. This is because the 'then' parts of the rules could suggest new atoms, which could be matched to the 'if' part of other rules, forming long rule chains towards a final conclusion. In the case of MYCIN, this conclusion would be a diagnosis of a blood disease and a recommendation for a dosage of an appropriate antibiotic.

This rule-chaining can be seen as facilitating something like means–ends analysis, reasoning-as-search, like the process in your satnav. Each rule is a road from one condition in the space of observed or inferred facts, to another position in that space. What the algorithm is doing is attempting to find a route from the observed facts about a patient, via the rules, through a set of intermediate locations, to a final destination labelled 'disease diagnosed, treatment prescribed'.

To make means–ends analysis fit the frame of diagnosis, there has to be a *quantity* to optimize, something similar to finding the minimum distance with the satnav. In MYCIN, this comes from the fact that no atomic observation is entirely certain, and that the drive is for the most certain diagnosis. This is the reason that 'heuristic uncertainty factors' appear in the paraphrased MYCIN rule listed out above. For each MYCIN rule, this factor is like the length of a road in your satnav. The algorithm in MYCIN was using reasoning-as-search in an attempt to optimize a 'route' to the diagnosis, by minimizing the net uncertainty.

With the physical symbol system hypothesis in hand, and the ongoing increase in available computer power, it seemed to many in the 1960s, 1970s, and early 1980s that this approach to AI was bound to render human expertise both redundant and inferior and yield great scientific and commercial achievements. However, this early faith in AI proved to be misplaced, due to two significant and persistent challenges. The first is what is known in AI as *brittleness*. Simply stated, expert systems, if asked a question even marginally outside the frame that their programmers had intended, fail, and fail rather dramatically, when compared to human experts.

If MYCIN was asked a question about something that was not a blood infection, it had no answer to return, because that question was outside its frame of 'expertise'. It could not speculate 'intelligently' based on its general knowledge of medicine or experience, because it had no general knowledge of medicine, or anything else. Its 'knowledge' was bounded by the atoms of its representation. An even worse scenario was if MYCIN was asked a question about something that at first appeared to be a blood infection, but was, in fact, something else (perhaps a poisoning). In that case the program could deliver an answer that was misleadingly, or even dangerously, wrong.

On the face of it, the obvious solution to this brittleness would be to expand what an expert system 'knows': to give it more 'atoms', and more rules that indicate their relationships. But this is, of course, combinatorially explosive. However, Simon and Newell's work suggests that arming an expert system with sufficient heuristics might overcome that problem. After all, human beings (some of whom aren't even 'experts') often manage to come up with reasonable solutions even when faced with questions for which they don't have complete domain knowledge. But the human atoms and heuristics that made these solutions possible proved hard to find.

This led to the second problem faced by expert systems: it turned out that extracting knowledge from people about what actually goes on in their heads when problem-solving, and then trying to fit that knowledge to a frame designed for reasoning-as-search, is exceedingly hard. Some of the limitations were merely practical, as experts are notoriously hard to physically pin down. They are of course amongst the busiest people in any organization. Blood-infection doctors were off saving infected people and had little time to talk to expert system programmers (known as *knowledge engineers* at the time). But even if you could get the time with them, the subtle reasoning and experience they deployed proved difficult to capture in the frames of expert systems.

This second problem is particularly vexing when coupled with brittleness. To overcome brittleness, you had to not just extract more knowledge atoms, but incorporate them into an existing frame. And it turns out that the subtle incorporation of more general knowledge with existing, rote procedural knowledge is incredibly difficult. Moreover, it seems that it is this ability to integrate experience, knowledge and rote procedure that enables people to fail gracefully when asked a question outside of their expertise, and occasionally turn those graceful failures into wild successes. Consider the seemingly tangential observations that often save the day in the TV drama *House*. While the show is fiction, anyone who has been through the treatment of a complex illness will be familiar with the process of false leads and educated guesses often involved in real-world diagnosis of a human condition.

At the end of the era of expert systems, one thing was sure, the 'knowledge acquisition bottleneck', the problem of transferring expert knowledge into formal frames of computer representations, was extremely expensive and time-consuming. If you could get the time to sit down with real experts, it was the most expensive time possible, and gathering sufficient knowledge (data) from them was explosively difficult. This made the implementation of the physical symbol system hypothesis, and reasoning as search, commercially unviable, leading to complete failure of the AI enterprise in the 1970s and the dawn of what is now known as the 'AI winter'.

Seeking to evaluate what the UK was getting for its investment in AI research in 1973, Sir James Lighthill reported to Parliament that there had been an utter failure of the field to advance on its 'grandiose objectives'. Soon afterwards in the USA, ARPA (Advanced Research Projects Agency), the agency now known as DARPA (Defence Advanced Research Projects Agency), received a similar report from the American Study Group. As a result, public funding for AI research was dramatically cut, and, by the end of the 1980s, almost all of those early AI start-ups had collapsed.

It would be wrong to say that expert systems died completely in the AI winter. In reality the term 'expert system' was simply replaced with the moniker 'decision support system' in reports and research proposals. This was a (perhaps conscious) effort to shift the role of the machine into the position of an aid or support to the less-brittle human decision makers. This re-branding also reduced the overhyped 'grandiose objectives' of AI and the techniques used in expert systems were simply absorbed into the expanded repertoire of programmers.

Today, the typical procedures and representational tricks in 'expert systems' are a part of day-to-day computing techniques that we all use everyday (like the satnav in our car). While these devices are wonderfully useful, brittleness and the corresponding, necessarily shallow, limited frames of knowledge are still embedded in their algorithms. That's fine when people understand the limitations involved (most everyone has learned to cope with the sometimes bone-headed suggestions of their satnav), but dangerous when those limitations aren't understood, and are employed autonomously, in complex human situations.

Algorithms must use frames with limited sets of concrete, symbolic atoms to represent things and concepts in the real world. And frames, by their nature, are brittle. Overcoming this brittleness means adding more atoms. Even as far back as the thirteenth century Ramon Llull discovered that the number of combinations of atoms explodes combinatorially. This is an unavoidable fact of life. Not being able to determine the one true solution because of such explosions isn't rare; it is stunningly commonplace. Problems that are terribly easy to describe can be terribly hard to solve in reasonable time. Using heuristics to overcome this combinatorial complexity doesn't really solve the problem. Heuristics only do the best they can, within brittle frames and limited time. In addition, the heuristics employed in algorithms often have little to do with the human reasoning. The 'good enough' results delivered by algorithms must be evaluated in light of their constrained abilities, and the fact that their coping mechanisms aren't like our own.

Moreover, technical complexity is only a part of the challenge, as Zuckerberg noted. Consider again the strange and subtle meanings of the word 'truth', with its linguistic history fusing the concepts of fidelity and veracity, in a way that is unique to English. Witness that the website Politifact, dedicated to fact-checking US politics, has to place truth into six categories (only half of which are definitive) and provide a detailed, written analysis to explain the nuances of the verity of each statement it examines. Human truths and falsehoods are not as simple as 0s and 1s.

The *Oxford English Dictionary* contains around 50,000 nouns, and at least 10,000 verbs, under conservative estimates that ignore obsolete and derivative words. Most of these have complex meanings, some even more complicated than that of 'truth', and the inter-relationship of words in human communication take these subtle differences and expand them combinatorially. In addition, the concepts embodied in every single word will translate into the frame of other cultures in very different, subtle ways that will also vary over time and place, building the complexity of words' meanings even further. And of course, words are only a part of communication.

Llull's *Art* involved only tens of symbols from which the statements he evaluated were composed, and he had the convenience of his Christian faith as an engineering principle for the simplifying frame he constructed. The algorithms in use today have far more symbols, and our faith in them is usually either based on a lack of awareness of the details involved, or a misplaced belief in the power of quantifying human concepts and reducing them into computational models. This faith, without understanding the technically necessary, but often limiting, simplifications involved, can obscure significant algorithmic biases or even basic errors, which may, intentionally or unintentionally, be misused. Finding a route with your satnav is intrinsically different from finding a route to the Truth.

3

The Death of Uncertainty

I think that the people of this country have had enough of experts.
MICHAEL GOVE, UK Justice Secretary, 2016

The ability to forecast an uncertain future and to choose the best course of action from among alternatives lies at the heart of contemporary democratic societies. Hence the heated debates surrounding the UK's 2016 referendum on whether the UK should remain in the European Union or, after more than forty years, depart from the political and economic coalition (now grown to twenty-eight nations) and forge a new destiny on its own. Experts from all fields – economics, trade, education, health, manufacturing, farming and government – weighed in strongly, the majority of them dismayed at the prospect of departure and predicting catastrophic consequences.

Appearing on a Sky News question-and-answer session on 6 June 2016,[1] Michael Gove dismissed the concerns of all those experts with the above comment. To be fair, Gove was specifically talking about experts 'from organisations with acronyms saying that they know what is best', his point being that many economic experts had failed to accurately predict the financial crisis of 2008 and, therefore, couldn't possibly pronounce on the impending impact of Brexit. Journalists seized on the abbreviated form of his comment, because it reflects the increasingly populist spirit of today. Gove has a point, in that statistically averaged 'user-generated' content and 'citizen journalism' has now gained greater acceptance than the opinions of 'so-called' experts. One could argue that the joint opinion of the masses has taken the place of experts, government officials and the defamed mainstream media. This point of view is highlighted by Gove's concluding comment: 'I'm not asking the public to trust me. I'm asking them to trust themselves.'

This is only one illustration of how people appear to have lost faith in experts in favour of popular opinion. Back in 1987, the Pew Research Center reported that trust in the US government was around 50 per cent.[2] Today it stands at under 20 per cent. Gallup also reports drops in confidence versus historical averages for institutions as varied as banking, criminal justice, medicine, organized labour, big business, police, print media, broadcast media, public schools and organized religion.[3] Meanwhile, faith in the opinion of the masses is soaring. What was once derided as 'lowest common denominator' is now hailed 'the wisdom of crowds'. This 'wisdom' isn't only being exploited by populist politicians; it is the life blood of today's AI.

The fact that expertise proved hard to fathom for expert systems is exactly what led to the AI winter. Since then there have been no significant technical breakthroughs on modelling how smart people reason. While modelling the reasoning process of a single human expert proved overwhelmingly expensive, the Internet heralded in a new era whereby the great mass of people in the emergent online world offered up a sea of information *for free*; and, in many cases, even *paid* (sometimes explicitly, but largely through subscriptions and views of advertising) to have their data monitored and mined.

The resulting 'big data' proved a game-changer, providing a new wave of technology companies with the ultimate data set. The massive, contemporary growth in AI speculation, development and exploitation could not have occurred without it. People input their information online largely free of charge, which provides the data that algorithms need to create demographic 'packages of people' that are then automatically sold to advertising customers, thus solving the intractable economic problem faced by expert systems. What's more, the data provided enables algorithms to make decisions about how to stimulate people into generating and sharing more data, thereby creating a never-ending cycle of supply and demand.

All that remained was to figure out a reliable way of sifting through the data's enormity and complexity in order to make sense of it. How, after all, were we to understand the explosive online data generated by millions of people in the vast, ever-evolving system that is the Internet? In almost all of the new AI we see today, this is done using probability theory, a form of mathematical modelling that allows for the quantitative analysis of complex data based on statistics. In AI development, statistical analysis of big data has nearly completely taken the place of attempting to understand the complexity of an individual human's thinking.

However, the idea that probability and statistics are the best way to cope with complexity and the uncertainty it creates is something of an act of faith for the AI community. That act of faith remains largely hidden from everyone outside that community by a cloud of seemingly impenetrable mathematics. This obscures the dangers inherent in using statistics and probability as a basis for reasoning about people via algorithms.

Statistical models, after all, aren't unbiased, particularly when, as is the case for most algorithms today, they are motivated by the pursuit of profit. Just like expert systems, statistical models require a frame within which to operate, which is then populated by particular atoms. That frame and those atoms are subject to the same brittleness (limitations) and biases. On top of that, the probabilities drawn from these statistics, which become the grist for the statistical algorithmic mill, often aren't what we think they are at all.

If you just looked at things statistically, you'd probably overlook some of the deeper history of my hometown – Birmingham, Alabama. The city was founded in 1871 when it was discovered that it was the only location on Earth where the minerals necessary for iron and steel production could be mined in one place. This industry-promoting coincidence created a boomtown that attracted migrants from all over the world, including Scots, Jews, Greeks and Italians. It'd be incorrect to say that this led to an integrated community, particularly since people of colour, only recently freed from slavery, were segregated by law, but despite the city's history of division, there has always been an undercurrent of diversity and people who were exceptions to the norm. This is part of the reason I got my first real-world lesson in probability from a local jazz guitarist and part-time, down-home bookie called Mickey. My ancestors were Scottish miners, and Mickey's were Italians who ran grocery stores and gambling in the Magic City, but we met in a place that defied convention in 1980s Alabama – a record store called Floyd's Live Catfish.

Floyd had been my college roommate, and his eponymous store was a magnet for the young people of the city who were seeking something different. The store was a local scandal, because it specialized in alternative music, art, literature, fashion and window displays that freaked out the locals. For instance, on the day I talked to Mickey about probability, there was a Halloween display in the window, featuring female mannequins with Hazmat suits and flamethrowers waging a pitched battle with plastic rats. It was driving the local league of blue-haired church ladies (who occasionally wandered in to ask why the store didn't sell catfish) to distraction. I loved the place, as did a multitude of other alt-Birminghamians.

Mickey and I were both hanging at Floyd's that day, talking about guitar and riffling through the albums, but despite my attempt at a break from my PhD studies, the back of my mind was still puzzling over something from an advanced course on random processes. So, I posed a question to Mickey, since I thought he must know lot about probability, given his sideline taking bets. He laughed at me, with precisely the same amusement he had when I (a hack rock guitarist) brought up the 'mathematics' of jazz. After his guffaw, he told me that bookies didn't have to know anything about probability; they only had to know about money.

Mickey informed me that being a bookie had absolutely nothing to do with the maths of probability theory. Consider, he said, the upcoming annual Iron Bowl, the culmination of the annual arch football rivalry between the University of Alabama and Auburn University. He told me that to make a living out of events like The Big Game, a bookie only had to look at two piles of money: the pile of bets for Alabama (a pile of A dollars) and the pile of bets for Auburn (a pile of B dollars). As bets come in, and the piles change sizes, the bookie sets the odds, the amount that gets paid out if Alabama wins (α dollars for every dollar bet) and the amount that gets paid out if Auburn wins (β dollars for every dollar bet). Those odds aren't set based on probabilities, they are set to make sure that he makes money *regardless of the game's outcome*. This is called 'balancing your book'.

Mickey watched as I sketched out my college-boy mathematical interpretations of balancing his book on Floyd's receipt pad:

If Alabama wins:

$$A + B - \alpha A > 0$$

If Auburn wins:

$$A + B - \beta B > 0$$

He nodded at my scribblings and said, 'Or in other words, after the game, you want to put the two piles of money together, pay out, then make sure you've got some profit left. That's all the math a bookie needs, Smith.'

With two engineering degrees under my belt, I wasn't willing to be told on this as easily as I was on the mathematics of jazz. 'Let's assume you don't make a profit, so I can turn those inequalities into their limiting equalities' I said, and scribbled:

$$A + B - \alpha A = 0$$

$$A + B - \beta B = 0$$

$$\alpha = \frac{B}{A}\beta$$

'The pay-out rates and the probabilities should have a reciprocal relationship,'[4] I said, writing:

$$\frac{1}{\alpha} = P_A, \quad \frac{1}{\beta} = P_B$$

$$P_B = \frac{B}{A}P_A$$

'To be real probabilities, they have to add to one, so let's put that in,' I said, writing:

$$P_B + P_A = 1$$

$$1 - P_A = \frac{B}{A}P_A$$

$$1 = P_A\left(1 + \left(\frac{B}{A}\right)\right)$$

$$P_A = \frac{1}{\left(1 + \left(\frac{B}{A}\right)\right)} = \frac{A}{A+B}, \quad P_B = \frac{B}{A+B}$$

'Now that looks right to me,' I said proudly. 'The percentage of money you've got on Alabama is the probability that Alabama wins, and the percentage of money on Auburn is the probability that Auburn wins. If you use this as a basis, the odds you give are fair, and reflect the true probabilities of winning, as measured by your bettors, as long as you don't make a profit.'

Mickey puzzled over my equations a bit, and then pushed them aside. 'I don't care about all that math, Smith. A bookie sets the odds to make what he needs. And why shouldn't I make a profit? I'm providing a community service here. And trust me, the bettors have no idea about the probabilities of Alabama or Auburn winning.' He then provided the weeks-in-advance odds he was giving for either side to win the Iron Bowl. They sounded widely skewed towards an Alabama victory, as one would expect in Birmingham, a largely Roll Tide town. Moreover, their related probabilities didn't sum to one.

About that time, Floyd walked over from re-sorting the magazine stand (tattoo mags together with sci-fi poetry). 'You guys gotta shut up. I got enough trouble with the local Living Word Baptists without getting busted for gambling. Thus far I'm just a local weirdo, but they'll shut my ass down if they find out I know real criminals like you,' he said, pointing at Mickey.

Mickey laughed and replied, 'That may be true, but the pastor at Living Word called me just last night to put two grand on the game.'

My conversation with Mickey revealed a fundamental confusion at the heart of probability, which lies in our understanding of the word itself. In the sixteenth century, when Galileo was writing about Copernicus' theory of the earth revolving around the sun, he called the idea 'improbable', because it contradicted what people could see with their own eyes (i.e. the sun revolving around the earth). Inherent in the word was the idea of ap*prob*ation or approval. Copernicus' theory, in this case, was improbable because it did not meet with approval or acceptance given the apparently observable facts.

By the seventeenth century, when Leibniz was revisiting Copernicus' theory, he described it as 'incomparably the most probable', meaning the hypothesis was the most credible theory given the evidence. The German word for probable, *wahrscheinlich*, conveys the meaning better, as it translates literally to 'with the appearance of truth'. This subtle shift in the meaning of the word reveals a tension at the heart of probability theory between what is approvable (i.e. what we actually know from past experience) and what is credible (i.e. what is *believable*). This subtle semantic confusion may seem insignificant, but it goes right to the heart of probability theory and the statistical reasoning that we use to model our increasingly complex and uncertain world with algorithms.

There's no doubt that probability theory is a powerful mathematical tool that has helped us to organize, interpret and analyse information in an increasingly complex world. These days probability theory guides us over a vast range of decision-making, from allocating wealth to public health policy, from waging war to setting insurance premiums, from planning agricultural subsidies to selling commodities. But it is one thing to create a mathematical model of the world and another to reconcile it with our lived experience, the daily struggle of life, the constant trial and error as we experiment with new ideas and ways of doing things, and the ambiguity of the facts themselves.

Human beings have been wrestling with the unpredictability of the world for millennia, but up until the Renaissance it seems that people, even in the classical period, were largely unconcerned with developing any scientific method for analysing the world's uncertainties or dealing with the inherent risks in making even the smallest of decisions. For them, the future was unknowable, and man wielded no influence upon it. The best read on the future was to consult the oracle or seer who would divine a vague idea of the possibilities by casting lots, reading Tarot cards or consulting the I Ching. Divination devices like these can be found in almost every ancient world culture from the Mayans to the Native Americans, from the Greeks to the Chinese.[5]

The oldest known divination device is an *astragalus*, the knucklebone from the hind leg of a sheep or goat. Egyptian tomb paintings dating back to 3500 BC depict them, and astragali from 500 BC have been found near an altar dedicated to the goddess Aphrodite in Athens. Astragali were also used in popular gambling games. Given that both activities involve an attempt to 'predict future outcomes', links between gambling and divination also appear across cultures from the very earliest times. Casting dice, spinning a wheel, drawing lots, dealing cards, and a whole range of actions were all used both to gamble and to divine. Modern, regularly shaped dice (which first appear about 2800 BC) probably descend directly from astragali. Mongolians still play with the knucklebones, in some games that are like craps, and others that are like what Americans call Jacks. The sticks thrown in American Jacks games are like those thrown in some Native American divination, or those thrown in the Chinese I Ching. Playing cards and dominoes have similar ancient origins that combine playing with randomness and prediction of fate.

Yet despite being ancient, commonplace and connected to games of chance, there is no classical mathematics that attempts to systematically describe the uncertainty associated with the random roll of these devices. The Greeks and Romans lacked a numbering system that would have enabled them to efficiently calculate with (instead of just record) their results, and they lived in a world circumscribed by the behaviour of a pantheon of fickle gods. Greek dramas tell tale after tale of the helplessness of human beings at the mercy of the Fates. While the gods were embodiments of various human characteristics which you might appeal to, the Fates were inhuman and deaf to entreaty. The Fates represented persistent uncertainty and couldn't be bypassed or overcome.

That is until Christianity did away with the Fates and a new omnipotent and omnipresent God changed the way Europeans saw the world and their place in it. Now men could put more faith in the future, at least in the afterlife, if they committed to live by a new moral code made clear to them via a hierarchy of priests. Proselytising Crusaders set out in the world to spread the good news and collided with the sophisticated Arab Empire. Although they failed to convert many Muslims to their cause, they returned home with some invaluable ideas, including the Hindu numbering system, which the Arabs had adopted following their invasion of India, and which, through works by scholars like al-Khwārizmī, had enabled them to race ahead of the rest of the world in the fields of mathematics, astronomy, navigation and commerce, all activities requiring sophisticated calculation.

In this more orderly Christian universe, armed with an effective numbering system that did away with the algorithmically cumbersome letters used by the Greeks, Romans and Hebrews, abstract mathematical ideas became possible, and the proto-scientific work of men like Ramon Llull emerged. As mysticism gave way to emerging scientific enquiry in the early days of the Renaissance, the mysteries of the world's workings and man's role within it became the subject of intense speculation. Although people still played the astragalus in the streets of Milan, Pavia and Bologna, Italy's big university towns, new games of chance and business opportunities were tempting Renaissance men to try their luck at taming the goddess Fortuna.

One such man was mathematician, scientist, philosopher and physician Gerolamo Cardano,[6] who was born in Pavia in 1501. Gerolamo was one of the greatest intellectuals of Renaissance Italy, but from the outset the Fates dealt him a difficult hand, and despite his many talents and achievements his life was beset by unfortunate circumstances beyond his control. He was the bastard son to a mathematician friend of Leonardo da Vinci, Fazio Cardano, who held a chair of mathematics at Pavia University, one of the oldest institutions of higher learning in the world. One might think connections like that would have given him a lucky leg up, but that wasn't to be.

He was a sickly child and his father bullied him, until he finally escaped to university at age nineteen. Just then war broke out and the school closed. He transferred to the far away University of Padua, where he took up gambling to offset school debts. Fortunately, he excelled at the gaming tables, managed to pay his way, and at twenty-four he earned his doctorate. He immediately applied for a position at the College of Medicine in Milan, but he failed to secure a place. This was partly because he was a bastard by birth, and partly because he was a bastard by disposition. He had an arrogant and abrasive personality that rubbed the medical establishment the wrong way, particularly when questioning the medical conventions of the time and promoting some of his more radical ideas (for instance, that regular bathing should be promoted as a means of better public health). Rejection by the establishment meant that he was forced to take up a post as a doctor in a small town outside Milan, where he just scraped by enough money to marry and have two sons and a daughter. He continued to gamble to supplement his income, but his luck turned sour; he lost all of his wife's jewellery and their household furniture, and he and his family were consigned to Milan's debtors' prison.

In 1536, just when all seemed lost, Cardano had an unusual stroke of good luck, and was given his father's old post in mathematics at the University in Milan. This restored the family to respectability and enabled him to resume his doctor's practice, but his eleven applications to the Milan's College of Medicine were still all rejected. Despite this, his reputation as a physician began to grow, because he side-stepped the medical establishment through the use of new media.

Cardano credited Johannes Gutenberg's printing press as one of the three most important inventions of his time, and this early mass-media machine allowed him to distribute literature on his ideas, and gain a popular following as a new kind of doctor. Without the Gutenberg press, radical ideas from a fringe individual like Cardano couldn't have been widely distributed. Consider that in Ramon Llull's day, books had to be laboriously hand copied at a maximum of sixteen pages per day, but by Cardano's era, a single printing press was able to produce 3,600 pages in that time. A writer like Llull would also have had a very limited audience, since almost everyone in Europe was illiterate when he created the *Art*, but in Cardano's time, while general literacy across Europe was 5 to 10 per cent, in major merchant cities like Milan, it is possible that up to one in three people could read.

Cardano published *On the Bad Practices of Medicine in Common Use* the year he gained his mathematics post. It became a popular book and was the beginning of a grand career in writing. Cardano would become one of the most read authors of the Renaissance, writing on mathematics, medicine, astronomy, hydrodynamics, physics, morality, natural law, gambling, music, horoscopes and dreams. During his lifetime, Cardano wrote well over a hundred printed works, claimed to have burned more than 170 and left 111 in manuscript form at his death.

Three years after the publication of *Bad Practices*, the Milanese medical establishment realized that they could no longer resist Cardano's popularity and accepted his twelfth application to the College of Medicine. Cardano had finally achieved the fame, reputation and financial security that was to turn his life around. This began the two great decades of his life, when he would establish himself as a physician of international acclaim with the credibility to promote ground-breaking ideas. Amongst his many accomplishments, he cured the Archbishop of Scotland of his asthma by recognizing he was allergic to his feather pillow, and he was one of the first people to advocate that the deaf could learn to write, without first having learnt to speak.

He also became a leading mathematician of the age. In 1545, he published his own *Ars Magna* (Great Art), in a (coincidental) titular echo of Llull's work, which contained the solution to cubic and quartic equations. He also published the best-selling *De Subtilitate Rerum* (On the Subtletly of Things), a work of science and philosophy, which ran to six editions. By this time he had become one of the most heralded thinkers on the Continent, holding the position of both rector of Milan's College of Medicine and Professor of Medicine at the University of Pavia.

But despite all Cardano's success, his personal life continued to play out like a soap opera. His daughter Chiara died of syphilis (on which he had, ironically, written the first treatises), contracted while allegedly plying her trade as a prostitute. His daughter-in-law extorted money from him, and flagrantly cuckolded his beloved eldest son, Giambatista, who then poisoned her with arsenic-tainted bread, for which he was arrested, tortured and executed in 1560. Now the father of a convicted murderer, Cardano had to resign his post in Milan and retreat to a more obscure post at the University of Bologna. There, his other son, Aldo, who had inherited his love of games, gambled away all their possessions, forcing his father to have him banished in 1569.

Then, Cardano himself was imprisoned for impiety by the Inquisition in 1570, possibly because he had computed a horoscope of Jesus Christ. Although he served only a few months in prison, he was forced to abjure his professorship and was forbidden from publishing any more of his work. His autobiography,

De Vita Propria, was published posthumously in Amsterdam after his death in 1576.

What a ride! With all those twists of fate, it is highly ironic that it was Cardano who wrote the first systematic theory of probability in games of chance, in his book *Liber de Ludo Aleae* (Book on Games of Chance), written around 1565, but only published posthumously in 1663. In it, he set out to define, for the first time, a mathematical system that could determine random events, anticipating many ideas encompassed by 'modern' probability theory, the most important of which is the classical definition of probability itself:

> So there is one general rule, namely, that we should consider the whole circuit, and the number of those casts which represents in how many ways the favourable result can occur, and compare that number to the rest of the circuit, and according to that proportion should the mutual wagers be laid so that one may contend on equal terms.

This is the first attempt to circumscribe random events, such as the throw of a dice, with mathematics. In it, the 'circuit' Cardano refers to is a round of a game. He assumes a game with well-made, cubicle dice, which don't change their shape over time, because implicitly he's saying that favourable faces of each die are as likely to turn up as the unfavourable faces. This isn't true in all games: imagine an astragalus, with an uneven organic shape. However, it only takes a little tuning of Cardano's definition to make it handle this general case: to find the probability of a favourable outcome (or any outcome), look at a series of n outcomes, take the number of times that the favourable outcome comes up, and divide it by n. For a game with perfect die, this is the same as Cardano's definition.

Despite establishing probability as mathematics and declaring he had 'discovered the reason for a thousand astounding facts', Cardano understood the theory's limits, acknowledging: 'these facts contribute a great deal to understanding but hardly anything to practical play'. This hard-won truth is a valuable insight from a man who had experienced so many twists and turns of fate. Cardano's life itself is a study in uncertain and unpredictable events, and it boggles the mind to consider what sort of reasoning system would allow one to figure a path from his ignoble birth to his eventual success and ultimate downfall. Rusticated to Rome in 1570, and having lost everything (career, fortune, reputation and family), in one last flourish he publicly predicted the date and time of his own death on 21 September 1576. He then ensured the outcome by drinking a glass of poisoned wine.

The usual way of describing probability theory of the kind Cardano articulated is to call it a *frequentist* view of probability. This is because the ratio of winning rounds to played rounds in a well-defined game can be thought of as a kind of frequency of winning. However, the word *frequency* implies a regularity to the universe that simply isn't there. While an archaic meaning of 'frequency' derives from the Latin *frequentia*, meaning 'an assembling in great numbers, a crowding; crowd, multitude, throng', the modern interpretation is related to the Latin *frequens*, meaning 'often, regular, repeated', in the sense of the swaying of a pendulum or the vibrations of a guitar string. The implied certainty of probabilistic calculations is undue, since random things are, by definition, not regular. A less suggestive term is to call the ratio of wins to rounds a *statistic*. That term means precisely what is being considered in these ratios, in that a statistic is a fact taken from a large number of observations. Cardano's ratio implies observing past rounds and taking a ratio of outcomes as a statistic.

The first lesson in seeing that probabilities often aren't what we think they are is to realize that we often talk about the probabilities of things that have never happened before, and not happened yet. We will talk about the probability of one team winning a football game against another, when those two teams have never faced one another before. We will talk about the probability of a car collision on a certain street corner, when the two cars that might collide have never passed that corner at that same time before. We will talk about the probability of an unborn child committing a crime, based on that child's forebears and circumstance, when the experiences of that child's lifetime are yet to happen. We talk about the probability of recidivism. We talk about the probability that a yet-to-be-invented technology will take a person's job. Each of these events has never happened before in quite the same way, and are yet to happen. This confounds the idea of probabilities as a projection of past statistics of well-defined games into future rounds, which Cardano described and which his theory of probability fits. This disconnect between the frequentist idea of probability and the broader use of the concept is the reason that American logician and philosopher Charles Sanders Peirce in 1910 introduced another way of interpreting probabilities. Peirce thought probabilities were less like frequencies or statistics, and more like *propensities*.[7] Making a distinction between statistics and propensities makes clear the hidden heuristic that is assumed in all probabilistic reasoning. I call it *the statistic heuristic*: the assumption that *the statistics of some past events reliably indicate the propensity of some future events.*

The mathematical laws of probability come from situations, like well-defined games, where statistics of past events can be utterly relied upon to predict future events. Since they are ratios of the kind Cardano defined, probabilities must always be between zero and one, as they are a number of possible outcomes (*events*) divided by the number of all possible outcomes (the size of the *event space*). For instance, if in a game with two die you can win with any roll that generates a seven, the probability is the number of ways to get a seven (there are six ways) divided by the total number of dice rolls (there are $6*6 = 36$, so the probability of a seven is 6/36, or 1/6). The probability of *any* of the events in the event space occurring (the probability of *any* dice roll) is by definition one (all the 36 dice rolls divided by 36). Reasoning from the size of these 'spaces', the probability of an event *not* occurring is always one minus its probability of occurring. The probability of not rolling a seven is $(36 - 6)/36$, or 5/6.

Only slightly less obvious is the fact that the probability of one event or another event occurring is the sum of their probabilities, minus the probability of them occurring at the same time.[8] A Venn diagram can help to make this clear (see Figure 3.1).

The area of the white circle is 1, because it's the probability of any event at all (out of the universe of possible 'atomic' events) happening. A and B are other events, and we calculate probabilities by considering the sizes of areas in this figure (the number of events in each subspace of the event space). Therefore, the probability of A or B is the sum of the two circular areas, minus the almond-shaped overlap to avoid counting it twice, thus giving the formula shown. This almond-shaped area is called the joint probability of A and B, P(A and B). For instance, consider the probability of getting a 6 on one of the dice in a dice roll. The event A is one die rolling a 6 (which happens 1/6 of the time), and the event B is the other die rolling a 6 (which also happens 1/6 of the time). The event of both dice rolling 6 is P(A and B), which only happens one way, and thus 1/36 rolls. So the probability of rolling a 6 on one die is (1/6) + (1/6) – (1/36) or 11/36. Taking out the (1/36) avoids counting boxcars (two 6s) twice.

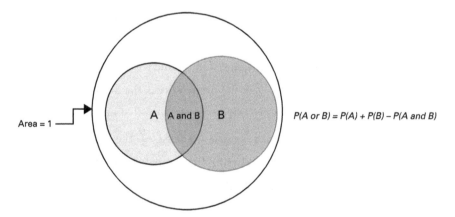

FIGURE 3.1 *Probability theory relates the chance of two things occurring together to the chance of either of them occurring by adding and subtracting areas whose sizes are assumed to represent the range of things that might happen.*

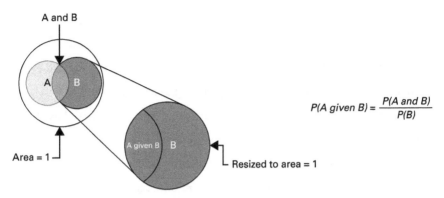

FIGURE 3.2 *Since it is all based on the size of 'event spaces', probability theory translates the chance of one thing happening given that another has happened via 'zooming in', and dividing to rescale the space that represents everything that might happen.*

This leads to the final, fundamental, most abstract and most important of the capital T truths of probability. A little staring at Figure 3.2 should make it clear.

Let's consider A to be the event that one die turns up the side with one dot, and B to be the event that the other die turns up its one-dotted side, as well (snake-eyes). What the figure is showing is that once we roll the first dice and see that its one-dotted side is face up, that event (which we'll say is event B), along with any remaining uncertainties in the world (the fall of the other die), becomes the entire universe of possibilities, resulting in a dramatic re-sizing of the event space.

This is because there are only six uncertain things left to happen (one of the six sides of the other die has to turn up). Thus, we zoom in, and rescale B to be the entire, new event space, which has to be of size one. That means that the almond-shaped portion gets zoomed by the same factor. We call this the conditional probability of event A *given* event B, P(A given B) or (A/B). This is given by the size of the almond-shaped area 'zoomed in', since that zoomed in area is a fraction of the new event space, B, which is zoomed to size one, since it is the new event space. The probability of both dice showing one, P(A and B) is 1/36 (there is only one way to roll snake eyes). The probability of one of the dice rolling a one is 1/6. Therefore, the probability of snake eyes, given that one dice has already turned up one, is the obvious value (1/36)/(1/6) = (1/6). This 'zoom' rescaling is at the heart of all reasoning that's based on probability theory, and it all comes down to the ability to completely enumerate the event space, to *know* all the atoms of what might happen in an uncertain future. This is easy in a dice game, as there are only six faces on each die. It's even easy for a game with thousands or millions of dice; you just have to do the calculations that are a bit more involved. Where it gets hard is in situations where it's difficult to find all the necessary atoms to describe what might happen in the future. In that case, the problem of finding the right atoms is just like the knowledge acquisition problem that made expert systems so difficult to perfect.

The analogy to expert systems becomes even stronger when one realizes that conditional probabilities are really just rules, precisely like those used in MYCIN. For instance, *P(A/B)* is precisely a statement of the rule:

If B *then* A, with heuristic uncertainty factor *P(A/B)*

The only addition to the constructs used in MYCIN is that the heuristic uncertainty factor of *P(A/B)* is assumed to be a number that follows the laws of probability. Probability offers a mathematically based way of manipulating and combining heuristic certainty factors when considering a chain of such rules, as we go through any process of reasoning, such as reasoning-as-search.

This is precisely how probabilistic reasoning occurs in many of the algorithmic systems being employed today. For instance, probabilistic reasoning is at the heart of algorithms that label images, make search engine suggestions, determine ad placements in social media feeds, and suggest mates on dating sites. In each case, reasoning from big data statistics (about your online profile, and those of many other people) are determining probabilities that are used to derive a desirable outcome. But most of these algorithms also involve an additional probability rule, which was furnished in 1761 by London Presbyterian minister Thomas Bayes.

Little is known about Thomas Bayes other than he was a Fellow of the Royal Society and he wrote two papers on mathematics, one of which, *Essay Towards Solving a Problem in the Doctrine of Chances* (published after his death in 1761), laid out the final foundational rule of modern probability theory. Bayes' rule follows trivially from the event-size-and-zoom-based arguments presented below, as shown in Figure 3.3.

$P (A \text{ and } B) = P (A \text{ given } B) \, P (B)$

$= P (B \text{ and } A) = P (B \text{ given } A) \, P (A)$

$P (A \text{ given } B) \, P (B) = P (B \text{ given } A) \, P (A)$

$P(A \text{ given } B) = \dfrac{P(B \text{ given } A) P(A)}{P(B)}$

The basis for Bayes' rule is that you can zoom on either A or B to make new event spaces. In dice games, this leads to usually quite trivial conclusions.

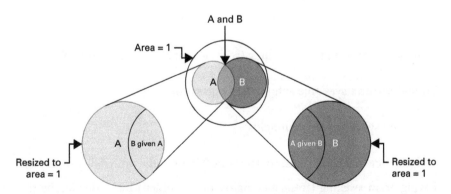

FIGURE 3.3 *Bayes' rule can seem almost mystical, with talk of prior and posterior 'belief', but actually it's just a calculation based on zooming and rescaling two different ways.*

For instance, the probability that the first dice shows 6, given that the other shows 1, is the probability that the second dice shows 1, given that the first shows 6 (this is simply 1/6), times the probability of the first dice showing 6 (this is also 1/6), divided by the probability that the second dice shows 1 (again, 1/6). That's Bayes' rule, which in this example yields 1/6.

In most simple and well-defined games, Bayes' rule is pretty banal. It only becomes interesting when we start applying it to events in the wider world, outside well-defined games of chance; for instance, in algorithms that use conditional probabilities as rules, like those from MYCIN. In these situations, the kind of reasoning Bayes' rule allows is the most important for algorithms, particularly those that deal with human data.

The neat thing about Bayes' rule for algorithms is that it allows you to do reasoning-as-search, in *both* directions. If you have a rule

If B *then* A, with heuristic uncertainty factor $P(A|B)$

Bayes' rule automatically gives you the rule

If A *then* B, with heuristic uncertainty factor $P(B|A)$

along with a calculation to get the heuristic uncertainty factor that is 'correct' for this new rule (under the laws and assumptions of probability theory).

For instance, consider the rule

If meningitis *then* brain swelling (with heuristic certainty factor 0.9)

From this rule, Bayes' rule automatically gives you

If brain swelling *then* meningitis

with the new heuristic certainty factor of 0.9 times the probability of anyone having brain swelling (from meningitis, or any other cause), divided by the probability of anyone having meningitis at all, regardless of whether their brain has swollen.

How does this apply to human data? Consider an analogy to the route finding that was discussed previously. In a satnav, Bayes' rule is sort of like being able to figure out where you came from by looking at your destination. More precisely, if you find yourself at a destination, it gives you a way to calculate the heuristic uncertainty factor for any given place you may have come from. In terms of the statistic heuristic, it allows you to reason from propensities (which you calculated based on the statistics of past events), back to the events that may have *caused* things that you have actually observed. Bayes' rule allows you to apply probabilistic reasoning from the present back to the past.

In human problems, this implies, for instance, that you could figure out the probability of a person's internal mindset (the analogous point of origin in their map of thoughts) based on what you've observed them doing. For instance, one could reason backwards from a social media user's presidential approval to whether they are disgruntled from being out of work. All you need is a model of how reasoning *forward* (from disgruntlement to presidential approval) takes place, with appropriate heuristic certainty factors along the relevant chain of rules.

Of course, this relies on two assumptions. The first assumption is that you can get a MYCIN-like model of that person's *forward* reasoning process (from being out of work to approving of a president, for instance). As we know from the history of expert systems, in all but the simplest cases, such models of human reasoning are hard to come by, at least without brittleness. The second assumption is that the probabilities (heuristic uncertainty factors) in that model are like the probabilities in Cardano's well-defined games, with their assumption of enumerable event spaces that you can 'size' and 'zoom' to make the maths make sense. These two assumptions aren't unrelated. They are both assumptions that the model of the problem being addressed contains the appropriate 'atoms' (which, in probability theory, would be atomic events, the 'A' and 'B' in the Venn diagrams). The final assumption is that the heuristic uncertainty factors (the probabilities) are in some sense 'correct'.

Since most of the algorithms operating in people's lives aren't dealing with well-defined games of chance, the probabilities they use can't really be viewed as frequencies. Many of them don't even derive from the statistic heuristic (from the analysis of past statistics). Instead, they are subjectively assigned (usually by the algorithm's creators). One point of view holds this as perfectly reasonable. In particular, Bayesian reasoning is often related to a *subjectivist* view of probability, which posits that probabilities shouldn't be thought of as frequencies at all, but as subjective *beliefs*. This is the reason that the mathematical terms in Bayes' rule are often called *beliefs*; P(B|A) is called 'the prior *belief*' and P(B|A) is called the 'posterior *belief*'. This language reflects the idea that if people aren't doing probabilistic calculations to cope with the uncertainties of the world, they should be, as it's the most rational way to *compute* beliefs. Of course, this begs the question, if the probabilities aren't Cardano ratios, why is maths that comes directly from those ratios, and their behaviour in those Venn diagrams, the most rational way to process them? Isn't this just a heuristic? And is it one that people actually use?

Faith in the rationality of probabilistic calculations comes from the commonplace belief that there *must* be some set of atoms that provides an adequate description for any uncertain situation (the weather tomorrow, the likelihood of getting cancer, the success of an IVF treatment). If you know all those atoms, you can calculate the areas of the circles in those Venn diagrams, and then all the math of probability theory follows. Belief in this theoretical set of atoms is belief that uncertainties exist *out there in the world* and if we just have enough information (data) they can be captured and enumerated in a technical frame. All we have to do is find the right frame and the right atoms. However, uncertainty isn't out there in the world; it is *a state of mind*. Things themselves aren't uncertain; it is people who are uncertain about the things. Will Brexit be good or bad? *We* simply don't know. We don't know how to find the atoms, the things to measure and calculate with, that will answer that question, either. It's unclear that such atoms even exist. But the uncertainty does exist, in our own minds. Viewed this way, we have to ask what the atoms of uncertainty might be within our minds? And, what's more, given the only nebulous tie between the uncertainties of the real world and those of Cardano's well-defined games, we also have to ask whether humans process those atoms probabilistically at all.

In 2005 the economists David Lane and Robert Maxfield published a paper[9] that considered a taxonomy of how uncertainty might exist as a part of human thought, rather than as some external reality. To demonstrate Lane and Maxfield's theory, let's consider an ill-described, real-world 'dice game' that many of us have played: seeing the results of a home pregnancy test.

Imagine that a + appears in the window of the test stick. That does not mean with certainty that the person doing the test is in fact pregnant, because there are unreliable elements in the test: it could be a false positive. If you have a look at the test instructions, it will report (in some form, probably a table) four IF/THEN rules, with uncertainty factors

If + *then* pregnant with P(pregnant|+)

If − *then* pregnant with P(pregnant|−)

If + *then* not pregnant with P(not pregnant|+)

If − *then* not pregnant with P(not pregnant|−)

where the four P values are probabilities. This situation reflects what Lane and Maxfield call *truth uncertainty*, where there is a clear true or false outcome in the case of a well-understood question or a well-posed problem. In this case, it is entirely appropriate to use the statistic heuristic, and that is in fact precisely what the probabilities in the rules above reflect. In the formulation of those rules and probabilities, a large population of women were tested, and Cardano's ratios were computed from the statistics derived for those women, with their pluses and minuses, pregnancies and not pregnancies. The statistic heuristic applies here. These past statistics clearly and reliably indicate the propensities of future events, like the event of a false positive when a '+' appears in the little window.

But, consider a second scenario, with the same + appearing in the test's little window but, in this case, you have lost the instructions and you can't remember for the life of you whether + means pregnant or not pregnant. As many of us will have experienced, your desire for the test to indicate pregnancy is liable to vary wildly based on your situation at the time. That situational desire, along with a host of other predispositions, are liable to colour how you remember or misremember the meaning of the + symbol. This is what Lane and Maxfield call *semantic uncertainty*, uncertainty about the meaning of symbols.

In this case, if one were to use probabilistic thinking, relying on the statistic heuristic, one could simply accept an average of raw statistics from a population of people remembering one way or the other about a pregnancy test that returns a + as a probability, a measure of their own uncertainty. At first sight, this approach seems unlikely to provide any meaningful results, since the predispositions of this crowd of people are likely to vary in critical ways (e.g. university students tend not to want to get pregnant while middle-aged couples do, etc.). So, one would have to devise a model, possibly a complex one, of how people remember and forget such things, perhaps including biases based on a user profile. One could then go on to infer the heuristic uncertainty factors from this model and employ probabilistic algorithms (possibly using Bayesian reasoning) to infer your particular mindset and help you determine the probabilities of what a + means. Of course, such models are liable to suffer from brittleness, since we know that conditional probabilities are simply rules. This is the hidden reality of using probabilistic systems for modelling human uncertainty: they have exactly the same modelling challenges as expert systems.

Finally, there may be an outlandish situation where neither a + nor a − appears in the window, but instead you see a skull and crossbones! This is a completely unforeseen circumstance, and it is what Lane and Maxfield called *ontological uncertainty*: uncertainty about the things that actually exist in the world. Perhaps the pregnancy test is a practical joke set-up by mean friends, perhaps it has malfunctioned in some way not documented in its instructions, or perhaps it isn't a pregnancy test at all. Regardless, what you are seeing represents a completely unforeseen symbol, something outside the expected event space, representing a break from the atoms of the universe, a completely unforeseen atom, a place for any reasoning system to suffer a brittle break.

However, while a shocked reaction might occur when a death's head appears in your home pregnancy test, human beings generally won't suffer a brittle break in their ability to reason under such unforeseen circumstances, just like real-world experts treating blood infections don't suffer the brittle failures of expert systems like MYCIN, and just like people at large don't suffer reasoning failures when faced with ontological uncertainty in their day-to-day lives.

The algorithms in most AI, from those that determine your Facebook newsfeed to those that offer you date matches or jobs, to those that determine your health premiums or pension plan, treat all uncertainty with probability theory. But that theory originates from a gambler's speculations, created for well-defined games of chance. What's more, relying as they do on the statistic heuristic, they assume that past statistics can predict future propensities. That assumption clearly isn't always true for real-world uncertainties (particularly semantic and ontological uncertainties) that people have to deal with every time they encounter a situation they've never seen before, from a novel failure of new technology, to a person from a previously unencountered culture.

Probability theory isn't some magic formula that can predict the future like the casting of lots or the toss of a die. Quantifying the future by reducing complex human problems into neat frames filled with assumed atoms like some well-circumscribed game is just as hard as creating expert systems. It's just that the problems of brittleness and complexity that exist in probabilistic systems are veiled in a fog of mathematics, and the commercial potential of analysing freely available big data. These factors also hide additional limitations in probability-based reasoning. To what extent can we rely on the past events to tell us what the future is like? What atoms should we use to divine what post-Brexit Britain will look like?

That's not to say probability theory isn't an incredibly useful modelling tool in discrete challenges, from aircraft-wing failure rates, to determining risk factors for cancer, to evaluating the effects of new technologies on the climate, and much more. Probabilistic analyses are useful so long as everyone understands the frames and atoms being used, and the limitations of these representations. But we need to beware our blind faith in these models when applied to complex human interactions by lightning speed algorithms in human-centred areas such as economics, sociology, health and media – particularly when many of the algorithms in question are driven by a desire for power, or profit. As Mickey said, 'A bookie sets the odds to get what he needs ... And trust me, the bettors have no idea about the probabilities.'

4

Scientific Pride and Prejudice

50,000,000 Elvis fans can't be wrong.
Album cover, spotted at Floyd's Live Catfish, 1984

Given the cold computational underpinning of AI, there is a widespread assumption that algorithmic decision-making is objective and without bias. With big data analysis, this assumption has become married to the 'wisdom of crowds'. Like those Elvis fans, there is a feeling that a great mass of people (or conclusions based on great masses of people) can't be wrong, if unbiased algorithms are mining their statistics. Such population-based conclusions can only cause society to positively evolve.

In many areas of society – policing, defence, law, education, health, childcare, transport and the media – this implicit belief has led to billions being invested in research and development for the application of big data analytics (US$20–30 billion in 2017, according to McKinsey[1]). In many cases, these programs are about understanding the propensities of individual people, based on the statistics gathered from great masses of people in the past. In the US, a program called Correctional Offender Management Profiling for Alternative Sanctions (Compas) has been used to inform the decisions of judges when assessing the likelihood of defendants reoffending, by comparing the big data of many past defendants to features of the individual facing time behind bars.[2] The Los Angeles Police Department worked with data scientists at UCLA and Santa Clara University to develop PredPol, a predictive policing program that maps out 'crime hotspots' where police should concentrate their presence, patrols, intelligence-gathering exercises and other efforts to prevent crime from happening, because according to Modesto Police Chief Galen Carroll, 'burglars and thieves work in a mathematical way, whether they know it or not'.[3] In each case, it's assumed that the evaluation of data about what *some* people have done in the past can predict the propensities of what *other* people will do in the future. All the analysis involved is based on features of those people, but it is assumed that any biases, for instance those based on the features of race, religion, gender or socio-economic factors, can be factored out by unbiased computations.

But those computations look biased. An investigation by ProPublica showed the Compas program returned results heavily biased against black defendants (45 per cent to 24 per cent for white defendants).[4] A study by the Human Rights Data Analysis Group (HRDAG) demonstrated how the PredPol programme became stuck in feedback loops over-policing black and brown neighbourhoods.[5] In addition, civil rights organizations, including the American Civil Liberties Union (ACLU), are starting to take up issues in areas such as housing or hiring practices, trying to pass city-level policies requiring police to disclose any technology they adopt, including the use of AIs. As Virginia Eubanks, the author of *Automating Inequality*,[6] points out, if there are holes in the data or the data set is incomplete or overly focused on one group, then it will not only reflect societal biases, but amplify them. More than that, the very nature of algorithmic reasoning about people is always based on computation over simplified features, drawing on the statistic heuristic, and those computations will always contain biases. People pick the features; it's extremely difficult for those people to avoid biases in their selection, and all feature-based models of complex phenomena contain biases. Therefore, the amplification Eubanks suggests is not just about biases in data, it's about the whole presumption of algorithmic understanding of complex human issues.

Algorithmic bias is certainly a huge and hidden civil rights issue, because it will not be the wealthy who will have their job or loan applications assessed by a computer (or their child care, mortgage or medical insurance). It is not the white-collar criminal who will be evaluated en masse by an algorithm for parole, or white-collar suburbs that will be targeted as areas that must be patrolled by police cars and surveillance in a search for potential *financial* crimes. It is highly likely that more privileged groups will continue to receive the services of real people, while everyone else will have to contend with algorithmic reasoning from big data to make big decisions in their lives. This isn't the only reason to be concerned with our growing algorithmic infrastructure. Nor is it because machine learning from simplifying features risks perpetuating stereotypes and discrimination, or even because of the lack of diversity in tech firms, or the lack of transparency in private companies offering AI solutions to civic challenges (although all of these are enormous social challenges in themselves). At a fundamental level, it is because flawed, historical philosophies underpin the entire algorithmic endeavour, and we need to re-examine them urgently. This examination will involve some soul searching, because some of the ideas involved are those that scientists, like me, hold most dear.

When I was growing up in Alabama, belief in Darwin's theory of evolution was *the* identity issue for anyone opposed to the fanatical religious fervour of the American South. Even decades after I completed my primary education, in 1995, 2001 and 2005 Alabama's Board of Education repeatedly voted to place stickers on biology textbooks instructing high-school students that evolution was a 'controversial theory' and that 'any statement about life's origins should be considered as theory, not fact'. When I was in elementary school in the early 1970s, there was no need for such stickers on textbooks. Most teachers, and in fact society at large, made things clear enough, particularly with regard to religion. Racism was similarly endorsed by authority figures in any young white Alabamian's life. Anglo-Protestantism's moral and civic superiority – a phenomenon with a centuries-long tradition that incorporated both anti-Catholic and anti-Semitic prejudice – was a tacit assumption, and barely hidden from view. In the years before I reached school age, it wasn't hidden at all. Intimidation and dehumanization of other minority groups took many forms, but it was the government of Birmingham's brutal response to the Children's Crusade, which took place a few days before my birth in May 1963, that finally caught the world's attention.

Over a thousand African-American school children skipped school to join this protest, an attempt to march to City Hall to speak to Birmingham's mayor about segregation. In response, Eugene 'Bull' Connor unleashed attack dogs and high-pressure fire hoses on the protestors, and hundreds of children were jailed. All of this was broadcast on national television, and the day after I was born, civil rights leaders and Birmingham business people came to an agreement, stopping the protests (and, more pointedly, the international embarrassment), and allowing African-Americans to dine, try on clothes, drink from water fountains and use restrooms in the same places as their white countrymen. Four months later, Birmingham's 16th Street Baptist Church, the rallying point for the children's protest that led to this agreement, was bombed, injuring twenty-two worshippers, and killing four black schoolgirls.

But by the time I reached elementary school, the protests were largely over; the civil rights movement was ostensibly victorious, at least as a matter of law. In response to legally mandated desegregation orders, black kids from a poor area of the Birmingham outskirts were bussed to the all-white elementary school I attended, but, while the law appeared to have settled the race issue, my school remained a place of obvious division and conflict.

At the time, I was a bullied, nerdy kid, and given the racial prejudice I'd grown up around, I was afraid of the new kids from Airport Heights, a slum at the end of Birmingham's runway. But to my surprise they didn't bully me at all. They barely even noticed me, as they had more important things to worry about. In fact, once bussing started, the usual white bullies laid off me a bit, and focused most of their attention on the black kids. One of these kids was Loretha Jackson, a tall, lanky, tough girl. She was a good student, but much of her energy was taken up defending the smaller black kids from the bullies. She was in fights all the time, and she could whoop the ass of any bully that said anything to her or to one of her friends that she thought wasn't Sunday-go-to-meeting polite.

Plenty of impolite things got said in that classroom, but Mrs Grady never seemed to notice the white kids who uttered a racial slur or pushed some small black kid to start a fight. She only saw the transgressions of Loretha, who got more smacks from Mrs Grady's thick wooden paddle than any other kid. The paddling went on outside the door while the rest of us waited and listened to the sharp loud strikes. Loretha held her head high when led back in by Mrs Grady, though there were silent tears. Even after these beatings, she politely raised her hand high to answer questions, while Mrs Grady relentlessly ignored her.

The paddlings weren't the worst thing, as I recall. On a day when Loretha came to school with a horrible, hacking cough, the kind that made me think of the hospital where my grandmother died, Mrs Grady made her eat a finger-scoop of Mentholatum, the smelly petroleum jelly cold cure that my mom would sometimes rub on my congested chest. Loretha had to run out to throw up, and sit alone all day in the nurse's office, because her parents couldn't get the time off work to fetch her home.

Around the same time, a lunchtime bully pushed me over a fence chain, and I fell on my backside pretty hard. Humiliated and hurt, I retreated to the back of the lunch line with the black kids and a few other nerdy bully targets. I'd never before spoken with an African-American peer, until Loretha, who happened to be in front of me in line, turned and said, 'You always go 'round lookin' at your feet'. She must have been looking directly at the top of my head, because what she said was true, I always walked with my eyes down, as it felt safer. When I looked up, she told me, 'If you don't start holding your head up, people gonna beat you down your whole life'.

That is one of the most important pieces of advice I've ever received, and I'm thankful for it to this day. Before it, I had no idea that this physical posture affected not only the perceptions of others, but my perceptions of myself. The next time I was bullied, I pushed back, and my assailant fell hard and flat on the concrete sidewalk. It was universally declared that I 'won the fight', and after three years of almost constant bullying the harassment finally stopped.

I tell this story not to demonstrate my personal awakening or my prowess in the playground, but because it is important to acknowledge the ugliness of real-world prejudice perpetuated by people against each other (even on and among children) and it is an ugliness that we do not want to unwittingly codify into our global digital infrastructure. With its rational arguments and methodical observations, experimentation and proofs, the scientific endeavour has done much to dissipate the worst aspects of racism, bigotry and religious intolerance and move the world onto a more egalitarian footing. It is a big part of the reason I became a scientist as, in many ways, it appeared a safe haven from the religiosity and prejudice I grew up around.

Why did I select science as the belief system around which I built my identity? One motivation was surely that I was a natural-born science geek, but another reason that is firmly cemented in my mind is a film I watched right around the time Loretha gave me that life-changing advice. The battle between science and religion is at the heart of the gripping 1960 Hollywood classic *Inherit the Wind*, which I saw for the first time on WTCG, Ted Turner's 'superstation' in Atlanta. The film is a dramatized version of the 1925 Scopes 'Monkey' Trial, in which John T. Scopes, an elementary school teacher in Tennessee, was arrested for teaching Darwin's theory of evolution. For me the film fit right in with Mrs Grady's illegal school prayers, rants against Yankee godlessness and condemnation of our science teacher, who was teaching us about evolution at the time.

Scopes became the centre of a national political drama, reported on by satirist and journalist H. L. Mencken, prosecuted by the evangelical, populist politician Williams Jennings Bryan, and defended by famous lawyer and agnostic Clarence Darrow. In the real world, the triumph of religion over reason in the Scopes trial was a foregone conclusion in conservative Dayton, Tennessee. Scopes was found guilty and fined $100, which was later overturned on appeal. But the broader judgment in the court of public opinion was a resounding success for Darwin and Darrow, and is one of the great liberal milestones of twentieth-century America.

Just as his case seemed hopelessly lost, Darrow had the idea of inviting Bryan to take the witness stand, whereupon he grilled him on a series of biblical events that could be seen as irrational, unreal or both. Bryan was caught between defending the literal truth of the whale swallowing Jonah and admitting that some things in the Scriptures might need alternative, rational interpretations, such as the number of days during which the Earth had been created. As the cross-examination continued, Bryan seemed flustered, inconsistent and even ridiculous, and Mencken wrote that God had aimed at Darrow but hit Bryan instead. At the end of the trial, Darrow concluded with a rousing speech on the connection between ignorance and bigotry, which Spencer Tracy delivered nearly verbatim in the film:

Ignorance and fanaticism is ever-busy and needs feeding. Always it is feeding and gloating for more. After a while it is the setting of man against man, and creed against creed, until with flying banners and beating drums we are marching backwards to the glorious ages of the sixteenth century when bigots lighted faggots to burn the men who dared to bring any intelligence and enlightenment and culture to the human mind.

The speech moved me as a boy, and much of the film is consistent with the progressive values that most scientists of today recognize. However, the details of the Scopes case are less familiar and more shocking from a modern scientific standpoint.

The textbook from which Scopes was teaching his evolutionary lessons when he was arrested was George W. Hunter's 1914 *Civic Biology: Presented in Problems*, which was inspired by the work of Charles Benedict Davenport, who (with funds from the Carnegie Institution) founded the American Eugenics Records Office (ERO) in 1911. As its title suggests, *Civic Biology* did more than just discuss the origin of our species; it had a specific social agenda, explicitly dividing humankind into five distinct races, with European and American Caucasians conveniently and predictably at the top of the developmental tree. In addition, the book explicitly supports the eugenic ideas of the ERO, including the parasitism of unfit individuals on society, and the 'remedy' of killing or breeding them out.

This was a cutting-edge, 'scientific' schoolbook for children, and it was defended by some of the most progressive liberals of the time. It is easy in retrospect to call this a mistake; to say that back then rational people didn't anticipate the consequences of such ideas; and, that with a bit more knowledge, or a more informed scientific perspective, they'd have behaved differently and supported more modern values. But the reality is that there are assumptions in the common interpretation of Darwin's theory that lead inevitably to these sorts of conclusions, because the theory itself is strongly connected to Victorian ideas of social evolution and the moral, social and physical perfectibility of mankind. Those ideas, while perhaps initially benign, have absolutely no scientific foundation, and are all too easily connected to malignant and extant social biases – biases that are now re-emerging in algorithms.

In many ways, the originating context of Charles Darwin's theory is social, not biological, and derives from the work of his grandfather, Erasmus Darwin

(1731–1802). It was Erasmus Darwin who most famously suggested the idea that 'populations' inevitably evolve towards better states. He first presented the idea in his scientific poem 'The Temple of Nature', which was published in 1803, six years before Charles's birth, and half a century before the discovery of the key concepts of biological evolution. The poem is presented in four cantos which, in modern terms, move from the big bang, through the origins of life, the emergence of sexual reproduction, the development of the human mind, and finally to the development and perfection of society. The connection between evolution and the inevitable improvement of civilization was clearly Erasmus's main intent, as an earlier draft of the poem was called 'The Progress of Society'.

Erasmus was undoubtedly a progressive thinker in his time, taking radical positions opposing slavery and promoting the rights of women, but he was also a man of his age, steeped in the ideas and culture of the Georgian era. It was a period in which Britain was undergoing massive political upheaval, technological progress and social change. Mass migration to cities and new colonies was disrupting centuries of settled rural life. Britain was at war constantly and lost its thirteen American colonies in the Revolutionary War (1775–83). It also had a front row seat on the French Revolution (1792–1802) and became embroiled in the Napoleonic Wars (1803–15), whilst also fighting a rear-guard action in Ireland, putting down the Irish Rebellion of 1798. Religious evangelism and political radicalization were also on the rise, and feminism was an emerging phenomenon with Mary Wollstonecraft penning her ground-breaking work *A Vindication on the Rights of Women* (1792). All around there was an air of questioning and debate, and a prevailing belief in social evolution towards something better.

A contemporary philosopher who held similar beliefs to Erasmus Darwin was Wollstonecraft's husband, William Godwin. In 1793, he wrote the following about the perfectibility of mankind: 'perfectibility is one of the most unequivocal characteristics of the human species, so that the political as well as the intellectual state of man may be presumed to be in the course of progressive improvement'.

The romantic poet Percy Shelley drew on this idea when, in 1813, he wrote his first large poetic work, *Queen Mab*. It combined ideas from Godwin (who was Shelley's mentor and later became his father-in-law) with notions of democracy and proto-evolutionary thinking, likely gleaned from Darwin's 'Temple of Nature'. The result was a revolutionary work that became wildly popular and marked Shelley out as one of the most radical intellectuals of his time. *Queen Mab* suggested that the perfect society would not arise through the violent revolutions of the time, nor through old notions of established aristocracy and nobility, but through Rousseau-like individual freedom and natural evolution, leading to increasing numbers of virtuous men who would ultimately improve and perfect the world. It was a comforting idea in an era of profound uncertainty, violence, disruption and dislocation.

Furthermore, it was an idea that chimed perfectly with the spread of democracy in the late eighteenth and early nineteenth centuries. Although democracy was an ancient political idea, it only truly took root in England with the founding of the first Parliament of Great Britain in 1707. Democracy's emphasis on individual rights fit neatly with the 'priesthood of the individual' doctrine at the core of Protestantism, the official religion of the country since the sixteenth century, and which by the eighteenth century was a distinguishing aspect of English thought, in contrast to more collectivist, Catholic Europe. This emphasis on individualism also found an echo in the emerging academic discipline of economics. In 1776, Adam Smith published *An Inquiry into the Nature and Causes of the Wealth of Nations*, in which he wrote:

> It is not from the benevolence of the butcher, the brewer or the baker, that we expect our dinner, but from their regard to their own self-interest. We address ourselves, not to their humanity but to their self-love, and never talk to them of our own necessities but of their advantages.

Thus, one of the founding principles of economics is self-love, and what we now call Smith's 'Invisible Hand', the idea that societal good emerges not from attempts to control an economy, but from the actions of a *population of self-interested individuals*. Thus, individual action, self-improvement and self-love were seen as the motivating forces towards personal and social improvement in religion, politics, philosophy and economics.

The only trouble was the prevailing misery and poverty of the times did not reflect this evolutionary utopianism. And, the idea that mankind could work towards a perfect society on earth ran counter to traditional Christian thinking that held that man was innately sinful and the only way of overcoming the present misery was through religious salvation, and a paradise after death. Perhaps because of this, in 1798, curate and academic Thomas Malthus wrote *An Essay on the Principle of Population* in response to Godwin's theory that society and universal suffrage would lead towards a perfected world. In the essay, Malthus argued that humankind's improvement was bounded by a harsh reality: populations could only increase until they exhausted their food supplies, which resulted in poverty, and constrained the vast majority of people in a sub-perfect equilibrium of tolerable starvation. Malthus had an undeniable point, but ironically it was his idea of natural constraints and limitations that provided the necessary frame for Charles Darwin's biological theory.

Interpreting Malthus' essay in 1858, Charles Darwin – along with biologist and naturalist Alfred Russel Wallace who was developing similar ideas thousands of miles away in the Malay Archipelago – saw the constraint on resources not as a limit on advancement, but as the actual *cause* of evolutionary improvement. Both Darwin and Wallace realized that all living populations bred beyond the capacity of their environment, which caused some *weaker* population members to die without reproducing. This meant that stronger members survived and reproduced, and passed on the traits that had made them successful. The result, therefore, was not a limiting equilibrium, but a continual progression of population improvements not unlike the selective breeding practised by farmers and horticulturalists for millennia. Thus, they named the phenomenon *natural selection*.

Darwin and Wallace realized that under the inevitable action of natural selection, instead of heading towards the miserable, Malthusian equilibrium, limited resources actually caused populations to evolve their features, and thus themselves. Neither had any idea that they had both come to the same conclusion, until Darwin received Wallace's papers for review. Thus, early papers on evolution were published under Darwin and Wallace's names, but the most memorable statement of the theory was Darwin's thanks to his revolutionary book *The Origin of Species*, published in 1859.

The Wallace/Darwin synchronicity is not surprising given the prevailing zeitgeist of evolutionary utopianism, particularly given that the keystone idea, that of *variation*, which allowed Darwin and Wallace to make the leap beyond Malthus, was also in the wind at the time. Thirteen years before the publication of *Origin*, Belgian statistician and sociologist Adolphe Quetelet published *Letters addressed to H. R. H. Gotha, the grand duke of Saxe Coburg on the Theory of Probabilities as Applied and to the Moral and Political Sciences*. This work addressed 'moral and political sciences' by examining the distribution of the chest measurements of 5,732 Scottish soldiers. Quetelet's idea was that the variations in the chest sizes of these men illustrated deviations from a single *ideal* soldier. He imagined that the soldiers were reproductions of an ideal man, copied with 'considerable probable error', in particular 'deformity by a host of accidental causes'. Deformities, in this sense, could make a man have a weedy lack of girth, or an unnecessary bulk around his ribcage, when compared to the ideal. For Quetelet 'the average man' (a phrase he invented) was an archetype, an idealization, like a Roman statue of a Gladiator, and deviations from this average indicated imperfections, of both physical and moral kinds:

If the average man were completely determined, we might ... consider him as the type of perfection; and everything differing from his proportions or condition, would constitute deformity and disease; everything found dissimilar, not only as regarded proportion or form, but as exceeding the observed limits, would constitute a monstrosity.

Variance and natural selection were the key to Darwin and Wallace's innovation. Taken together, they suggest the complexity and diversity inherent in biological life. But when coupled to ideas about perfectibility and limited resources, they can take on more sinister connotations, which, along with the revolution caused by Darwin's theory, have had their own ongoing historical impact. Where there is perfection, there must by default be imperfection; and, if there are limited resources, then how they are deployed in the pursuit of perfection becomes a pressing social consideration. No wonder, then, that the full title of Darwin's famous book was *On the Origin of Species by Means of Natural Selection, or the Preservation of Favoured Races in the Struggle for Life.*

If you are going to engineer society towards perfection you need some sort of reliable method of *measuring* what is ideal and what is not. Thus, to prove his theory of deviation from the ideal, average man, Quetelet needed to show that the size of the soldier's chests were distributed in such a way that reflected *natural* errors. As an idea of what a natural error was, he drew on ideas that came from astronomy, which, despite ties to science that is as far away from human realities as the stars are from Earth, are still in use for similar purposes today.

The scientific need to understand natural error distributions dates back to Galileo's *Dialogue Concerning the Two Chief Systems of the World—Ptolemaic and Copernican* (1632), where he observed that human errors in measuring the physical world required a formal, scientific treatment. He commented that while there is only one true value for the distance from the centre of the Earth to a star (for instance) errors from faulty instruments and fallible human observers were inevitable in the process of measuring that distance.

Astronomers in the time of Galileo had various procedures for managing errors in the quantities they measured. They certainly all took multiple measurements, and observed that the measurements were often different when their models of the universe said they should be the same. In such cases, they may have taken the median of the values they measured (the measure that fell in the middle of all the measures when they were ordered smallest to largest). They may have simply thrown out measurements that they subjectively found suspect. Given that we now live in a world awash in the statistic heuristic, it may seem a strange fact, but in the time of Galileo, the idea of *averaging* several, error-fraught measures to get the 'best answer' was not an automatic assumption. For this idea of averaging over errors to become dominant, it needed probability theory.

Building on the works of Cardano, Fermat and Pascal, Swiss mathematician Jacob Bernoulli (1655–1705) determined a general formula for the probability of k wins in n rounds of a game of dice (assuming that the probability of winning any one round is a constant p). This number is given by an expression known as the *binomial distribution*. This distribution, which is based on combinatoric calculations very much like those used by Ramon Llull, may be the first probability distribution anyone bothered to write down or draw. If one plots the probability *versus* k, it looks like the diagram in Figure 4.1.

This distribution is really useful, as it generates some convenient conclusions, like the famous 'Rule of Three', which states that if you play a game and you don't lose in n rounds, then you can be pretty confident that the probability of losing in future rounds is $3/n$ or less. Students of statistics would learn this rule for hundreds of years after Bernoulli. It's an illustration of one of the great advantages of calculations like this: they provide easy rules for understanding complex things.

But when simple rules like this are applied to complex human systems rather than games of dice or measurements between physical objects, it's all too easy for the computational conveniences to provide results that confirm

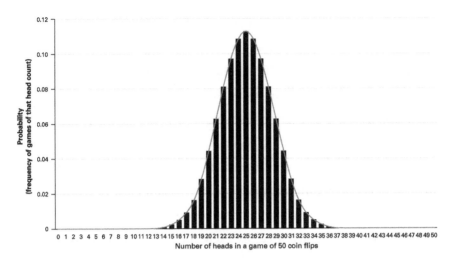

Figure 4.1 *An example binomial distribution, showing the probability p of k heads out of n = 50 coin flips.*

pre-existing beliefs. Take, for instance, the Dutch mathematician Willem 's Gravesande, who in 1712 attempted to prove the existence of God by using binomial statistics and big data. Gravesande did this by considering whether God was manipulating the great gender coin toss: whether any given baby would be a girl or a boy. He tested the hypothesis that male births and female births are simply the result of pure chance, rather than divine order, by analysing the records of births in London from 1629 to 1710. He reasoned that if one were to assume that the child's sex was a random event, like the flip of a fair coin in a game of chance, maths like those in the binomial distribution should determine the probability of the facts observed in the London birth data, and the observed data should nicely fit a few of the columns in a figure like the one in Figure 4.1.

Gravesande's computations involved combinatorial explosions that strained the boundaries of what could be computed, but he overcame this problem by inventing clever approximations that indicated the binomial probability of the observed baby genders in the data was (approximately) 0.00000000000000000 000000000000000000000000001. Gravesande felt that this was too improbable an event, and thus the sex of a child couldn't be a random event. The maths clearly showed that God played a role in determining the sex of children in some non-random, divine way. If you assume otherwise, he reasoned, you have to ask how such a low probability event could have ever occurred.

There are several plausible explanations. For instance, consider that home births would remain common in London until the twentieth century, with 80 per cent of children born at home until 1920. Thus, record keeping on births was poor in the eighteenth century and biased towards those of better means. With the differing social and legal statuses of boys and girls (particularly with regard to inheritance law), it seems likely the figures can't be trusted for accuracy. Two of every three children died before their fifth birthday in London at that time, and it is impossible to know if female infanticide, a commonplace practice amongst many impoverished people throughout world history, was a factor. The data might, therefore, contain significant socially motivated bias, rather than statistical signs of divine intervention.

The situation is like many others involving statistical analysis to this day, including those being conducted algorithmically in our day-to-day lives. Gravesande thought he was examining one question, when he was actually examining another. He thought he was looking at the number of girl and boy babies being born in London, when actually he was looking at what *the records showed* as the number of girl and boy babies being born in London. The latter is a *representation* of the former, and one which may have contained many errors and biases.

Regardless, Gravesande's experiment was prototypical of the general utility of the approximations to the binomial distribution for any problem involving large numbers. There were many such applications, ranging from the failure of wooden wheel spokes in a massive factory, to patient survival after a new medical treatment. To measure, understand and control mass production, mass medicine or any other mass-scale activities, one had to face down the combinatorial explosion of many unforeseen situations in the future. This compelled mathematicians to refine the estimation of the binomial distribution for large numbers, culminating in the provably-best-possible approximation, given by De Moivre in 1733:

$$P(n,i,j) \approx N\left(\frac{j-np}{\sqrt{np(1-p)}}\right) - N\left(\frac{i-np}{\sqrt{np(1-p)}}\right)$$

where the key term is the function $N(z)$:

$$N(z) = \frac{1}{\sqrt{2\pi}} \int_{-\infty}^{z} e^{-x^2/2} \, dx$$

This formula follows the smooth grey line given in Figure 4.1, sketching out a shape that, particularly to an eighteenth-century eye, looks like a bell, hence it's more common name, the Bell Curve.

The Bell Curve proved so mathematically convenient that its use spread far beyond factories and patient surveys, to the point where it began to be considered a virtual natural law, particularly once maths prodigy Carl Friederich Gauss determined that a distribution of scientific measurement errors was given by $N(z)$, the Bell Curve. This is the reason for the distributions second common name: the *Gaussian*.

Gauss's proof also emerged from an astronomical context; in this case, the hunt for the dwarf planet Ceres, which had been spotted by Giuseppe Piazzi in 1801 before falling into the sun's glare and out of sight.[7] Piazzi, operating alone with only one set of equipment, recorded just twenty-four measurements of the planet's position. Given this limited and surely error-prone data, the rest of the scientific community attempted to predict where the planet might emerge again based on this data with no success. That was until young Gauss innovated by using the Bell Curve to model the distribution of errors in Piazzi's measurements and came up with the correct solution, successfully predicting the planet's re-emergence on New Year's Day 1802, and simultaneously gaining academic celebrity that persists to this day.

Implicitly, Gauss's idea considers any measurement to comprise a base truth and an infinite number of infinitesimal 'atomic errors', like micro-tremors of the measurer's hand, each with a fixed probability, like the toss of a coin. At random, some of the tremors will move away from the true value, and make the measurement worse, and some will get lucky, winning the infinitesimal error game, making the measurement better. The distribution of these tiny atomic errors is of course binomial, and the best approximation of a large number of such errors is then given by the Bell Curve. Gauss's new use of the Bell Curve was an inspired idea, but it must be evaluated in the context of Galileo's critical point: in the case of physical bodies, there is *only one true value* for the distance from the centre of the Earth to a star.

Gauss's theory was so seductively simple it appeared to offer an almost magical way to predict previously unknowable things with startling accuracy. Perhaps it could be used to illuminate truths in other complex physical, social and economic phenomena in the increasingly complex industrial world of the late eighteenth century? It was Pierre-Simon Laplace (1749–1827) who, in 1785, found a way to broaden the application of the Bell Curve with the publication of his *Central Limit Theorem* (CLT). This theory establishes that *measurements* of all sorts of phenomena tend to be distributed according to a Bell Curve, *even if the variations of the thing being measured aren't distributed by a Bell Curve.*

To understand how CLT works in the real world, let's consider its application in presidential approval polls. Let's say we ask Americans to rate approval of their president's performance on a scale of 0 to 100. In the derivation of errors in finding the position of the planet Ceres, Gauss assumed that errors were equally likely to be high or low, but the same symmetry of distribution may not hold true for presidential approval. Like Marmite, people tend to either hate or love the president, so the distribution of approval is likely be fat near 0 and 100 and thin near the middle values. The sample may have other humps and lumps, or it may not be symmetrical at all. What the CLT says is that this underlying complexity and uneven distribution *doesn't matter*, if what you are trying to find is a practical way of getting a statistic (for instance, the *average*) approval rating.

The reality is, there are too many people in the USA to practically conduct a complete presidential approval poll. However, we can poll a *sample* of the people. A sample is a kind of measurement, taken by random queries of a population. Let's say we call 100 random people, get their individual approval ratings, take the average approval, and find this value is 60. We've only sampled a few citizens, so how do we know that this value is right in any way? We don't, so we call another 100 people, and find the average of their ratings is 45. We don't know that this value is any better than 60, so we just keep repeating this process, calling 100 people, and taking their average approval rating. In a process like this, what can we conclude about the results, and their relationship to some 'true' approval rating?

What the CLT tells us is that the distribution of the *average* approval ratings from these repeated polls will be distributed by the Bell Curve, and that the centre of that curve will be the *average* approval rating of *all the people of America*. CLT says the Bell Curve turns up in sampling *regardless of the distribution of the thing being sampled*. Even if this distribution is highly skewed towards haters and backers, the distribution of the averages of the polls will be a Bell Curve around the average of all the voters. The more people you poll, the easier it is to see that average in the Bell Curve.

But what the CLT actually tells us is a lot simpler than it first appears. Let's say the 'real' average approval (what we'd get if we really asked every American) is 52 out of 100 or 52 per cent. What CLT says is not that 52 per cent of Americans approve. It says that the average poll will have the value 52, and that the distribution of polls around that average is a Bell Curve. The variance of the other values of the polls taken will provide the width of that Bell Curve, and will relate to the size of each poll, and the variance of public opinion. Since CLT says that curve will have the shape given by $N(z)$, a statistician can talk with confidence about the *probability* that any given poll will come out to give 52 per cent approval, or thereabouts. This, of course, assumes that nothing changes during this polling, including that the repeated polls have no effect on the people being polled.

Despite its obvious flaws, the CLT appeared to offer a 'scientific' (that is mathematical) way to model complex phenomena that couldn't be measured completely or accurately. Since science was about observation and measurement, this extended the reach of science far beyond what was feasible via direct measurements. And, it advanced the use of probability theory from a way of explaining games of chance and astronomical calculations, to a way of describing all complex phenomena in the world. The universal faith in the Bell Curve as a natural law gave scientists confidence in the statistics that it generated.

However, there is another way to view the Bell Curve: not as a natural law, but as an artefact of trying to see complex and uncertain phenomena through the limiting lens of sampling and statistics. The CLT does not prove that everything follows a Bell Curve; it shows that when you sample in order to understand things that you can't observe, you will always get a Bell Curve. That's all.

Despite this reality, faith in CLT and the Bell Curve still dominates in statistical modelling of all sorts of things today from presidential approval ratings to reoffending rates for criminals to educational success or failure, to whether jobs can be done by computers as well as people. What's more, faith in this mathematical model inevitably led to its use in areas where it was ill-suited and inappropriate, such as Quetelet's *Theory of Probabilities as Applied and to the Moral and Political Sciences*. Quetelet indirectly used the idea of CLT in his measurements of Scottish soldiers and his proof of an ideal man. Just like Gravesande, he concluded that if the Bell Curve was a natural law then the deviations he saw from the average man indicated natural variation around an ideal. This is an astoundingly dangerous conclusion, and implicit in it is a denial of diversity and difference and an apparently scientifically sanctioned method of discrimination. In reality, the calculations presented by Quetelet poorly match the Bell Curve, and the chest-size data he used was badly extracted from the 1817 *Edinburgh Medical and Surgical Journal*, which contained numerous transcription errors, to the extent that even the number of soldiers is incorrect. But these errors, and the initial conceptual errors in Quetelet's thinking, did not prevent his work from becoming an important part of prevailing scientific thinking.

In particular, Charles Darwin read Quetelet and was explicitly influenced by his idea of natural variation. However, in Darwin's theory, average did not mean ideal. The distribution of human features included better and worse, and Darwin theorized that natural selection would sort the former from the latter, leading to inevitable improvements towards an evolutionary ideal over time. For Darwin, deviations could be both good or bad, but evolution would always drive ultimately towards good.

Darwin's theory emerged from the marriage of evolutionary utopianism and mathematical modelling based on statistical analysis of complex populations, but his theory was (at least initially) strictly biological. It was Darwin's contemporary, Herbert Spencer, who interpreted (or perhaps returned) the theory of evolution to a social context. Spencer was one of the leading intellectuals of his time, who introduced the term *sociology* to the English lexicon, and wrote a lifetime of material on the idea that evolution was the driving force behind biological, social, political and economic systems. But perhaps his most lasting legacy was his coining of the phrase 'survival of the fittest'.[8]

Before Spencer, Darwin's evolutionary theory spoke only in neutral terms of natural selection, but Spencer's 'survival of the fittest' phrase was so resonant with the evolutionary utopian ideas of the time that Wallace implored Darwin to substitute the phrase for natural selection in later editions of *Origin*. While Darwin did not make a direct substitution (for fear that the change would be confusing to the growing number of people working in the field), he did include Spencer's phrase in the fifth edition of *Origin* (published ten years after the first), with the following comment: 'The expression often used by Mr. Herbert Spencer of the Survival of the Fittest is more accurate, and is sometimes equally convenient.' This apparently simple change in language brought with it a host of assumptions and implied meanings with significant logical difficulties that persist to this day. Gone is the suggestion of random variation; instead 'survival of the fittest' implies Quetelet's idea of deviation from an ideal 'fitness'. This, in turn, implies that there exists something objective and external, likely something quantitatively measurable, called 'fitness'. But this idea is no more scientific in reality than Quetelet's assumptions about chest sizes. 'Survival of the fittest' is at best a tautology and at worst a reversal of the order of evolution's actual mechanism. In natural selection, features that survive and are reproduced are *by definition* fit. There is no objective fitness other than survival. Spencer himself was troubled by this logical difficulty, writing:

> very often that which humanly speaking, is inferiority, causes the survival. Superiority, whether in size, strength, activity, or sagacity, is, other things equal, at the cost of diminished fertility; and where the life led by a species does not demand these higher attributes, the species profits by decrease of them, and accompanying increase of fertility. This is the reason why there are so many cases of retrograde metamorphosis. When it is remembered that these cases out-number all others, it will be seen that the expression 'survivorship of the better' is wholly inappropriate.

Comments like Spencer's have obvious implications in social and political spheres and would eventually lead evolutionary utopians to certain inevitable and dangerous conclusions, in terms of how society should act politically. If 'fit' was not explicitly 'better', then it was probably a good idea to attempt to make it so, by any means necessary. By coupling the Bell Curve with evolutionary theory, the now measurable characteristics of men – such as physique, skin pigmentation and, even, intelligence – could theoretically be tweaked and improved upon through natural selection, pushing up the mean by reducing any 'deviations' at the tail ends of the distribution. From here it was a short step to George Hunter's racist *Civic Biology* textbook at the centre of the Scopes' Monkey Trial, and it explains why such a book was defended by men considered science-loving liberals of their time.

These deep-seated philosophies are also embedded in the genetic algorithms (GAs) that I've built my career on. They are the most current manifestation of centuries of mathematical modelling based on probability theory. These algorithms are most often applied in optimization problems (like the aircraft-wing example I used on the blind date, finding decent solutions to the TSP, finding the safest route of an aeroplane through hostile airspace, and millions more). GAs exploit populations of solutions in a search to find the optimal value of some calculation that can be performed on every population member. This calculation is unsurprisingly referred to as that population member's *fitness*. In these powerful and effective algorithms, fitness is literally a number that is higher for some individuals than it is for others. While GAs are a particular class of algorithm, the ideas in GAs can be applied to any algorithm that exploits populations. Thus, they are a way of looking at nearly every online algorithm of massive complexity and scale.

In a GA, fitness is a number, and in most algorithms there is usually some quantity which is being optimized. With appropriate understanding and caveats this is fine for technical applications, but using numbers to describe people and complex human issues such as crime, justice, health, news and economics is another matter entirely. Understanding the difference between an algorithm's quantitative view of the world and the real-world reality of how people interact and co-operate in real populations is vitally important today. But to do so means overcoming a long-cherished utopian belief that populations will inevitably optimize and that people and their behaviour can be reduced to simplistic, quantifiable features.

While necessary to overcome the simplifying quantitative interpretations of that theory applied to people, and their negative historical impacts, this change in perspective is difficult for those whose convictions about Darwin's theory are a part of their deeply personal identity. Even more so for those who have benefited from many of those quantitative interpretations. Like me.

5

AIQ

I have no faith in anything short of actual measurement and the Rule of Three.
CHARLES DARWIN

This quote adorned the masthead of *The Annals of Eugenics*, and the editor's intent was (probably) the implication of Darwin's strong belief in probability theory. However, the quote is actually from a letter in which Darwin was discussing his study of some chickens he owned, and it's likely the 'Rule of Three' to which he referred was not the statistical one, but a schoolboy arithmetic principle, where if given four numbers in two equal ratios, knowing three of the terms uniquely determines the fourth. In fact, Darwin stated elsewhere that he was no mathematician, and that as a student the subject was 'repugnant' to him.

It is therefore unsurprising that there are no mathematics in Darwin's theory of evolution, as he wrote it. Instead, what the masthead quote from the eugenics journal demonstrates is how, time and again, scientific theories are used to justify unscientific social prejudices. None has been more impactful than Darwin's theory, particularly with regard to the application of the concept of natural selection to human heredity and evolution, via Spencer's catchy phrase 'survival of the fittest'.

Although Darwin's theory was not originally about human social evolution, it came from that context, and based on the work of Spencer and others, a set of ideologies termed social Darwinism emerged in the late 1800s. These ideas used Darwin's theory of natural selection to justify a whole range of political, social and economic views that were popular in the rapidly expanding Victorian British Empire. They included a laissez-faire attitude to free-market economics, a staunch antipathy towards any welfare assistance for the 'unfit' poor, a justification for imperialism, sexism and racism, and, ultimately, a growing enthusiasm for eugenics. The mathematization of the theory, through the introduction of statistics and probability, lent these social and racial prejudices the stamp of scientific respectability.

The most widely accepted and controversial tool of social engineering to emerge from the era was the intelligence quotient (IQ) test. In the opinion of the scientists who developed its application, if society was going to be improved, then there needed to be a 'scientific' way of determining better from worse, and there was no better quality of man's (and by that, Victorians did largely mean men) 'fitness' than their most idealized virtue, intelligence. Historically, IQ is a score obtained by dividing a person's 'mental age score', obtained by administering a standardized test, by the person's chronological age. The resulting fraction is multiplied by 100 to obtain the IQ score. Since the IQ testing procedure is looking at a complex phenomenon (human intelligence) through the lens of a sort of sampling (through a few questions asked in a standard test), it's unsurprising that it results in a Bell Curve. The average IQ is assumed to be 100, and the Bell Curve generated by a century of IQ testing indicates approximately two-thirds of the population scores between IQ 85 and IQ 115. About 2.5 per cent of the population scores above 130, and 2.5 per cent below 70.

This ranking system is terribly convenient for *categorizing* and *sorting* people into groups, and over the decades IQ scores have been used to segregate classes and races, set immigration policies, screen potential applicants for jobs and military service, and determine the treatment of criminals. Even today, education systems around the world use IQ tests (or other versions of intelligence testing) to help identify children for special educational needs and gifted programmes. Both SAT tests in the US[1] and the UK's eleven-plus entrance exam[2] are direct descendants of IQ testing methodologies.

IQ is the prototypical way of turning a complex, hardly understood quality of human beings (intelligence) into a number, so it's unsurprising that the underlying techniques of its development have a close connection to algorithms, many of which are widely used in the infrastructure of today's online world. It's important to understand the methods and flaws that originate with IQ, because they affect everyone's lives today, but they started affecting mine in particular when I was twelve years old.

My own place at Jefferson County Alabama's only gifted school was determined by an IQ test that I was invited to take when I was in the sixth grade, as part of a socio-economic diversification programme aimed at promoting the life chances of working-class kids in the American South.

I was let off school early to take the test, and I only missed one class, but it was one of my favourites, science with Mr Clement. Mr Clement was a part-time police reserve officer, and I was one of less than a handful of kids in the class that hadn't had brushes with the law. There were no girls in the class, and while many of the other boys were African-Americans, bussed in from Airport Heights, others were what were commonly called 'white trash' kids.

None of the boys were legally delinquents, or they'd already be in the fabled and feared juvenile detention facility on the other side of the Pinson Highway, but most of them had strayed close to the line, or had older siblings in juvey, or parents in jail. The class I shared with them was in the final timeslot of the day, probably to keep the boys from heading out early and into trouble, while providing them with some male mentoring. Mr Clement didn't teach much science in class; instead he told stories of his experiences in rough places, and his knowledge of the streets and prisons. When he wasn't looking (which he had a knack of doing at the just the right moment) I saw my first joint and my first switchblade in that class.

I hated to miss Mr Clement's class for the IQ test, as I was learning a lot of valuable life lessons in there, but results on a federally mandated achievement test had triggered a surprise phone call to my parents. The county board of education said that they wanted to test me, to see if I qualified for a special programme of gifted education, and so I headed down to an airless grey office in Birmingham to be tested.

Most of the test consisted of puzzles, which I really liked. My favourite was one where you looked at pictures of red-and-white geometric patterns, then had to reconstruct the same pattern with semaphore-marked wooden cubes. I'd gotten all of them right in no time, but some were just hard enough to make it fun. After the puzzles came general knowledge questions, such as: 'Who discovered America?'

This sort of question is typical of IQ tests, which have been roundly criticized over the decades for their cultural biases. As African-American critic Robert Williams pointed out:

> Is it more indicative of intelligence to know Malcolm X's last name, or the author of Hamlet? I ask you now when is Washington's birthday? Perhaps 99 percent of you thought February 22. The answer presupposes a white form. I actually meant Booker T. Washington.[3]

In addition, much of the test content favours white, male, middle-class test-takers with subjects weighted to science, politics and sport. In fact, in 1937, when the tests indicated that women were, on average, a bit more intelligent than men the test was changed to include more questions, mainly about sport, to correct what was seen as an error. And over the decades the tests have had to be made more challenging to maintain the average at 100 as we all appear to be getting too smart. Projecting back 100 years, IQ researcher Jim Flynn found that average IQ scores measured by current standards would be about 70, which nowadays would indicate serious developmental delay.[4]

But despite mountains of research questioning their validity, and even the morality of reducing people and their intelligence to a single number in order to rank them for opportunities, jobs or even the death sentence, IQ tests continue to be widely used as a method of social engineering.

In answer to the question about the discovery of America, I responded: 'No one knows the answer to that question.' My examiner, who had seemed absolutely enthralled with my semaphore cube performance, got a puzzled look on her face, and said 'What do you mean, Rob? Do you not know the answer?' Her words had a lilt of encouragement that was, I suppose, meant to nudge me to the 'correct' answer, Columbus. I responded: 'There were people in America already when Columbus got here, so what would it mean to say that he discovered America? There were Indians, and the Vikings had probably been to America already, so the question doesn't really make any sense.' She took down a note and moved on to other questions.

At the end of the test, she called my mother in, and told her I was smarter than 99.7 per cent of the people in the world. My mother looked elated. 'And he's highly verbal,' the examiner said. I was a chatty kid, so this gave them both a good laugh.

Early in the summer holidays came an offer from the school board, and I was invited to start eighth grade at a new school over an hour further away, on the other side of Red Mountain, Birmingham's dividing line between working-class neighbourhoods and suburbs where white-collar families lived. Most of the students at my new school were from a higher socio-economic class than my own. Bussing brought kids from places like Center Point, where I grew up, Graysville, a rural mine-and-farm community where my dad was raised, and Hueytown, the grease-monkey town of NASCAR fame, to the side of Red Mountain where parents were more likely to be doctors, lawyers and professors.

I didn't know it at the time, but this was intentional: the school wanted to expand its class spectrum, and it's likely the school brought kids from my school to take the IQ test precisely for this attempt at improving some of the social equity of the county's gifted programme. There's no doubt, my success at the IQ test and admission to the gifted school gave me new opportunities and opened a door to a bigger world. But the disparity in socio-economic background that bussing was attempting to correct by using the theoretically unbiased IQ test as the only admission requirement could not overcome the entrenched racial segregation of 1970s Alabama. None of the other children in Mr Clement's science class was even asked to sit the test, and although girls and boys were fairly evenly represented in the 250 or so students in my new gifted school, only one kid was African-American. This despite the fact that the school sat in a black neighbourhood and served the 600,000 people of Jefferson County, Alabama, which was (and is) around 42 per cent African-American.

Research has repeatedly shown that ethnic minorities are grossly under-represented in gifted programmes. This is because referral to these programmes often relies on social perceptions and expectations. Note that the IQ test I took was only offered after I excelled on the achievement test, which was much more like a standard test on the material we were being taught in school. Moreover, not much is expected of students, like my fellow class mates in Mr Clement's science class, who have backgrounds blighted by poverty, drug addiction, truancy and crime. Unsurprisingly, IQ testing has long been popular with ethno-nationalists and eugenicists who maintain that the historically lower IQs of non-white racial groups, poorer people and women provides evidence of their genetic inferiority, and that the inequalities we see in society are not structural, but are rather a natural result of the evolutionary process.

Unsurprisingly, since its invention, the IQ test has generated heated debate. There has been much excellent work done debunking the idea that such a complex and multifaceted phenomenon as human intelligence can be reduced to a single number, most notably by Stephen Jay Gould in his book *The*

Mismeasure of Man[5] (which itself has been strenuously contested). The intent here is not to revisit those arguments, but to take a closer look at how our desire to understand and measure intelligence is connected to a broader range of ideas that have important, deep, technical relationships to today's online, algorithmic society.

In 1869 Francis Galton drew on Quetelet, and wrote *Hereditary Genius*, where he sought to explain that human intelligence was a quantitative factor, just like the chest size of those Scottish soldiers. He further wished to show that this factor was inherited, and thus under the action of evolution. Galton was a strong believer in the evolutionary theory that descended from his grandfather, Erasmus Darwin, and had been made into real science by Charles Darwin, his first cousin.

At the time, no one had any knowledge of the mechanisms of genetics that determined simple things like eye colour, much less a complex phenomenon like intelligence. DNA was discovered in 1869, and the term 'gene' was introduced in 1905, but the fact that the former was the same as the latter wouldn't be clear until Watson and Crick's discovery in 1953. Thus, in order to prove his theory, Galton absolutely required Quetelet's variational reasoning, which said that the measurements of human factors must be viewed statistically, through the lens of probability, and the Bell Curve.

Like Quetelet's inference that variation from his ideal soldier was a deformity, Galton reasoned that a child's intellect was subject to 'deformity by a host of accidental causes'. Therefore, from parents of 'normal' intelligence, one would expect the birth of children who were also of normal intelligence with a high probability, but also the arrival of abnormal, stupid or genius children with some probability. From genius parents, you'd expect a similar outcome, but with the intelligence of the children skewed upward in general. With less intelligent parents, the skew would be downward. Galton reasoned, based on Quetelet's ideas, that the quantitative factor of 'intelligence' had to be distributed amongst these children according to the Bell Curve. Thus, it was Galton that gave the Bell Curve its third common-usage name. He called it 'the Normal Distribution'.[6]

This new name has powerful connotations. No longer is data simply just plotted on a curve; instead the introduction of the word 'normal' brings with it a host of value judgements and the assumption that there is, in fact, a norm. In addition, the word 'distribution' implies there is a quantitative scale from better to worse. Together the whole phrase 'Normal Distribution' seems to suggest something of a natural law. Galton was also making a leap of reasoning based on CLT – a methodology that was originally based on human errors made while measuring the *physical* position of stars – to natural variations in a complex human phenomenon that was *assumed to be* a quantitative factor without, at the time, having any knowledge of the basic mechanisms of the factor at all. He wrote: 'It will be remembered that these are to the effect that individual errors of observation, or individual differences in objects belonging to the same generic group, are entirely due to the aggregate action of variable influences in different combinations.' He goes on to restate the assumptions of Laplace in CLT, implying the idea that the integration of many underlying 'errors' should yield the observed Bell Curve of outcomes. Galton himself knew that his Normal Distribution was an artefact of reductionism, but the field of study he launched would find statistical means to not only ignore this fact but imply that the underlying human reality of intelligence was very simple.

Galton also took another important step beyond the assumptions of Quetelet, who saw the average man as ideal and deviations from this ideal as monstrous. Galton, drawing on the work of his cousin, felt that the average man could be *improved*, evolved, made less monstrous than the current manifestation, via morally and politically controlled evolution: that is, the promotion of the low probability genius children to become genius parents and, inversely, the discouragement of lower intelligence people from becoming parents at all. Via this active strategy, society could move towards the evolutionary utopian goal of physical, moral and cultural perfectibility, through the birth of a new academic field and social movement, which Galton called *eugenics*.

Galton spent the rest of his life advancing eugenic ideas as a positive force for change. He argued that social institutions such as welfare and mental asylums allowed inferior humans to survive. Their survival meant an increased chance that they could reproduce, possibly even at higher levels than their superior counterparts in the upper classes. He was not alone in his thinking. Initially, eugenics was enthusiastically embraced as a liberal, meritocratic movement, one aimed at freeing men, and to a lesser extent women, from being judged on arbitrary, superstitious grounds, particularly religious beliefs, thus facilitating the evolution of society, through meritocratic, technological interventions, towards a better world for all. It was *Queen Mab*, made into scientific political action.

The theory chimed perfectly with the Victorian age of enquiry, when men bestrode the world measuring, analysing and collecting a prodigious amount of data on their new colonies. Galton himself travelled extensively through Eastern Europe to Constantinople, and to east and southern Africa, where he carried out a surveying expedition in Namibia in 1850, which earned him the Royal Geographical Society's Founders Gold Medal in 1853. Having been a child prodigy himself, he had always been interested in intelligence and how this and other behavioural and character traits were transmitted from parents to child. And following the publication of *Origin*, he was the first person to attempt to systematically measure intelligence, inventing questionnaires, twin studies, the lexical approach, psychometrics (the science of measuring mental faculties) and differential psychology. At the same time, he was hugely influential in the fields of statistics and mathematical biology, having established the principles of correlation and regression to the mean.

In 1884, he founded the Anthropometric Laboratory, first at the International Health Exhibition and then at the South Kensington Museum. Its aim was twofold: first, to demonstrate how measuring physical characteristics (such as eyesight) regularly would help to identify any deficiencies early on; and, second, to collect data for his statistical studies so he could compare attributes across races, occupations, age and birthplace to determine how character, intelligence, aptitude and behaviour might vary. During the first year, nearly 10,000 people came to be measured, with thousands more in subsequent years. The amount of data collected by the Laboratory was so vast that it wasn't until the 1960s that there were computers capable of dealing with it. The techniques used at the Laboratory were seen to have potential for practical social applications, for instance, they directly inspired the first system of forensic anthropometry devised by French policeman Alphonse Bertillon (who would later develop the mug shot). The Bertillon System was specifically aimed at identifying recidivists via 10 key body measurements. Given his laboratory's fame and success, Galton sought the backing of an academic institution, and naturally he chose University College London (UCL), where I now hold a post in computer science.

Established in 1826 as the first secular institution of higher education in the UK, UCL was considered the cutting-edge scientific institute of its day and was the only British university that would grant degrees to non-Anglicans. The university's founders and supporters were some of the greatest scientists and philosophers of their time, men who believed the supernaturally based prejudices of religion should have no part in a modern education. It was here that Galton sought support for his anthropometric laboratory, and where, in 1904, the UK Eugenics Records Office was established as a centre for capturing biometric 'big data'. Galton was in his eighties by then, so to carry on his work he requested that his protégé Karl Pearson was made a Francis Galton Fellow, and later the Francis Galton Chair, a position Galton endowed at UCL on his death in 1911.

Like Galton, Pearson was a prominent liberal of his time, an outspoken freethinker, a lecturer on women's right to vote, and on the theories of Karl Marx (in honour of whom Pearson changed the first letter of his name). His political views encompassed economic conservatism and radical socialism to produce a unique brand of social radicalism. He was also unequivocal that while fair and scientific, the advance of humanity via evolution was not to be gentle under eugenics. Pearson wrote:

My view – and I think it may be called the scientific view of a nation – is that of an organized whole, kept up to a high pitch of internal efficiency by insuring that its numbers are substantially recruited from the better stocks, and kept up to a high pitch of external efficiency by contest, chiefly by way of war with inferior races.

Nor was his rigorous application of social Darwinism solely reserved for other races or weaker members of society. In his 1909 paper *The Problem of Practical Eugenics*, Pearson even argued that the reform of child labour laws had made children into an economic and social burden to their parents and society. Calling for a repeal of child labour and work laws he states, 'practical eugenics demands in the first place that the economic value of the child shall be restored [to pre-regulation status]'.

When he took over the UK Eugenics Records Office from Galton in 1907, Pearson renamed it the Eugenics Laboratory, which had a more scientific ring, and reflected how the facility's work moved from merely gathering data to creating a new science around data analysis, via statistics. Processing the lab's big data required statistical mathematics, so in 1911 Pearson (who already held a chair in Applied Mathematics at UCL) merged the biometric and eugenics laboratories to form the Department of Applied Statistics, the first university statistics department in the world.

Pearson went on to create the Pearson correlation coefficient, one of the most fundamental calculations in statistics. In fact, his work is so foundational to statistics that he was offered a knighthood (which he declined based on his personal commitment to socialism). The UCL building which once housed the Department of Statistics bears his name. Pearson also founded *The Annals of Eugenics* journal (which now exists as the prominent *Annals of Genetics*), the masthead of which originally included the famous (mis)quote from Charles Darwin.

Pearson's focus on advancing eugenics put him amongst the most liberal intellectuals of his time, not only in the UK, but throughout the world. Seven years after the British ERO was founded its American equivalent was established (by Davenport, who would inspire the *Civic Biology* text that Scopes would teach from). At the same time the Eugenics Education Society was created to include a broader range of intellectuals who supported eugenics as a positive social force. Galton was the first president, and upon his death it was renamed the Galton Institute (a name it still holds today). Prominent members have included economist John Maynard Keynes (who served as the organizations VP in 1937), British Prime Minister Neville Chamberlain, cereal inventor John Harvey Kellogg and Margaret Sanger, an American and the founder of what is now known as Planned Parenthood.

The Galton Institute, the Eugenics Records Offices, the UCL Eugenics Laboratory and other similar bodies existed to propagate the idea that eugenics was a fair and scientific way to advance human development, and was part of an august progression of liberal philosophical ideas, from Godwin's theory of necessity, through the social utopianism of Percy Shelley's *Queen Mab* to the belief that the Bell Curve reflects a natural law of normal distribution, and Darwin's theory. In the eyes of early twentieth-century intellectuals, the advances in science and mathematics finally provided the means to enact these utopian agendas through the new field of eugenics. Eugenics provided the means of ensuring that Spencer's 'survival of the fittest' became 'survival of the better'.

The question is, better how? Implicit in all this reasoning is the idea that humanity, subject as it is to survival of the fittest, has a *fitness*, which must be measurable. In essence, in order to apply the mathematics to the social tasks of eugenics, we have to have something to measure, like the throw of the die in a game of chance. While Quetelet implied that physical deviations, like variations in chest measurements, were connected to the moral character of man, Galton made explicit the idea that the complex, human phenomena of intelligence could be viewed as an aggregated, measurable phenomenon, subject to mathematical laws, just like the distances between the stars. Pearson, with his statistical abilities, sought to add mathematical rigour to the matter, using the data gathered in the Eugenics Laboratory, particularly with regard to quantifying human intelligence. He started much the way Quetelet did, by looking at things one could evaluate with a balance scale or a measuring tape.

For instance, the brain. Around 2000 years ago, Hippocrates, the father of modern medicine, wrote: 'from nothing else but the brain comes joys, delights, laughter and sports, and sorrows, griefs, despondency and lamentations'. By contrast, Aristotle believed the brain was a cooling device, a kind of fleshy radiator, that enabled people to overcome their hot-bloodedness in contrast to animals with smaller brains. By the Renaissance, thanks in large part to Descartes, the brain was seen as a surrogate for the soul, a separate entity divorced from the body where the higher functions of rational thought and moral behaviours resided. Therefore, if scientists were going to find a method to improve mankind, it made sense to start by measuring and gathering statistics on the size of brains.

The Petrie Museum of Egyptian Archaeology stands beside the UCL Computer Science Building, which houses my office. It is named for another eugenicist contemporary of Pearson's, Egyptologist Flinders Petrie (1853–1942), who was a staunch believer in the superiority of the Caucasoid races. He created and propagated the idea that the Pharaohs (and their kin) were not Africans but were instead a race of white people who long ago conquered and ruled over the indigenous people of Egypt, who were assumed to be 'mulatto'. During Petrie's African travels, he collected a huge number of skulls, which he presented to his friend Karl Pearson for biometric examination. At the time, across colonial territories, the collection of native remains and specimens was a widespread and accepted practice, as was the dehumanizing habit of measuring every aspect of living native peoples. The scientists, collectors and museum curators engaged in this mass act of desecration, graveyard robbery and humiliating measurement were, for the most part, believers in eugenics who thought the study of different human remains would yield important insights into the evolutionary genealogy of the human species.

Pearson added Petrie's African skulls to his collection of local head bones, which he sourced largely from plague pits in England, eventually creating a collection of over 7000 skeletal human heads. Pearson used these skulls in his work, creating his Coefficient of Racial Likeness, which involved measuring each skull and comparing it to statistics of other skulls, to establish a person's race. This interest in differentiating the so-called 'races' gave birth to craniology, a whole field of science devoted to the study of skulls to determine racial differences. By elaborate measurements of cranial capacity, this new field set out to assess brain size, relative development of different areas of the brain and thus, it was assumed, intelligence itself.

Naturally, it was clear that men as a group had more cranial capacity and, therefore, more intelligence than women, who generally had smaller skulls. And, unsurprisingly, it was soon discovered that on average the cranial capacity of the white race was greater than that of Africans, Asians and even Southern Europeans. As a popular new science, craniology added impressive new data to support the existing sexual and racial caste system, and reinforced racial segregation and the oppression of women.

But there were many illogical inconsistencies in the theory. What was to be done, for example, about whales and elephants, who clearly had larger skulls than homo sapiens? Should the ratio of brain weight to body weight be taken into account to deal with this inconsistency? But then that would make women more intelligent than men as a group. Or should the ratio of the brain surface to body surface be used? Except that would make men of some other races smarter than Caucasians. Or should the slant of the forehead be taken into account? But, then, what about anteaters? In the end, it was a female mathematician, Alice Lee, who demolished the theory in her paper 'A Study of the Correlation of the Human Skull', which was published in 1901.

Ironically, Lee worked in the UCL biometrics lab, and she came to work there via a vigorous disagreement with Pearson, the lab's head. In 1892, Pearson wrote an article in the *Pall Mall Gazette* suggesting the closure of the Bedford College for Women. The College, which was within easy walking distance of UCL (where Bloomsbury Publishing now has its offices), was founded in 1849 as the first institution for the education of women in the UK. Pearson suggested its closure not because he felt women should not be educated. On the contrary, Pearson was a strong defender of women's rights. He simply felt that Bedford had a lack of academic standards. Alice Lee, who had graduated from Bedford, and taught there, wrote Pearson a spirited letter refuting his assertions. It must have been a good one, as it not only changed his mind, it led him to hire her.

As a keen mathematician, Alice developed a clever way to measure the size of the brain within a living skull, based on external measurements, and some reliance on the statistic heuristic, thus overcoming the issue of each skull's unique thickness. She filled her dead skulls with sand, poured the sand onto a scale and recorded the weight. She then took other measurements of the same skulls' exteriors. Using these measures and some statistical maths, she developed a formula such that external measurements of living skulls could be taken and converted to the equivalent brain volume based on the dead skulls, with statistical validity demonstrated on the UCL collection of skulls.

This enabled her to conduct an experiment comparing the brains of female students at Bedford College, male faculty members at UCL and thirty-nine distinguished anatomists of the Anatomical Society of Dublin. She measured their skulls and used her formula to determine their brain volumes, and then presented the results in a ranked table in order of decreasing skull size, with each entry identified by name. The paper showed irrefutably that the eminent men in the study didn't have unusually large-sized brains at all. So unless they were willing to accept their lower ranking on the table as proof of their lower intelligence, they had to accept that the craniometric theory of intelligence was bogus.

Alice Lee's pivotal work demonstrated that gross physical measurements weren't going to provide a quantitative metric for intelligence. Looking back at craniology, it may seem absurd that it was ever considered a respectable field of science, but even today its dehumanizing othering of people of colour still casts a long shadow, particularly over indigenous peoples such as the Aboriginal peoples of Australia. Re-examining this history provides a useful lesson in how accepted, even popular, theories can turn out to be dramatically wrong. In the end, craniological proofs were found to be enormously biased, carelessly and fraudulently gathered, and largely based on deep-seated culture-bound assumptions. Likewise, forensic anthropometry was enormously error-laden and had dangerous social effects. The related field of criminal anthropology (also known as offender profiling), first devised by physician Cesare Lombroso around the same time as the Bertillon System, which advocated that criminal behaviour could be identified by physical defects, was scientific prejudice at its worst. This reminds us that we constantly need to question, test and re-examine current theories for their scientific validity in case they, too, ultimately turn out to be faulty.

While Alice Lee was busy putting the final nail in the coffin of craniology, in France the French Ministry of Education was seeking the help of psychologist Alfred Binet, in order to find a way to quantify intellectual fitness to distinguish children with learning difficulties and place them in a special classroom with additional support. Work of this sort had become necessary because the French had finally started compulsory education to age thirteen a few decades before, lagging behind most of the rest of Europe,[7] due to conflict between the Catholic Church and the secular state. In this modern educational setting, Binet sought a scientific way to measure the differences between normal learners and those with abnormal difficulties, and he described his methods in his 1903 book *L'Etude experimentale de L'intelligence* (*Experimental Studies of Intelligence*).

Binet believed that human intelligence was not necessarily innate, but malleable under the influences of education. He was interested in understanding human intelligence in order to see how education affected it. He first conducted tests of people who had extraordinary abilities in performing calculations, and masters of chess. Amongst the mathematical geniuses, he found that their aptitude was often at the expense of 'general' intelligence. By investigating how well chess players could play blindfolded, or play in multiple simultaneous games, he found that chess masters seemed to possess particular innate skills, but skills that differed from those who could calculate well. He also found that despite their innate abilities, mental training and exercise was also necessary.

Then, Binet examined creative genius, talking to dramatists about their thought processes. While no quantifiable findings came from this work, Binet did observe a great diversity in the workings of the imaginations of his subjects. Overall, Binet's studies of genius gave him the impression that rather than being a single, quantifiable factor, intelligence was a complex phenomenon, impossible to capture with simple tests and measurements.

It was when he took up the work with the Ministry of Education that Binet, along with his research assistant Theodore Simon, began to develop the first intelligence test. The test was specifically intended to identify children who were struggling and needed more help, and comprised a variety of questions and problem-solving exercises (based on years of observing children in their natural environment), which Binet and Simon thought were representative of the kind of tasks children had to do at various ages. They included very simple tasks such as repeating sentences, to harder mental-skills tests (such as puzzles) and some general knowledge questions. By scoring his tests on children of different ages, he expected that the distribution for any given age would be a

Bell Curve (he was, after all, sampling from a complex phenomenon), and that the centre of this curve (the average score for children of a given age) could be taken as the standard, against which individual children could then be given a 'mental age'. The ratio of this 'mental age' to chronological age would eventually become known as the intelligence quotient, or IQ.

It's important to note here that Binet was always clear on the limitations of his scale. He stressed the diversity of intelligence and the need to study it using qualitative, as opposed to quantitative, measures. Binet also stressed that intelligence developed at variable rates and could be influenced by environment and was, therefore, not solely based on genetics. As far as Binet was concerned, intelligence testing was subject to variability and was not generalizable, and always had to be viewed in context, comparing children with similar backgrounds. So long as all this was considered, Binet felt he had developed a tool to identify students who needed special help to improve their overall prospects through specially focused education.

While Binet was busy seeking a measure of intelligence to serve children with developmental challenges, back in England another researcher at the Eugenics Laboratory, Charles Spearman, was using the big data provided by the rise of universal education to prove a very different point. He postulated that good performance in all scholastic fields was related to a single factor, and that factor, which he called g (for general intelligence), could be shown to exist via analysis of the data that was coming from the England's new mandatory education system. Spearman's intent, like that of Gravesande and Quetelet, was to show that the g factor existed by using an appeal to big data statistics suggesting an underlying natural law. The big data set he was to employ was the tests being taken by English schoolchildren, who, like the children of France, had only started being mandatorily educated past age ten a few decades before.[8]

The statistical algorithm Spearman developed for his analysis of big test data is called *factor analysis*. Pearson, who was Spearman's colleague (and rival), developed a similar method called principal component analysis (PCA) in 1901, drawing on a neat relationship between data analysis and the shape and orientation of physical objects. Spearman's factor analysis isn't quite PCA, but the two are closely related, and it seems likely that Spearman made use of the same physical analogies in creating factor analysis in 1904. While Spearman is the inventor of the *g* factor idea, understanding Pearson's PCA is sufficient to grasp the inherent assumptions and biases in both algorithms, which are intrinsically related to many of the big data algorithms of today.

To understand how PCA (and in fact an entire class of widely used data reduction algorithms) transform big data into smaller, generalized descriptions of that data, imagine that the data is plotted as points in some space. It's easiest to think of this space as having three dimensions, and that the cloud of data in that space has some general shape, like a cloud in the sky. When a person looks at a cloud, they might imagine it to look like all sorts of things: a flying saucer, an ice-cream cone, the Great Pyramid in Cairo. We imagine these things by mentally removing all of the cloud's complex and fluffy detail in favour of a simple and familiar shape. For data reduction, we're going to take the data cloud and reduce it to a regular, mathematical shape, because that shape can be described with just a few numbers, which can be used in algorithms. To see how this works, consider a flat disc (like the shape of an extremely boring flying saucer), and think how you might tell someone the general form of the disc, and how it is oriented in space, with numbers. This description requires two things: the disc's diameter, and the three numbers indicating the direction of a single arrow, pointing perpendicularly from the disc's face. Now imagine the mathematical shape of a perfectly smooth ice-cream cone. Its shape and orientation could be described with three things: a single arrow (three numbers) along its central axis, the diameter of its opening and its height from its point to its opening. Finally, imagine a regular pyramid. Orienting it in space requires four things: the length of one side of the base, its height, a three-number arrow for direction for its tip and a direction for one of the corners of its base. In each of these cases, you can think of the directions and sizes as ways of turning each cloud shape into a set of numbers. We'll call these numbers *factors* that describe the cloud. Once you have the factors, and you know which category of shape they describe (whether it is a disc, a cone or a pyramid), you don't need any more information about the simplified shape. These factors are a complete model of those regular objects. The regular objects are simplifications of the cloud, which explicitly ignore those fluffy details, and give us just a set of numbers to compute with.

We have to ignore those details in this data-simplifying process, because a complex object, like a real cloud in the sky, is highly asymmetrical, with a complex surface, colours and densities, and it requires a spectacular number of numbers to be completely and accurately described. *In fact, one could say it is its own best model*, that we'd have to know the position of every particle in the cloud to really capture its details. But in practical scientific work, like big data analysis, it's useful to reduce a complicated shape that is its own best model to its nearest simplified equivalent, a shape that accounts for as much of the real object's detail as possible. Simply stated, doing so gives us fewer things to deal with, a simplified reduction of a complex reality and, in particular, one that reduces to numbers, such that an algorithm can find the 'best' shape by computing.

In the PCA algorithm, a cloud of data is reduced to a few numbers by using some maths to fit a smooth and regular bubble closely around as much of the cloud as is possible. This bubble is implicitly *ellipsoidal*, so in three dimensions it is the shape of a symmetrically flattened rugby ball. For example, imagine the scores of thousands of thirteen-year-old English students in 1904 on their tests (so we've got three dimensions, and can visualize this easily, let's say the tests are in maths, physics and literature). Think of each set of scores for a given pupil as a point in a three-dimensional space, and the set of points as a cloud of data in that space. Now imagine that these points are the true, complicated shape of the cloud. This cloud may or may not be nicely shaped like a rugby ball, and it certainly has lots of points not filled in, but you can imagine a rugby ball bubble that will fit around the data, regardless of its real distribution. What Spearman/Pearson's analytical technique did was to fit a symmetrical bubble around these points, then find the directions of the axes of this simplified shape (see Figure 5.1).

In higher dimensions (that is, for more than three exams), it's harder to imagine, but in those cases PCA is really shaping a higher-dimensional flattened rugby ball. Finding the size and orientation of the rugby-ball bubble

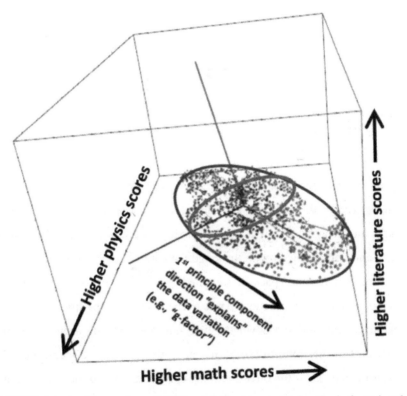

FIGURE 5.1 *An illustration of PCA and the argument for the 'g-factor'. Like many algorithms for understanding complex data, PCA roughly fits a shape around data (say, from test scores), then argues that the longest axis of that shape 'explains' the variation in the data. If it's long enough, it's considered a good explanation, like the existence of some underlying factor(s) that explain why student test scores correlate. That this is a single 'g-factor' is only a (biased) assumption.*

is precisely like specifying the orienting and scaling factors of the disc, cone and pyramid, and PCA provides a precise algorithm for finding the best possible rugby-ball-shaped bubble. By finding the relative size of the ball's three axes, and the directions that they point towards in this 3-D space, PCA reduces the potentially *infinite* complexity of a big data cloud down to just a few numbers that describe those sizes and directions. What Pearson, Spearman and all designers of data reduction algorithms do is precisely that: they reduce the complexity of a data set to a simplified model.

In the figure, the directions of the edges of the cube are the range of scores for the three different tests, and each of the black dots is a single pupil's scores on those tests. The two ellipses indicate the shape of the rugby-ball bubble that has been rotated and sized by PCA to best fit the data. The directions along the axes of symmetry of this rugby ball are each weighted combinations of the scores of those three tests. The 'first principal axis' of the shape is the one along the longest axis of the rugby ball. In the case of the tests, the weighted combination of test scores along this longest principal axis is often said to 'explain' most of the variation in test scores overall. However, that language must be used with care, as a less loaded description sticks to the realities of axes and lengths: the first principal axis is the one that has the longest length, and lines up nicely with the longest apparent distribution of the data in the three-dimensional space of weighted test scores. The second principal axis is a weighted combination that is perpendicular to the first, and second longest; imagine looking down the first axis, and drawing a line along the widest part of the cloud of scores, if you treated it as two dimensional. The third principal axis is the direction that is perpendicular to the first two. In a particular way, these axes (and lengths) can replace all the data in the cloud of test scores. The result is a *model* of the scores of three tests for thousands of thirteen-year-old English students in 1904, which requires far fewer numbers to describe their performance on their school tests than the actual results themselves. We can do analogous algorithmic steps for more than three tests;

it's just harder to imagine multi-dimensional rugby balls, but the process is the same. This is the way that, like all data modelling algorithms, PCA reduces big data to small data.

In Spearman's factor analysis, the weighted combinations (directions of axes) are the 'factors'. Spearman asserted that the first principal axis was so long that it 'explained' enough of the variation of test scores to 'prove' the existence of g factor as a 'real' phenomenon, rather than just an artefact of statistical analysis. This is in fact a self-fulfilling prophecy, in that any set of data that has correlations (has some shape) will have a set of principal axes, and in lots of cases it will have a dominant axis (a latent variable that accounts for more of the shape's spread in space than any other). In some cases, that dominant axis will be much broader than the others, and thus 'explain' a lot of the variation.

In the case of school tests, the fact that one weighted combination of test scores – the axis Spearman assumed was indicative of the real-world g factor – is larger than the others is actually the unsurprising result that kids that do well on one sort of test in school tend to do well on other sorts of tests in school. Like Gravesande measuring the *records* of boys and girls born in London, rather than the actual births, Spearman buried the fact that he was looking at the *test scores* of boys and girls, not the actual pupils themselves.

Some kids are good at school, and some are good at tests. Some kids are better prepared for those educational institutions based on life experiences, and may be better by inclination. That inclination could be labelled as 'general intelligence', but that's an assumption and, moreover, separating that inclination from other effects, such as lifestyle, nutrition, cultural and developmental variations, is inherently complex. Each of those effects is a possible bias, against the poorer, the less privileged, or those whose cultures differ from the norm. These biases in the representation of intelligence that exist implicitly in tests and schools are not only hidden in Spearman's argument; they are assumed from the start to be subsumed by a latent factor for 'general intelligence'.

Spearman was doing more than ignoring or burying those biases: by arguing from factor analysis of exams as a proof of the *g* factor's existence, he was turning those biases into a self-justifying truth.

That truth is made even stronger by the assumption that the Bell Curve is a natural law, rather than a ubiquitous outcome of reducing underlying complex systems. Tests, of course, are sampling and averaging procedures of complex underlying phenomena (human knowledge, intelligence, plus social and economic factors, and much more). They are much like polls, where simple questions mask complex opinions. The implications of the CLT are that a complex underlying phenomenon when seen through a lens of statistics will give a Bell Curve, regardless of the real dynamics of the underlying phenomenon. The Bell Curve is an artefact of using statistics to probe things about which we are uncertain, not necessarily an artefact of the thing itself.

Thus, tests generate Bell Curves, via the CLT, particularly when the underlying phenomenon being tested is complex, and the test is imprecisely measuring the thing in question. If you plot Bell Curves in multiple dimensions, they look very much like the nicely symmetrical cloud in the figure that was used to explain PCA, a distribution that a flattened rugby ball nicely fits, conforming to the assumptions of the PCA algorithm itself. The reductionist assumptions of these algorithms thus feed their apparent justification for big data reduction, becoming a self-fulfilling prophecy. In this case, that is not because we understand general intelligence, or because the *g* factor exists. It's because of the tools we are using to look for the factor in the first place.

Spearman published his *g* factor results in 1904, and Binet and Simon published the Binet–Simon IQ test a year later. Spearman's work lent great support to the idea that general intelligence could be tested, while Binet and Simon's test unwittingly provided a vehicle for doing such tests practically.

Although never his intention, the Binet–Simon IQ test had a devastating impact in the hands of eugenicists like American educational psychologists

Henry Herbert Goddard and Lewis Terman. Goddard came across the Binet–Simon test while studying abroad. On his return to the US he had it translated into English and distributed 22,000 copies across the country, advocating testing in hospitals, schools, the legal system and the military as a means of identifying undesirable elements in society and then eliminating them via institutionalization, sterilization, or both.

Similarly, Lewis Terman had a fascination with genius, believing it to be heritable. As a professor at Stanford University he revised the Binet–Simon test for America, creating the Stanford–Binet test. Unlike Binet's original test, the new test was not devised to help assess the specific educational needs of children; instead it was used for the opposite *exclusionary* effect. For example, Terman gave the Stanford–Binet test to people of many different ethnic groups in California, including Mexicans, Native Americans, Portuguese and Italians, and generally found these races to have low IQs. He expressed concern that their rapid reproduction was a 'grave problem' for society.

Goddard's best-known work, *The Kallikak Family*, was published in 1912. It was a study that traced the descendants of a Revolutionary War soldier, Martin Kallikak, who had two sets of children; one with his wife, a Quaker woman, and another with his mistress, a 'nameless feeble-minded woman'. Goddard's book showed that descendants of the former union were all normal, upstanding citizens, while the latter were criminals, 'a race of defective degenerates'. While his research methods were called into serious question not long after the paper's publication, the assumptions in its conclusion had a real social impact that reached far beyond Vineland, New Jersey, where Goddard was Director of Research at the Vineland Training School for Feeble-Minded Girls and Boys.

At the time, America was experiencing a second huge wave of Irish immigration. The first wave of desperate, undereducated and malnourished Irish people, who were escaping the Potato Famine between 1845 and 1849, had led much of the US public to adopt the commonplace racist view that the Irish were an inferior race and generally mentally defective. This provided a bigoted justification for the fact that, in America, Irish immigrants were largely poor, uneducated and overrepresented in prisons. Similar views were held against other non-Anglo immigrants, and in 1882 the US Congress passed a law preventing the entry of 'feeble-minded' people into the US, as the thinking went they might, through intermarriage and reproduction with Americans, lower the quality of the white, Anglo-American majority.

Enforcement of the law was initially arbitrary and difficult, as there was no easy or 'fair' way to determine the feeble-minded among the massive influx of people. That was until Goddard established his easily administered, 'scientific' IQ test programme on Ellis Island in 1913. Goddard's regime used a combination of visual screening (by his trained assistants), some 'obvious' rules (Goddard did not test people travelling in first or second class, and omitted the 'obviously' normal and 'obviously' feeble-minded) and administration of Terman's Stanford–Binet test.

Based on his Ellis Island testing, Goddard developed a new range of categories for people based on IQ. In this categorization Goddard took the next logical step in the use of big data analytics. If g was indeed a latent factor and the IQ test could quantify it, then PCA (under some questionable assumptions) provided the statistical 'proof'. Goddard's work translated this quantity into atoms of a new representation of human intelligence, which we can visualize as rules:

If $0 < x < 25$ *then* idiot (with probability given by the Bell Curve)

If $25 < x < 50$ T *then* imbecile (with probability given by the Bell Curve)

If $50 < x < 70$ *then* moron (with probability given by the Bell Curve)

If $70 < x < 130$ *then* normal (with probability given by the Bell Curve)

If $130 < x <$ infinity *then* gifted (with probability given by the Bell Curve)

This is precisely how big data analytics solved problems of expert systems AI – the problem of how very hard it is to find the right atoms of a representation. With big data analytics, first, you use data reduction (techniques like PCA) to find 'factors' in the data, like the *g* factor (usually while ignoring all the caveats and anomalies of the original information through the simplifying steps of data reduction). You do this, in one way or another, by reducing the data cloud to simple shapes. Then, you dice those shapes up along their easy-to-see axes, dividing the spread of data into ranges. Those ranges become *categories*, which are the atoms of your representation, the things you can use to classify things and make rule-based decisions about them (see Figure 5.2).

For instance, in this example 51–70 IQ range has become the symbolic atom 'moron', a word that Goddard himself invented from these statistics, drawing on the Greek word for 'foolish'. Once this categorization is complete, it's easy to make decisions about entire groups of people. For instance, at Ellis Island, Goddard was able to effectively and efficiently deny entry to around 80

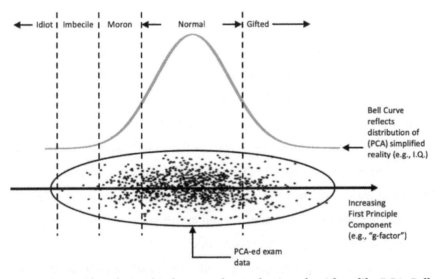

FIGURE 5.2 *The relationship between data reduction algorithms like PCA, Bell Curve quantifications and categorization 'atoms', with Goddard's 'idiot/imbecile/ moron/normal/etc.' classification as an example.*

per cent of the hopeful immigrants because of the categories into which they had been placed.

Through applying algorithms like PCA, the data itself dictates the quantities that can be turned into atoms of categorization, by rules, thus completely eliminating the challenges (and costs) of using human expertise to develop those rules. Bell Curve maths even provides the heuristic uncertainty factors. Of course, the representational biases, biased practices (like Goddard's concentration on steerage) and all of the previous assumptions are all still there. But like Spearman's bootstrapping conclusion that school-test factor analysis justified the existence of the g factor, these flaws in reasoning are obscured by the slew of mathematics involved, along with a voluminous fog of big data.

Despite categorical condemnation from Binet, who died in 1911, and Simon, who criticized the misuse of their test well into the 1960s, the 'scientifically designed', easily administered IQ tests were widespread by the 1920s and 1930s. The idea that each person could be evaluated and assigned a number that determined their societal value and destiny became an accepted cultural notion. Dedicated to quantifying the *differences* between people, the use of the test as a eugenics tool was inevitable, as it provided an efficient way to generate and categorize data, which could then be used to make so-called 'objective' decisions about whole groups of people (immigrants, prisoners, mental patients, deaf and blind people, alcoholics, indigents and 'promiscuous' women).

Given this historical precedent, it is more than a little worrying to learn of the new AI-powered Social Credit System (SCS) currently being developed in China, which will become mandatory in 2020. Its aim is to rate the 'trustworthiness' of every one of its 1.3 billion citizens, as well as corporations, assessing and evaluating all their online interactions in five categories: credit history, fulfilment capacity (i.e. does an individual honour contractual obligations), personal information (i.e. does a person have an address, phone number, etc.), behavioural preferences (i.e. shopping, travel, fitness, leisure, etc.

habits) and interpersonal relationships (i.e. what is the profile and extent of your friend network and what do your friends say about you). All of this will, via AI, be reduced to a single number, your so-called Citizen Score, which will be ranked publicly against the rest of the population and which will be used to determine your opportunities in life, such as eligibility for certain schools, loans or visas, your marriageability (higher numbers are already apparently status enhancing) or employability, or even whether you get fast-track check-ins at hotels or preferential treatment at restaurants. The government document[10] outlining the system says the system will 'Allow the trustworthy to roam everywhere under heaven while making it hard for the discredited to take a single step'.

America was the first country to enact significant negative eugenic practices as social policy based on IQ (including sterilization, institutionalization, segregation, birth control, forced abortions and rejection of immigrants). Many of these laws were authored or influenced by the work of Harry Laughlin, the Superintendent of the Eugenics Records Office from 1910 to 1936. He was an enthusiastic advocate for sterilization, authoring the Model Eugenical Sterilization Law and Virginia's Racial Integrity Act, which outlawed miscegenation.[11] Laughlin provided direct inspiration to the German Nazi Party, who also enacted sterilisation laws and zealously pursued the one-sided social utopianism at the heart of eugenics to its devastating conclusion in the Holocaust.

Given the devastating effects of the Second World War and the appalling consequences of the Nazis' eugenics programme, the idea of eugenics as a legitimate field of scientific enquiry was well and truly discredited by the war's end in 1945. But there was one area where the thread of eugenics thinking, stretching all the way back to the early days of Galton's Eugenics Laboratory, remained unbroken. That unbroken thread is IQ.

The year the war ended, American psychologist Raymond Cattell took an academic post at the University of Illinois. Prior to the Second World War,

Cattell had undertaken his PhD under the guidance of Spearman at UCL, where he had helped to develop factor analysis. Later, during the war, he served as a consultant to the US government, developing tests for selecting officers from First World War recruits. The tests were not dissimilar to the first mass experiment with IQ testing. Amongst the various questionable conclusions of this experiment was that Mediterranean races were inferior to Nordic races, and blacks were inferior to whites.

Since the *g* factor is a form of proto-big-data-analysis, it was inevitable that computing would be brought to bear on it, and with the installation of ILLIAC, the first university-owned, electronic computer at Illinois in 1952, Cattell became the first psychologist to use a computer to gather and analyse big data about people. Via computation, Cattell's later research used algorithms to greatly expand psychometric testing, finding more and more latent 'factors' from human big data. He created the idea of a 'crystalized intelligence factor', a separate 'fluid intelligence factor' and sixteen other latent factors describing human personality, all by using data analysis techniques like PCA to derive 'factors' from various test-based sources of big data. Cattell's work with ILLIAC was instrumental in developing the psychometric discipline into a legitimate field of study and, as a result, in 1997, the American Psychological Association offered him a Gold Medal Award for Lifetime Achievement. Though Cattell had distanced himself from his early work's relationships to race, the award was vociferously criticized by other members of the Association, who accused Cattell of being sympathetic to eugenics ideas, and Cattell subsequently withdrew his name for consideration and, in failing health, died a few months later.

Support for IQ testing and the analysis, quantification and ranking of diverse peoples survived in other quarters, notably those with mainly political, rather than academic, impact. For instance, the Pioneer Fund was established in 1937 by, among others, eugenicist and Nazi advisor Harry Laughlin, to support advocacy and research that promoted the cause of 'race betterment'.

The Fund's work continues to this day, although their banner has been modified to read '*human* race betterment'. Through the years, the Fund has supported repatriating African-Americans to Africa, opposed the civil rights movement, opposed desegregation bussing, and supported anti-immigration efforts, as well as financing academic publishing and research in anthropology and sociology, most of which is related to the issue of race. Perhaps the best-known work based on Pioneer Fund supported research was the 1994 book *The Bell Curve: Intelligence and Class Structure in American Life*, a book that has received renewed endorsement with the rise of the alt-right movement, and in turn revived Spearman's century-old ideas of the *g* factor. In the book, psychologist Richard J. Herrnstein and political scientist Charles Murray used meta-analysis (effectively analyses of many other analyses of populations of IQ tests) to assert that these tests categorically measure a real, underlying *g* factor. Their results purportedly indicate that high IQ is a clear indicator of positive social outcomes (like having a job, avoiding poverty, having legitimate children, staying out of jail, and having a positive, survey-based 'middle-class values index') and they, too, controversially conclude that *statistically* white Americans have substantially higher IQs than African-Americans, and that this difference is better explained by race than by socio-economic status.

Criticisms of *The Bell Curve*'s methodologies and intent are still hotly debated today, particularly given the recent rise of ethno-nationalism and the renaissance of so-called 'race science' among far right and conservative groups which espouse anti-immigration, neo-liberal and anti-welfare agendas. The intent of this book is not to revisit those arguments, but to point out the unarguable fact: that IQ testing and statistical analysis of intelligence represents a gross reduction of a complex human phenomenon to a single quantity. Moreover, the techniques involved in deriving not only this single number, but any set of reductive numbers about clouds of data, hide a host of complexities via a focus on data statistics. Data-reduction techniques hide the fluffy details of any cloud of data. Moreover, they hide biases that can be implicit in the design of the original data-gathering devices, in this case the tests that are used to determine IQ or the g factor. Arguments like those of Spearman (and the later writers who have reiterated his work) are precisely like those of Gravesande and Quetelet. It is important to remember that they aren't looking at the actual complex human systems they are considering, but data, which is always only a limited look into those systems, and then statistics, which are always a simplification of that data. An old quip, which upon reflection is more concerning than amusing, applies: 'Statistics are like bikinis. What they reveal is suggestive, but what they obscure is vital.'

6

Value Instead of Values

Power, like a desolating pestilence,
Pollutes whate'er it touches; and obedience,
Bane of all genius, virtue, freedom, truth,
Makes slaves of men, and of the human frame
A mechanized automaton.

From *Queen Mab* by PERCY SHELLEY

Pioneering educationalist Sir Ken Robinson has keenly observed that much of the modern, Western educational system is still modelled in the image and interests of the Industrial Revolution.[1] He points out how schools mimic factories in many ways, from the ringing of bells at the end of 'work sessions', to the division of knowledge into specialist subject areas, and the 'processing' of children through the system in 'batches' according to their age and ability. Standardized and aptitude testing, like the IQ test, are a part of this production line mentality, its aim being to evaluate and categorize children into the correct cohort, using simplifying metrics, and then funnel them through the system preparing them to become productive workers in the economy according to each person's intellectual capacity.

It is no coincidence that the invention and expansion of universal education took place during the rapidly industrialising eighteenth and nineteenth centuries. The new industrial economy needed workers with a certain level of practical and intellectual skill, and they had to be trained in sufficient numbers if the new economy was to thrive. As with our ideas of intelligence, some of our most dearly cherished economic beliefs are also shaped by the theories, philosophies and cultural norms of that era. And like IQ testing, these ideas contain a strong emphasis on metrics, simplification, mathematical modelling and an economic growth model predicated on Spencer's 'survival of the fittest' doctrine.

As a result, over the last 250 years, we have conceived of and created an economy in the image of a giant factory or machine that runs on the classical economic model of self-regulating markets, governed by supposedly *natural* laws of production and exchange, where prices and profits tend to a *general equilibrium*, famously captured by Scottish economist and philosopher Adam Smith's (1723–90) metaphor of the 'invisible hand'. We talk of 'market mechanisms', 'supply' and 'demand', and the image we hold in our heads of what the economy looks like was captured by economist Paul Samuelson in his 1948 Circular Flow diagram, whereby labour and capital go in one end and goods and services come out the other. Engineer and economist Bill Phillips even built a hydraulic machine called MONIAC (the Monetary National Income Analogue Computer), complete with transparent water tanks and circular pipes, to demonstrate how money flowed around Samuelson's system like fluids in a hydraulic mechanism.

But the modern economy is light years away from this simplistic factory-based model peopled by capitalists, workers and consumers. Now algorithms are also active, independent players in the market, though often their workings and motivations are obscure. These days high-frequency traders are more algorithmic rather than human, trading billions in milliseconds and causing inexplicable 'flash crashes' that even their own systems engineers can't explain because, as complexity scientist Neil Johnson has shown,[2] these algorithms are now operating in a new all-machine ecology. Furthermore, they remain 'unseen' and unrepresented in even the most complex models of our economic systems and they are barely understood at the highest levels of business and government.

And, yet, despite our woefully out-of-date economic model and bare grasp of how algorithms operate and interact with each other in our economic systems, we are now being told that robots and superintelligent AIs will soon displace not only the labour of human hands, but that of human minds in the knowledge and service economy as well. It is simply assumed that much of the thinking that people do can be broken down into simple, machine-friendly, task-oriented steps, which computers can execute with greater speed, precision and efficiency. But, just like the chasm that exists between handmade, artisanal objects and mass-produced products there are good reasons to suspect the quality of this computational 'thinking'.

Prior to the industrialized economy of the eighteenth century, Western European society was largely composed of five classes: noblemen, merchants, tradesmen, unskilled labourers and the rural peasantry. As members of powerful, organized guilds, it was the merchants and skilled tradesmen who powered the Renaissance economy from wool processing to shipbuilding and banking. Their guilds exerted considerable political and social power, setting standards of quality, limiting outside competition, training apprentices and providing charitable support to members' widows and children on their deaths. So, when William Lee sought a patent for his new 'stocking frame knitting machine' from Queen Elizabeth I in 1589, she refused him on behalf of the hosiers, saying the new technology 'would assuredly bring to them ruin by depriving them of employment, thus making them beggars'. The Queen didn't say this because she was a proto-champion of the proletariat, but because the hosiers' guild held real power. In fact, the guild was so strong that it influenced the denial of Lee's second patent application by James I, which prompted Lee to leave England for France, where he ultimately died in distress at his failed efforts.

It wasn't until the eighteenth century that Lee's idea of a mechanical knitting machine was revived in France, when in 1741 the talented inventor Jacques de Vaucanson was given the task of reforming the silk weaving industry, which was falling behind competitors in England and Scotland. The appointment must have seen as surprising to some, as up until that time Vaucanson was known for making *automata*. These mechanical simulations of animals and people had existed since ancient times, but up until Vaucanson's innovations they were largely just toys, often made from precious metals and used as decorative amusements for the very wealthy. However, Vaucanson had taken the devices to a new level, and gained international celebrity as a technologist, rather than merely a toymaker. His amazing machines included a life-sized, mechanical Flute Player that actually blew into and worked the valves of its instrument to create music, and a Digesting Duck, which to everyone's amazement could flap its wings, eat grain and even defecate (or so it seemed, although in reality the duck contained a hidden compartment where a mixture of breadcrumbs and green dye were stored for excretion). His devices were so awe striking that the philosopher Voltaire declared him 'The Modern Prometheus'.

Automata went from being toys to the AI of their day, with growing interests and efforts prompting speculation about their bearing on the future, along with actual technical advances, and gross manipulative frauds. The frauds included the 'Mechanical Turk', a device made by Wolfgang von Kempelen in 1769. This chess-playing figure of a man wearing Orientalist garb was able to mechanically move chess pieces, mysteriously managing to defeat many human players, including Benjamin Franklin. In reality, the secret to the Mechanical Turk's prowess at the game was the human chess master hidden inside the chess table, who moved the pieces on the board through the thin table top by using a magnet. Nevertheless, while Vaucanson's duck used some trickery to convey the impression of digestion, his mechanical innovations and skills were largely real, and by transferring his intricate knowledge from automata to weaving machines, he developed some of the first industrial technology that might be called 'automation', given its automata ancestors, though a less poetic term that was used at the time was *mechanization*.

Textile manufacture led the way in mechanization not only because of the industry's importance, but because of certain convenient characteristics of its nature. First, the raw materials involved, such as silk or cotton, are largely homogeneous, as is the yarn that is spun and the final cloth product. The manufacturing process that leads from one of these homogeneous artefacts to another is an extensive series of largely repetitive actions. Compared to products where things are less uniform, textile processes, organized step by step, were easy to replicate in machines. Vaucanson played a key role in creating the machines that did these steps, drawing on his experience with the intricate clockwork of automata.

The final step came in 1804 when Joseph Jacquard added one critical innovation to a Vaucanson-style weaving machine. Jacquard added a stack of cards with holes in them, which enabled machines to autonomously execute a sequence of loom configurations, such that the machines could create intricately patterned fabrics. Before this innovation, making complex, patterned fabrics required fiddly manual steps on something called a drawloom, with someone called a drawboy working beside the main weaver, configuring things called warp ends and heddles. These fundamentals of yarn work are all bits of arcana now, because variations on the Jacquard loom were adopted internationally, eliminating these last few skilled weaving jobs.

The elimination of essentially all high-skilled textile jobs by the eighteenth century meant massive job displacement, a devaluation of weaving skills and the degradation of working conditions for the remaining low-skilled workers who were retained to operate the machines. Similar effects were seen in other newly mechanized industries, leading to the destruction of the once powerful guilds. People soon realized that the craft skills they nurtured were no longer valuable in the nineteenth-century economy.

As the skill requirement dropped and wages fell in newly mechanized factories, women and children became the preferred workforce, as they could be paid less than men (who were often fired when they reached adulthood and then supported by their factory-bound families). Regardless of gender or age, workers laboured twelve- to fourteen-hour days, servicing, cleaning and resetting machines when they hit a snag. These jobs were dangerous and accident ridden, causing 40 per cent of all hospitalizing injuries. Factory air, polluted with the dusts of high-speed machine processing, caused a raft of new diseases for workers. Orphans and children from poor houses were conscripted into a new kind of factory-sponsored apprenticeship, which were very different from those of the guilds. A child working as a factory apprentice learned nearly no valuable and lasting skills, while living in barracks owned by their employer. As discipline, child apprentices were sometimes hung in baskets from high factory ceilings, or their ears were nailed to a table. These deplorable working conditions are what prompted William Blake's famous 1804 vision of England's 'dark, satanic mills', recounted in his poem 'And did those feet in ancient time', which is now preserved as the hymn 'Jerusalem', a song many have proposed as the English national anthem.

Shelley also took notice, and his political poem *Queen Mab*, with its references to frames and automata, was (amongst other things) concerned with the technological erosion of workers' rights and humanity's oppression in rapidly industrializing England. It was written in 1813 in the midst of the Luddite Rebellion (1811–16), when textile workers turned to destroying machines (in political acts called 'frame breaking') in a violent struggle for better working conditions. They named their movement after a legendry weaver Ned Ludd, who, tired of being whipped by his boss, smashed two of the machines that his labours serviced. Despite popular misconception that the Luddites were anti-technology and anti-modernity, at the core of the protest was a dispute around labour practices and well-founded concerns that the skills workers had spent years acquiring were being devalued, replaced by machines and cheaper and less-skilled workers.

The Luddites grievances were justified. The mechanization of the workplace not only resulted in the dehumanization of factories (quite literally, as fewer people were required to undertake the work) but the new work itself was dehumanizing. Broken down into smaller, simpler tasks, to match the operation of machines, work became mind-numbingly repetitious and required little skill. However, the cost of industrialization to people was no match for the increase in profit that mechanization promised. Eager to exploit these advantages and in no mood for disruption to their plans, mill owners took to shooting frame-breaking protestors on sight and, in 1812, the British government deployed 12,000 troops to extinguish the rebellion. It is a testimony to how powerful historical biases can be that we still refer to those with any reservations about technology or its deployment in human contexts as Luddites, with little understanding of what the real Luddites were fighting for.

While Shelley set up a fund to help support Luddite orphans, the British government moved to create a new law called the Frame-Breaking Act, to make the destruction of industrial machines a capital offence. In response, the twenty-four-year-old peer Lord Byron took up the Luddite cause in the House of Lords delivering a tub-thumping first speech to parliament, in which he compassionately argued for 'the rejected workmen'. Nevertheless, his efforts failed and frame breaking became punishable by death. On 2 March 1812, *The Morning Chronicle* published Byron's 'An Ode to the Framers Bill':

> Men are more easily made than machinery
> Stockings fetch better prices than lives
> Gibbets on Sherwood will heighten the scenery,
> Showing how Commerce, how Liberty thrives

Mechanization evolved to handle tasks outside of textiles, and spread quickly throughout industries and the world, nearly uniformly displacing jobs and degrading workers' rights along the way. Three decades after Vaucanson's marrying automata tech to industry, Adam Smith wrote *The Wealth of Nations*, the book which not only created the notion of the 'invisible hand', but foresaw the economic effects that mechanization would accelerate: *specialization*, and its inevitable consequence, *the division of labour*.

Imagine the making of a fine, eighteenth-century leather purse. A single person, working alone to make such a purse would have to know how to raise grain, feed livestock, slaughter them, skin them, tan those skins, and make tools to sew and work the leather (not to mention the finishing work). One person doing these tasks would be so woefully inefficient that the creation of the purse would be nearly impossible, and likely cost a fortune. But, Smith reasoned, if one person raised the corn, another the livestock, while still others did the tanning, etc., each could be efficient and effective in their work. These people would trade goods that they needed, and specialization of their labour (along with the 'invisible hand') would create products, not to mention an efficient and effective economy.

These ideas did not spring from Smith's head fully formed; they came from things he observed in the real world, natural outcomes of the evolution of people working together. There were well-established networks of farmers, butchers, tanners, leatherworkers and many others long before Smith's time. But Smith saw that new industrial practices would drive specialization to a far finer level, dividing labour into smaller and smaller tasks.

Smith's case in point was a pin factory he studied, where he observed that there were about eighteen distinct specializations, ranging from drawing out wire, through various cutting, sharpening, and finishing operations, to finally putting the sharp pieces of metal onto a paper card. Smith realized that while one worker probably couldn't have made a single pin a day, ten workers in these eighteen specializations could make about 48,000. The efficiencies of specialization were explosive, and thus the ever-finer division of labour was economically inevitable.

At least for pins. A pin of quality is like every other pin; in fact, that consistency is what defines its quality. Similar arguments hold for many other tools and machine parts. One might say that the opposite is true of a fine leather purse. That purse is made from organic raw material, which varies widely from batch to batch, because of its entire supply chain. The grain fed to the animals, the conditions in which the animals ate, were slaughtered and their hides tanned: all these factors could vary with a multitude of complex effects in the environment. An artisan would work with these varied materials responsively, as well as responding to other factors. The particular fashions of the time, knowledge of the in-the-moment needs of the end customer, and personal preferences and moods are also variable factors that would affect the artisan's craft and ingenuity. It is all of these contextual elements that make for a unique artisanal product. And we still value that uniqueness today as can be seen from the extremely high prices of handmade luxury goods.

Pins don't require this sort of artisanship, so they were a perfect illustration of Smith's theory. Smith saw that new industrial practices and mechanization would drive specialization to a far finer level, dividing labour into smaller and smaller tasks. However, he did also warn that the extreme division of labour could lead to 'the almost entire corruption and degeneracy of the great body of the people. . .unless government takes some pains to prevent it'. It was the same problem Shelley had foreseen in *Queen Mab*, when he noted that the unchecked power of industrialists 'like a desolating pestilence' turned the human frame into 'a mechanized automaton'.

Nonetheless, Smith's work laid the foundations of classical free-market economics and inspired legions of social scientists, economists and engineers. One such man was French mathematician Gaspard de Prony, who in 1791 went to work for the French Land Registry. The Registry were attempting to bring uniformity to the multiple measuring systems used throughout the country (in what would eventually become the metric system) and consistency to the calculation processes used in civil engineering. At that time, all complex calculations were done by using tables, not unlike those of Bell Curve values, which were created for computational convenience, storing calculations that came up over and over again in science, maths and engineering. With the right tables, engineers did not need to do those detailed and commonplace calculations; they only needed to find the right row in the right table in an engineering handbook. Many such handbooks, containing thousands of such tables, containing calculations like logarithms, trigonometric functions, and so on, were needed to power French advances in these fields. A typical table would store thousands of values, each calculated to between fourteen and twenty-nine decimal places. The resulting multitude of digits took massive time and skill to generate, and developing standard, quality tables for the Registry was the Herculean calculation task given to de Prony. He found a way to make it efficient and practical via direct inspiration from Adam Smith's division of labour. Prony decided that if he could divide up the calculation labour into a sort of computational factory, he 'could manufacture logarithms as easily as one manufactures pins'.

At the highest level of Prony's factory sat five or six skilled mathematicians with sophisticated analytical skills, who chose the formulas and specified the number of decimals and the numerical range of the tables. Then came a group of seven or eight lesser mathematicians who prepared templates and instructions, and the first worked row of calculations. Finally, there were sixty to eighty human 'computers' (this was a term developed for this new, human job at that time) who were not trained mathematicians and had only a rudimentary knowledge of arithmetic, but who carried out the most laborious and repetitive process following the templates and instructions. They even had available to them a fourth layer of ninety or so even less skilled computers, to whom they could further farm out the worst of this arithmetic drudgery. In fact, many of Prony's computers were out-of-work hairdressers who had fallen on hard times due to the guillotining of their clients during the French Revolution.

Mathematical table-making fit up against the division of labour even better than pin making, because almost all the complicated calculations needed could be reduced to a long, precise series of simple additions and subtractions, through techniques like 'the method of differences'. It's a mind-numbingly laborious way to get the right numbers, but it affords the efficiencies of Smith's pin factory. Human computer factories like this, enabled by the printing press, were soon distributing tables in a multitude of engineering reference books used by engineers building bridges and boilers, making looms and carrying out land surveys, and everything in between. Whenever a hard calculation was needed an engineer could simply turn the pages of a handbook to find the right row in the right table.

The next step in the evolution of computing factories was to come from an Englishman whose career was partially inspired by an automaton not unlike those created by Vaucanson decades before. In the last year of the eighteenth century, eight-year-old Charles Babbage saw a silver automaton of a naked woman in a Covent Garden amusement shop. When writing his autobiography over sixty years later, Babbage recalled the moment he first saw The Silver Lady, saying that the automaton 'attudinized in a most fascinating manner. Her eyes were full of imagination, and irresistible'.

Charles Babbage grew to become a mathematician and mechanical engineer whose accomplishments are vast and span everything from modern economics to the pricing of postage stamps, but his most famous accomplishment evolved from his realization of the one great flaw in de Prony's human computer factories. Regardless of the mathematical checks that the many human computers could place on one another to insure the validity of their digits, those digits had to be typeset by printing press workers who had no knowledge and likely no understanding of the calculations involved. There was always some probability that a digit would be typeset wrong. Babbage found such instances in standard tables, did a rough calculation of the probabilities of other errors and the impact on vital engineering calculations, and came up with an alarming probability of buildings collapsing, bridges falling, boilers exploding and looms mis-weaving that was far too high for comfort. It is said that in looking at one set of erred numbers, Babbage exclaimed: 'I wish to God these calculations had been executed by steam'.

Babbage would build on the idea of computing by steam for the rest of his life, starting in 1822 with a concept for a machine he called the Difference Engine. Like de Prony's factories, the machine broke calculations apart into many simple mathematical operations (specifically via 'the method of differences'). It conducted the fundamental arithmetic in much the way that a Pascaline (fitted with Leibniz wheels) did, using mechanisms of brass gears and levers, but Babbage's machine did these operations autonomously, and was on a much larger scale than any of its eighteenth-century predecessors. Crucially it was also fitted with a 'printer' at the end, which stamped out soft lead type to eliminate the errors of the human typesetter.

Babbage's Difference Engine was the most complex machine anyone had ever conceived, and while he was a great thinker and engineer, he was not the best possible manager for such a project. He relied on parliamentary grants for the expensive work, but his abrasive personality and poor politics dogged the project from the beginning. The scale of the effort was massive, so Babbage had to farm out the work to contractors. This prompted him to develop a precise system of drawings and mechanical notations, carefully breaking the machines into specialized parts. But as the build dragged on, the ever-inventive Babbage compulsively modified the drawings, making numerous innovations to the idea, many of which delayed its completion.

A positive side effect of Babbage's tinkering led to his ultimate breakthrough. He realized that by borrowing the idea of Jacquard's punched cards from the weaving loom, he could make a machine that was *programmable*, and thus able to do many different computations. Just as the loom cards created the pattern of a textile, they could change a pattern of arithmetic steps in a computational engine, and by simply changing the card deck, one could change what the machine did.

The result was a design for Babbage's second-generation computing machine, the Analytical Engine, the first (at least theoretical) general-purpose computer. But despite the brilliance of Babbage's ideas and designs, his engine couldn't actually be made to work. Problems in managing the massive project were part of the reason, but ultimately the Engine was doomed, ironically, by the limited technologies of the time: brass parts were too heavy and friction-bound to make for effective computers. But the years of managing the huge project with its complex work flows and endless design iterations were not to be wasted. Throughout the years, Babbage travelled extensively around England's industrial districts, noting the underlying principles of manufacture and the various technologies deployed in factories.

Along the way, Babbage realized that the very structure of his machines suggested how jobs might develop in the post-industrialized world. At the front end of Babbage's Engine were the Jacquard cards, the computer's programs, which, like the programmes made by de Prony's top-level mathematicians, required well-educated humans for their construction. In the middle was an autonomous machine that did laborious but simple computations, over and over again. At the far end was the printer which (once the engine was made to work) could spew out typeset numbers at a previously unrealizable rate. Babbage realized that all industrial machines have a similar structure: they require designers and operators at one end, making sure that the machine is set up to perform the required tasks; in the middle they displaced artisanal jobs by executing simple, repetitive operations; and at the end they turn out products at a rate that had never been seen before.

Babbage captured his division of labour and work-flow theories in his popular 1832 book *On the Economy of Machinery and Manufactures*. It is arguable that this book, rather than his un-completed computer engines, contains his most impactful legacy. In it, he transformed Smith's theory of the division of labour from a mere observation to a design tool for the economic future of the world. He did so by articulating the mathematical advantages for production afforded by specialization of tasks, and the related design of systems of human work in factory flows. Babbage also cited the 'advantages' of the division of labour in making it possible to insert women, boys and girls at very low pay into jobs formerly performed by men, thus reducing the cost of labour.

The mechanically driven scale-up principle he articulated is known as the 'Babbage Effect', and it specifically influenced two of the most enduring books on economics ever written. One was John Stuart Mill's 1848 *Principles of Political Economy*, which was a primary economics textbook in capitalist countries well into the twentieth century. The book drew on Babbage and offered the first systemic treatment of increasing returns on large-scale production. The other was Karl Marx's *Capital*, in which Marx's primary criticisms of capitalism rest largely upon Babbage's efficiency-driving division of labour, particularly the dehumanizing effects of greater and greater specialization:

> In handicrafts and manufacture, the workman makes use of a tool, in the factory, the machine makes use of him. There the movements of the instrument of labour proceed from him, here it is the movements of the machine that he must follow. In manufacture the workmen are parts of a living mechanism. In the factory we have a lifeless mechanism independent of the workman, who becomes its mere living appendage.

The other upshot of the Babbage Effect was the requirement of a more educated workforce to design, 'program' and operate industrial machines in order to turn out unprecedented volumes of products, which would then need more consumers. This new class of worker could perform roles at both ends of the machine, and create an entirely new economy. Hence the late-nineteenth and twentieth-century drive towards mandatory education throughout the Western world as governments realized that a more educated populace would result in a more productive economy, which in turn would generate greater prosperity and consumption, thus driving an apparently virtuous, work-earn-and-consume, tax-educate-and-work economic cycle.

This economic model is still with us today, and Babbage's ideas about the economy as a factory and the division of labour in the manufacturing industry are now deeply embedded in developed economies around the world. It is hardly surprising, then, that since the 1950s, when electronics finally enabled the realization of Babbage's nascent ideas of general-purpose computation, we have begun to question whether or not computers can substitute for the thought-work of people, enabling another massive escalation in productivity via the Babbage Effect.

This is another way of looking at the central question of AI: is it possible to divide the labour of human decision-making (in general, or even in a particular expert domain) into a set of computational atoms and mechanical rules to process them, such that they can be performed on a Babbage-style computer which was, after all, built on the concept of the computational division of labour? Given the potential economic advantages, finding an answer of 'yes' may be a self-fulfilling prophecy. However, the AI winter of the 1970s and 1980s seemed to demonstrate that atomizing human decision-making was simply too complex and expensive for practicality, and that the answer was a firm 'no'.

But the advent of the Internet, with its web-like social structure, cheap crowdsourcing potential and explosive scalability, has heralded a paradigm shift, much like steam technology did in the eighteenth century. Now it looks very possible that big data algorithms could replace a slew of white-collar intellectual jobs ranging from clerks, social workers and lawyers to general practitioners, policemen and judges. In fact, the process is already under way as increasing media reports and high-level policy conversations indicate, most notably at the 2016 World Economic Forum at Davos, where the focus was the 'Fourth Industrial Revolution' and whether intelligent automation might lay waste to a slew of human jobs. Or, in other words, for every given job someone holds today: 'Can the tasks of this job be sufficiently specified, conditional on the availability of big data, to be performed by state-of-the-art, computer-controlled equipment?' This was the central question of research on the subject of human job displacement by computers that has been broadly referenced in many articles and colloquia, including at Davos in 2016. The research, conducted at the Oxford Martin School in 2013, has led to a broad consensus that, yes, a great many of the jobs people do today will be taken by machines.[3] However, these results are themselves based on algorithmic big-data processing, so it's instructive to have a look at the realities of that processing. The central result is shown in Figure 6.1.

As can be seen from the legend, jobs in this graph are categorized into groups. These groups are shown as layered bands, with each band's varying

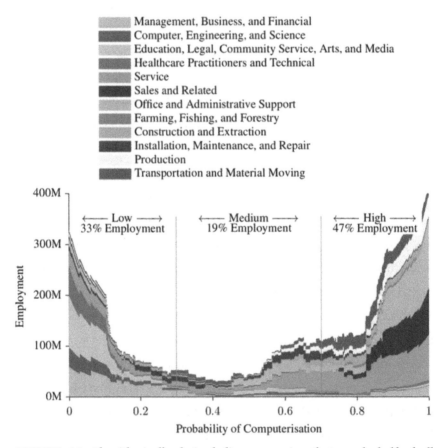

FIGURE 6.1 *Algorithmically derived diagram saying that nearly half of all human jobs can probably be done by computers, and only a third probably can't. Reprinted with permission.*

thickness at a given position left-to-right indicating the number of people holding certain jobs in that group. The left-to-right positioning reflects the varying *probability* that particular jobs will be taken by machines in the near future. Sliced into three neat vertical sections, the chart concludes that 33 per cent have a low probability of computerisation, 19 per cent are somewhat computerizable and a staggering 47 per cent are highly-computerizable. This graph covers 702 occupations, which employ 138.44 million Americans, or 97 per cent of the US workforce. Similar percentages can be extrapolated for workers throughout the world.

The graph delivers a dire and serious conclusion, but as with the results of all algorithms, we need to take a closer look under the bonnet to understand and evaluate those conclusions. This analysis used data made available by the US Department of Labour, in an online data set called O*NET, which divides the requirements of occupations into features, each of which has a written description, and rating number for each occupation. For any given job (say, dental assistant), feature ratings have been gathered by polling employers and employees in the field (in this case, dentistry), asking them to provide a number for each feature. Statistics of these numbers are used to determine to what degree features like 'creativity' and 'manual dexterity' (and 250 or so more) are required in any particular occupation. For instance, for a dental assistant, 'medical and dental knowledge' would have a requirement score 87 out of 100, 'English language' 81, 'customer and personal' service 76, 'clerical' 47, etc.

Referring to this data, the researchers at Oxford Martin used workshops to evaluate (through human consideration) the computerizability of just seventy occupations, while all the other jobs were evaluated by an algorithm. This was done specifically *to avoid human subjective bias* in the categorization of jobs, and it is instructive in how delegating jobs to algorithms is itself a sort of division of labour, dividing that labour into simplifying features, and how that division might hide biases of its own.

The jobs that were selected (by the human workshop participants) as fully computerizable included accountants, bus drivers, cashiers, fast food cooks, dishwashers, file clerks, casino dealers, sheet metal workers, technical writers, and twenty-eight more. That gave a total of thirty-seven jobs that computers, enabled with big data, could surely do, in the opinion of the workshop participants. In addition, some jobs were selected as not computerizable at all, even if one employed modern computers, AI and big-data analysis. Those occupations included athletes, chief executives, the clergy, dentists, economists, hairdressers, hunters, physicians, physicists, registered nurses, wait staff, zoologists, and twenty more, for a total of thirty-three. Together that gave seventy human-categorized jobs.

The computerizability of the remaining 632 job categories were determined by a machine-learning algorithm called a Gaussian Process Classifier, that used the seventy jobs categorized by the researchers as the basis from which to 'learn'. Like PCA, this algorithm constructs a simplifying shape that tries to best fit data points in a space, in this case the seventy jobs. But the Gaussian Process Classifier (GPC) can construct a far more complex shape than the flattened rugby ball of PCA. It can wildly warp a multi-dimensional Gaussian around the data points. This is hard to visualize, particularly in more than three dimensions, but the following thought experiment helps understand the algorithm. Imagine all the 702 jobs are in a data cloud in a three-dimensional space, like in the rugby ball example in the previous chapter. Now imagine taking away all but the seventy human categorized jobs, and that the computerizable jobs appear in one tight cloud together, widely separated from the other cloud of non-computerizable jobs, which are also tightly grouped together. Now imagine you have your flattened rugby ball, and that it's very rubbery: it can be stretched and warped in all sorts of directions. Take the ball, and stretch and bend it such that one of its pointy tips is over the cloud of the computerizable jobs, and the other tip is over the cloud of the non-computerizable jobs. Then add back in the other 632 jobs, which will appear somewhere inside and around the warped, flattened rugby ball. This is roughly what the GPC process is doing mathematically, except the rugby ball in this case is a cross section of a multi-dimensional Bell Curve: the fat part of that curve is the fat centre of the ball, and the skinny parts (what are called the 'tails' of the Bell Curve) are its pointy tips. What GPC is doing in this application is warping the Bell Curve to put its opposite (low-probability and high-probability) tails over the computerizable and non-computerizable jobs.

But to do this process, as is typical in big-data processing, some human decisions have to be made about what data to include, and what to exclude, to make the processing possible. Some of these decisions are often made by the availability of data; for instance, Spearman chose to focus on school exam results precisely because mandatory education had made that data available. Similarly, O*NET made the job feature data available, so it has been used as the basis for data analysis in this study. But often additional human decisions are made to prune the data down to features that are perceived by the algorithm's designers to be those that matter to the application at hand. For instance, in this application, from the more than 250 features of jobs that are scored in O*NET, only nine features were chosen by the creators of the study, because they felt these were features that were indicative of an underlying computerizability factor in the jobs. The researchers placed these nine features into three groups.

The first group has to do with perception and manipulation, and it included the O*NET metrics for *finger dexterity*, *manual dexterity* and *cramped work spaces (or awkward positions)*. The second group has to do with creative intelligence, which includes the O*NET ratings for *originality* and *fine arts*. The third group has to do with social intelligence and includes the O*NET numbers for *social perceptiveness*, *negotiation persuasion* and *assisting and caring for others*. Only these nine numerical features are used by the algorithm to determine whether a machine can do a human being's job.

After the GPC algorithm's Bell Curve is warped around to best fit to the seventy jobs into its tails, that curve (acting very much like a IQ test relative to

Spearman's *g* factor) naturally provides a 'probability' of computerizability for all the other 632 jobs, simply by putting the scores on these nine metrics into the warped Bell Curve (that mis-shaped rugby ball) that the algorithm has 'learned'.

Implicit in this approach is the assumption that the Bell Curve is somehow a natural distribution from which one can (and should) determine such probabilities. Moreover, the fact is that the resulting numbers aren't really probabilities under any definition that relates to the foundations of probabilistic maths at all. It's hard even to call them propensities. Despite the stated intention to use an algorithm to avoid subjectivity, these 'probabilities' are only *subjective ratings*, which are based on a very speculative form of statistic heuristic. That heuristic assumes that past poll numbers from the O*NET survey, reduced to nine features, processed through the workshop-and-feature methodology outlined above, and a machine-learning algorithm, can provide effective, Bell-Curve-based numbers that reflect the computerizability for these jobs. The graphic is the result of all these assumptions and processes. Labelling its x-axis as 'Probability of Computerizability', and then drawing conclusions about percentages of human jobs that will be lost in the future to computers, is highly speculative, at best.

Despite the realities behind these algorithmic ratings, there have been many quantitative conclusions drawn from the 'probabilities', job categories and employment statistics represented in this graph, and people seldom look beyond the resulting infographics to the specific conclusions for specific jobs. However, those results are provided in the study, in an appendix table where the jobs are ranked from 0 to 702, with the highest number being the most computerizable category of job. That job is Telemarketer, with a near certain probability of computerizability of over 0.99. Right behind Telemarketers, with the same probability to two decimal places, are Hand Sewers.

One would assume that given that their jobs were largely eliminated by Lee's and Jacquard's weaving frames in the 17th and 18th century, Hand Sewers occupy some tiny fraction on the far right of the layer labelled in the legend as "Production." Behind Hand Sewers, again with the same probability, are Mathematical Technicians, reminding us how Babbage's Engine design was expected to eliminate most of the human computers in de Prony's factories. One would expect that their jobs are some tiny fraction of the far right of the layer labelled "Computer, Engineering and Science" in the legend, since their jobs have been gradually eliminated since the realization of general-purpose computers in the 1950s. Insurance Underwriters are the next most computerizable job. There's every reason to expect that there are lots of those in modern employ, and that those jobs occupy some part of the layer labelled "Office and Administrative" in the legend, which is so fat on the right-hand-side of the graph.

There are quite a few other modern jobs that are interesting to consider. While Athletes were human-categorized as completely non-computerizable, the algorithm only manages to squeeze them in at the 0.28 'probability' level in the warped Bell Curve tail. However, the job of Umpires and Referees was ranked as computerizable with a 0.98 probability. Apparently, enforcing the rules of the games *people* play is almost entirely doable by a machine. Perhaps the most amusing result in the study is the computerizability of Models (as in Fashion Models), who also have a 0.98 probability of being replaced by computers coming in at ranking 669 out of 702 jobs.

It is an absurd conclusion, but one can't actually fault the simplified reasoning of an algorithm for drawing it, given the processes and nine features within which the question has been framed. Reflecting on the nine features it's clear that the job of a fashion model rates low for all of them. Modelling doesn't require finger dexterity, or manual dexterity, or working in cramped spaces (though the mention of awkward positions may prompt a giggle). If we looked carefully at the data, the assignment of numbers for creative intelligence or fine arts might insult many models, but these numbers are after all drawn from a human populace, and include associated commonplace, sexist and

Zoolander-prompted biases relative to that profession. While assisting or caring for others is a stretch as a job requirement for modelling, social perceptiveness, negotiation and persuasion are thoroughly debatable points. However, the underlying data, with its survey-based sources, is likely to rate all these features as low for Models. Thus, it is only logical that the algorithm ranks Models as highly replaceable by machines, even though it defies human-judged credibility.

Human models are not machine-like in any way, which is why it seems so laughable that the Gaussian Process Classifier could assume that any sort of automata could take their jobs. The work of Models is intensely subtle, involving a very human form of attraction, expressiveness and communication. Modern technology has not only not achieved the replication of those abilities, it even has a difficult time replicating the *human-like* charm of old-world toys like the Silver Lady, which are the products of lost, artisanal craftsmanship. These kinds of human factors, which are not easily divided into a list of features, and not easily divided into a series of mechanical steps, are not just employed by Models and craftsmen, they are an aspect of a multitude of jobs, particularly those where people interact with each other.

Just like we fashioned our economy to look and work like the machines that inspired it, we currently look set on fashioning our future digital economies and algorithmic infrastructure on out-moded models based on the extreme division of labour, the simplification of tasks and the atomisation of workers into low-skilled, low-paid 'machine support' jobs (for tasks that machines simply can't do due to a lack of dexterity) and mind-numbing mental service work (to fill the intelligence gaps of not-so-smart AI).

The reality is algorithms, while useful modelling tools, are statistically simple-minded, rigid representations of highly complex phenomena and should not be relied upon solely when making socially impactful decisions. Fashioned conceptually in the Industrial Revolution, their flaws reveal the limitations of the statistical and economic theories that underpin them, wedded as they are to simplification and decontextualization. AI's *codify* that simple-mindedness and drive it to a logical, mechanical extreme.

One of the most illustrative examples of where this is leading the modern economy is in the configuration and operation of Amazon's vast distribution warehouses. In these enormous windowless structures 'stock pickers' (they are not called 'employees') are monitored by cameras, while electronic wristbands algorithmically control their movements by telling them where to go and what to select from the millions of algorithmically ordered products placed to optimize workers' movements between shelves. Toilet and lunch breaks are timed, emails are constantly monitored and employee performance is measured. Although since dropped, in 2016, the company even patented a *cage* atop a trolley to carry workers into areas of the warehouse where robotic workers operate.[4]

It's hard to imagine a more dehumanized or dehumanizing vision of a workplace, but at least in the real world we can see and identify abuse and exploitation and hopefully correct it. But what happens when we can't actually see what's going on, much like the trick Vaucanson played on the public with the hidden guise of his Digesting Duck, or the fraud committed by von Kempelen with the chess master hidden inside his chess playing Turk? Without a hint of irony, in 2005 Amazon launched a crowdsourcing Internet marketplace called Amazon Mechanical Turk, the object of which is to crowdsource human intelligence to undertake micro-tasks that computers are currently unable to do.

Amazon's Mechanical Turk is a sort of post-irony imitation of its eighteenth-century predecessor. It is accessed through the Internet through an *API* (application programming interface), precisely as if its internal operations were those of Internet software. Employers can use this interface to formally specify a simple task called a Human Intelligence Task (or HIT). Those tasks aren't done by software; they are undertaken by a largely hidden, distributed army of lowly paid people, informally known as *Turkers*, who deliver the results programmatically. Tasks include things like answering simple surveys, selecting words to describe images from multiple choices and transcribing text from blurry photos of documents, which is then largely used by companies to train AI machine-learning algorithms, which then deliver results to end users who believe the task has been accomplished via artificial intelligence! As Ayhan Aytes observed in *Return of the Crowds*,[5] just as with Kempelen's 1770 Mechanical Turk: 'the performance of the workers who animate the artifice is obscured by the spectacle of the machine'. Rather than reducing human labour to mere step-by-step tasks, MTurk (and other similar services that have sprung up) allow programs to use human brainpower for mind-numbingly simplified tasks that have proved irreducible to computation. Such services allow such work to be done on a massive scale, very cheaply. By 2011 there were a reported 500,000 Turkers located in 190 different countries and as *The Atlantic* reported in 2018 most of these workers are isolated and living in areas where traditional employment has dried up.[6] Employed as contractors, Turkers have no labour protections and aren't subject to minimum wage laws. Turkers are the poorly paid backstop for algorithmic imperfections, in much the same way workers in the early industrial era were paid poorly to service machines.

Throughout the new 'gig' economy, there are people working with limited protections, responding to algorithmic management. The drivers of services like Deliveroo and Uber have their work assigned by algorithms and do the part of their task that the algorithms simply cannot do: speedy delivery to the door, in navigation situations (on bike and on foot) that are unlikely to be effectively addressed by autonomous vehicles anytime soon (although that, too, is wildly promised). Likewise, Amazon warehouse workers select products from shelves that would be difficult for robots to identify or handle, but feed an otherwise mechanized system of sales, order and delivery (excepting those final delivery steps, which are also increasingly done by algorithmically controlled humans). Everything in these systems is managed algorithmically with incentives and punishments hard-wired to performance metrics. Deliveroo riders who do the most drops get benefits (like the most lucrative time slots), but those who fail to meet their targets get a lower rating and a less lucrative shift next time. Marx's vision of people as the 'mere living appendage' of a mechanism is fully realized here.

The number of people doing this simplified, but difficult to computerize, Victorian-style piecework is growing rapidly, having increased at least by a factor of ten in just the last three years. That's because the distributed 'factory model', whereby workers are rebranded as self-employed contractors (Deliveroo riders are called cycling micro-businesses), offers a way to further reduce labour costs: paying per job rather than per hour, eliminating the need for overtime, holiday pay, sick pay, parental leave or pensions. And in each of these jobs, the erosion of workers' rights has started to become a serious social concern, resulting in the unreliable availability of work, depressed wages as low-skilled workers are interchangeable, dangerous working conditions, and denial of basic human comforts in the workplace.

In the case of food-delivery service Deliveroo, the *Guardian* reported in 2017 that the company is now investing in 'dark kitchens',[7] which take the form of windowless metal boxes not dissimilar to shipping containers kitted out with industrial kitchen equipment, where chefs frantically prepare meals to feed the increasing demand for takeaway food. Projected to grow tenfold by 2030, a report from investment firm UBS in 2018 entitled 'Is the Kitchen Dead?', described a perfect case of the Babbage Effect:

> Assuming a progressive shift to dark kitchens and declining delivery costs, the economic benefits of one hour spent cooking [relative to ordering a meal via an app] could decline from £13 per hour to £8 per hour ... i.e. lower than the median wage.

The UK's Skills and Employment survey revealed that nearly a third of workers now have to work at very high speed 'all' or 'most of' the time, while the share of people who have 'a lot of discretion over how they do their job' has crashed from 62 per cent to 38 per cent.[8] Instead of the proletariat we now have the precariat: a class of people with insecure jobs afraid to ask for pay rises or improved working conditions. And, just like the Luddites before them, workers insist that they are not against innovation, technology or flexibility, they just want some basic rights and security. From dark kitchens it doesn't seem like such a large step to Blake's 'dark, satanic mills'.

While there are currently no signs of online services nailing children's ears to tables, the dehumanizing effects of quantification as it reaches into the far corners of our cognitive and affective worlds is already painfully evident. In an attempt to bring the dark corners of the digital economy and digital systems into the light, organizations like AI Now Institute are undertaking pioneering work to help us see some of the physical, cognitive and natural costs of AI technologies. As authors Kate Crawford and Vladan Joler write in their insightful study 'Anatomy of an AI System': 'Digital labour – the work of building and maintaining a stack of digital systems – is far from ephemeral or virtual, but is deeply embodied in different activities.'[9] And to help us visualize the extraordinary complexity of the global factory AIs now depend upon, they offer an arresting graphic, which with its geometric, machine-style structures and factory-like work-flow looks strikingly like Babbage's elaborate Difference Engine designs (see Figures 6.2 and 6.3).

With the illusionary promise of frictionless efficiency and explosive scalability, it seems inevitable that increasing areas of work will be automated, resulting in the literal dehumanization of the workplace. In many ways this seems remarkable in a post-industrial era apparently committed to historically hard-won worker's rights and replete with ideas of employment as a means of personal fulfilment.

Consider the role of Receptionist, which in the Oxford Martin jobs study is considered to be highly computerizable, ranked at 628, with a probability of

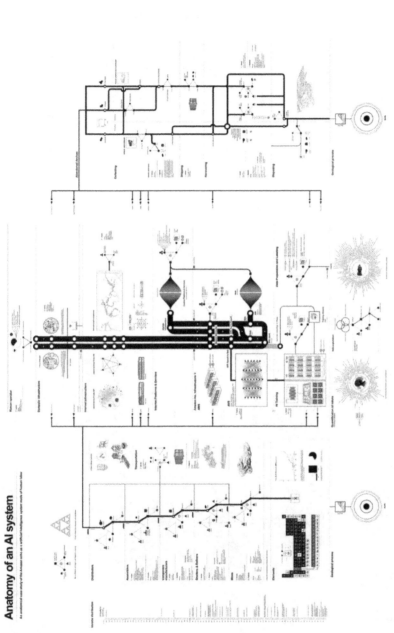

FIGURE 6.2 *A diagram of the global factory that produces and supports Amazon's Echo (the device commonly known by the name of its disembodied AI, 'Alexa').*

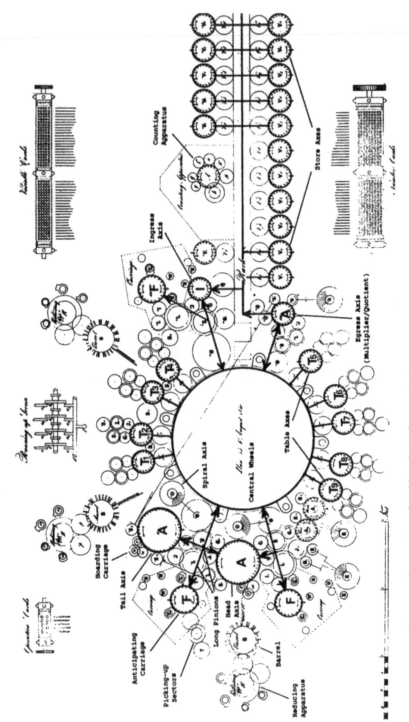

FIGURE 6.3 A diagram of a portion of Babbage's Difference Engine.

computerizability of 0.96. It is certainly possible to imagine certain elements of a receptionist's work might be computerizable, but there is clearly more to a good receptionist than this set of simplified tasks. A good receptionist is a person's first contact with an organization. They must greet people, keep them at ease when inevitable scheduling conflicts arise, or even brush someone off when their scheduled meeting has been pointedly but covertly cancelled. But this does not mean that receptionists aren't already being replaced by computer equipment. Kiosks that do most of the tasks listed above have begun to replace receptionists in many situations, including the UK's National Health Service. Checking in for appointments is now automated in many surgeries and while a human receptionist currently remains nearby, that person's efforts are, ironically, liable to be directed at a computer screen, where they carry out other duties, to best exploit the efficiencies the kiosk is providing.

In the O*NET data, receptionists are lumped in with 'Informational Clerks' and all manner of other clerking which is considered highly computerizable. Only Judicial Law Clerks were hand categorized as non-computerizable, though the Gaussian Process Classifier put them at a probability of 0.41 and Court, Municipal and License Clerks survived as less computerizable than not. Travel Clerks, Stock Clerks, Correspondence Clerks, Expediting Clerks, Loan Clerks, Mail Clerks, Office Clerks, Rental Clerks, File Clerks, Timekeeping Clerks, Credit Clerks, Auditing Clerks, Shipping Clerks, Procurement Clerks, Order Clerks, Brokerage Clerks, Processing Clerks, New Accounts Clerks, and a few others, are all ranked as more likely to be done by computers than not. Though Clerks are likely scattered throughout the graphic, many of them are probably concentrated in the layer that is largest on the right-hand side of the chart (the one labelled "Office and Administrative Support" in the legend), indicating a significant number of people's jobs at risk of computerisation.

Given the common perception of jobsworth clerks this may seem like no bad thing, but even here it is important to sound a note of caution. The role of a clerk may be unglamorous, but organizations rely heavily on administrative clerks to receive and process information about customers, suppliers, products and services. Clerks need to be reliable and organized, and have good attention to detail. And quite often a long-serving clerk will know the inner workings of a company better than anyone else.

Edmund Morel was just such a clerk at the Elder Dempster Shipping firm in Liverpool, where he secured a position in 1891. Thanks to his command of French, Morel was often sent to Belgium to view the accounts of the shipping contract the company held with Congo Free State. In doing this, Morel noticed that ships leaving for the Belgian Congo carried only guns and ammunition, and those returning only contained rubber and ivory. Morel estimated that the value of goods coming from the Congo was five times that of the armaments being shipped there, and he correctly deduced that the difference was being extracted by force. Morel's revelations and subsequent activism exposed what was to become known as the 'Congo Horrors', the Belgian genocide that saw the death of 13 million Congolese between 1885 and 1908 in the effort to exploit the country for its natural resources.

Now imagine Edmund Morel's job being done by an algorithm. That algorithm would most certainly be programmed with an economic imperative, as profit is the goal of most companies and shareholders and is also the quantitative feature that is the easiest to program. As a result, an algorithm would simply never notice the discrepancy in the accounts that Morel saw as long as the money continued to flow in the right direction. And, it certainly could never extrapolate from the numbers to the human catastrophe, much less communicate the horror to the outside world with the compassion Morel demonstrated in his subsequent activism.[10]

There's a lesson to be learned here from what really happened in the earliest history of industrial mechanization. The reality is that the skills of respected seventeenth- and eighteenth-century artisans were not bettered by mechanization. Artisanal products did not cease to exist then, or in fact cease to be superior to the work of machines, even in the highly homogeneous activity of textile manufacture. Handmade silk, hand-embroidered fabric, hand-cut and tailored suits all still exist, and are all still considered to be vastly superior products to the machine-made textile goods that the vast majority of people consume. This is because the 'Babbage Effect' relies on breaking human labour into simpler tasks, and inevitably that means overall simplification of complex effects, of the sorts that humans best perform.

The difference today is that the human craft being taken over by machines is not just product based, it is about our fundamental human interactions with our GPs, lawyers, bank-account managers and so on. Inevitably, the economic pressures will begin to yield the same effects in these social contexts that they had in manufacturing, resulting in the rising expense of human-to-human interactions, making them less a part of common life and more a luxury for the better off. Moreover, because human work exists within a system where machines are likely to economically displace jobs, many more people will be driven into isolating work environments, like the Turkers.

The merging of profit-maximizing economic and metric-optimizing scientific objectives, driven by and driving technological progress, forms a Gordian knot at the heart of AI. Perceived optimality and the efficiency of specialization drives economic progress, but with it we lose the art of the craftsman and the benefits of synergistic working. Simplification is a convenient skill in scientific modelling, and is the great driver of efficiency, but by its reductive nature it often obscures rather than illuminates the complexity of what we seek to understand. Algorithms that divide complex human capabilities into simplified features are not only a catalyst for dehumanization, they are the mechanism that causes it. To overcome this, we need to think again about AI's role in the economy and society from the point of view of the welfare of humanity rather than the overriding efficiency of the machine.

7

Women's Work

Essentially, all models are wrong, but some are useful.
G.E.P. BOX, 1976[1]

With much of the current focus on the socio-economic impacts of AI, what has largely gone unasked is whether algorithmic models really are models of intelligence, or in fact models of the world around us. Obvious errors, like the classification of fashion models as highly computerizable, or racist image searches for unprofessional hair, are usually put down to inadequacies in the data, or the algorithmic methodology used to process it. But what if there's something more fundamentally wrong with the approach overall?

Whether by the classical logic of 'if/then' rules-based expert systems or the statistical modelling of big data, all algorithms have at their core *models*. These models consist of frames and atoms; narrowing of scope to a particular concern, and quantifying it with an enumerated set of features. In problems of real complexity (like those that deal with human beings or human societies), these models are always simplifications, and it is combinatorially explosive to try to de-simplify them.

All models of complex things are sure to succumb to their own brittleness and fail in some situations that weren't foreseen by the modeller, the person who created the algorithms involved. The question, which the quote from statistician George Box prompts, is what do we do when our models are found to have errors? Do we disregard them as outliers, or do we see them as useful prompts to rethink the assumptions of our models?

History shows us that when these erroneous assumptions are based on existing social norms and prejudices, we tend to treat them as outliers, best ignored. Given the embedding of assumptions in the complex algorithms of our social infrastructure today, it's even more likely that exceptions to accepted models will fall by the wayside, as the assumptions become hidden in mathematical and computational fog. There's a peril to this reality, one revealed by more careful study of what Box's famous quote was about.

George Box (1919–2013) was one of the greatest statistical minds of the twentieth century. He was a specialist in Bayesian inference, the statistical technique at the heart of many of the sophisticated algorithms of today. Originally a student of chemistry, he was assigned to the British Army Engineers during the Second World War, where he was given the task of determining the effects of poison gas which might be used as chemical weapons. His experiments yielded test results that were so varied he couldn't make sense of the data, so he asked that a statistician be assigned to help him. None were available, so Box bought some statistics books and taught himself to analyse the data, and did work that provided some insights into the effects of gas on soldiers and how they might best be treated.

After the war, Box was awarded the British Empire Medal for his contribution, and returned to school to formally study statistics, later earning his PhD from UCL under the supervision of Egon Pearson, the son of Karl Pearson, the founding father of statistics. Over the decades, Box made an enormous contribution to the field of statistics and yet, despite being a specialist in modelling strategies, he is most famously remembered for the cautionary quote that all models are wrong, and some are useful.

Box made his iconic statement because he understood that modelling complex phenomena *requires* simplification. Therefore models – and, by extension, the algorithms built upon them – always offer a *selective view* of a problem or situation, based as they are on the selection of fixed features (such as the nine variables in the job computerizability study) and statistical techniques (like the algorithmic details of the GPC), which jointly form the particular model of the problem at hand.

These often-detailed differences of models are why algorithms studying the same problem can sometimes turn up different conclusions, as in the case of Dr Jane Green's and Dr Chris Cardwell's opposing conclusions on whether osteoporosis drugs cause cancer of the oesophagus.[2] If the frame (perspective) of a model is different, if the 'atoms' used are different, or if the dataset being analysed is different, then the outcomes can be different. This example, and literally millions of others that litter the scientific literature, are precisely what Box meant when he said 'all models are wrong'.

Nevertheless, given the complexity of the real world, the scientific process depends on simplifying models, as do algorithms. When scientists are faced with a complex problem they first need to devise an experiment based on a simplifying model in order to progress their knowledge. That model inevitably involves some initial assumptions that need to be tested against observations in the real world. Observations that fit the model are gratifying, but those that don't are perhaps the most important part of the scientific process. They should prompt the evolution and innovation of assumptions. Unfortunately, this isn't always what happens, particularly in models that simplify people, and even more so when errors go up against established social biases, the models we have of society and how simple features of people determine their roles within it.

Like many social and philosophical ideas revived in the Age of Enlightenment, *the separate spheres model* of society dates back to the ancient Greeks, when Aristotle, in his work *Politics*, described two distinct social spheres: *oikos*, the home and the domain of women, versus *polis*, the city, the public arena, which was populated by men. But, like eugenics science, the separate spheres notion of biologically determined gender roles kicked into high gear during the Industrial Revolution, when droves of men first left home to sell their labour in newly constructed factories. The theory conveniently matched these socio-economic changes, holding that men are best suited to work outside the home (earning wages) while women are best suited to working (unpaid) in the home, managing child rearing and domestic affairs.

Before the Industrial Revolution, the majority of men and women worked at home in agricultural roles. As nascent industries emerged in the Renaissance, those with valuable skills, such as carpentry and sewing, were able to supplement their incomes via the original cottage industry,[3] whereby the agents of large companies 'put out' work– such as firearms, furniture and textile manufacture – to home-based craftsmen and women in an early, proto-mass-production model, before the rise of mechanized factories. Similarly, before the rise of de Prony's computer factories, the work of calculation was put out to cottage industry. This included the most important calculation of the day, that which allowed the life blood of commerce to flow through the navigation of ships on the sea.

Finding one's position on the Earth is hard, because the Earth is spinning. The stars in the sky can help you tell where you are from North to South (latitude), but not from East to West (longitude), because the Earth spins East to West under the canopy of stars. For centuries, this fundamental fact of life meant a substantial risk that merchant ships laden with valuable cargo might go astray, or warships might not arrive at the scene of battle on time, because they couldn't accurately tell where they were East to West. Modern GPS fixes this longitude problem by placing satellites above the Earth that spin in geostationary orbit so that we can measure against their fixed position (relative to Earth) to determine our location and plot our routes. But there were no objects in the sky fixed relative to Earth when the blood of commerce flowed through the world on ships at sea. So while we now view astronomy as a niche hobby, up until the nineteenth century it was one of the most important fields of human endeavour, business as serious as building B-52s during the Cold War, or big-data algorithms today. Finding a computational solution to the longitude problem was the most important challenge in that vital endeavour. English Astronomer Royal Nevil Maskelyne was charged with this challenge, which made him the most important technologist of his time. Maskelyne developed a system for determining one's longitude, but unfortunately it required the computation of massive tables.[4]

The secret to Maskelyne's longitude system is that it is relatively easy to know what time it is in a particular location on the spinning surface of the Earth, because no matter where you are on Earth, as long as weather allows you to see the sun, you can determine the local time (particularly at midday, when the sun is at its maximum height). If you also know what time it is in a particular place on Earth (in the UK, the reference location was chosen to be the location of the Royal Observatory and Royal Naval College in Greenwich), you can measure what your longitude is (relative to Greenwich Mean Time) by subtracting the time at Greenwich from the local time. The problem is knowing what time it is at Greenwich. Maskelyne knew that the moon's distance from various stars in the sky is unique to a given time of day, for any given day in a year. So, if one had a *table* of those distances, one could determine the time at Greenwich by looking at the moon's position relative to those stars.

The challenge was computing that table, which required significant amounts of maths. In the mid-eighteenth century, machines like the Pascaline were the only computational devices available, and there were precious few of them in the world. A single mathematician, even one armed with a Pascaline, could spend a great deal of time making calculations and still never produce the quantity of calculations that were needed. So Maskelyne did what was done in many other industries at the time. He used cottage industry.

In 1765, funded by the British Admiralty, Maskelyne wrote a detailed programme for mathematicians, who could work from their own homes computing the necessary table entries for the Nautical Almanac, the navigational reference for every British ship at sea. Maskelyne gave this vital computational work to friends and associates he knew were good mathematicians and in need of supplemental income. One such man was John Edwards, who had been introduced to Maskelyne by a professor of theirs at Cambridge, who now served with Maskelyne on the Board of Longitude (the organization charged with solving the longitude problem by Parliament). Maskelyne gave Edwards the extra work, which nearly doubled the Edwards family income, and allowed John to continue his official work as a Shropshire clergyman, while also supporting his hobby, astronomy.

Unfortunately for John Edwards his hobby was to prove fatal when, in 1784, he inhaled arsenic while coating a telescope mirror with metal. This left his wife Mary a widow with two young daughters to support. Furthermore, the family were rendered homeless on John's death, as they lived in a rectory owned by the church. On top of that John's astronomical hobby left his family substantial debts. With nowhere else to turn, Mary was forced to go to Maskelyne and ask for help, revealing a surprising fact. She was the family's home computer and had been supplying the computations for the Nautical Almanac for over a decade.

Given her desperate circumstances, Mary asked Maskelyne not only to continue her employment, but to give her even more work. He must have been convinced of her abilities, because he changed the name on the contracts from 'John' to 'Mary', and eventually gave Mary half of all the Almanac's computer work with the remaining half shared by two other computers, both men. Through these strange circumstances, Mary Edwards became the most important computer on Earth for forty critical years of the British maritime era. She was still working on the Almanac when she died in 1815, by which time she had trained one of her daughters to take over the work. Thus, the Edwards ladies provided a substantial part of the computation that ensured Britain's supremacy at sea during the country's most powerful period in history, enabled the defeat of France in the Napoleonic Wars and paved the way for the British Empire's domination of nearly half the world in what is considered the largest empire in history.

All this, despite the prevailing separate spheres model that said Mary should have been focused on childcare, housework and religious education, and should have been *incapable* of attaining the intellectual heights of her male contemporaries. Furthermore, Mary's talents appear even more extraordinary in light of the fact that she almost certainly did not receive a formal education in mathematics (at the time, even upper-class girls, if they did go to school, attended 'dame schools' where the focus was on training to be a good wife and mother), which begs the question of how she learned to do what she did. Did she learn maths at home as a child from books studied by her father or brother? Did John teach her? Or was she just a gifted prodigy who took to the computations with little help from others, perhaps learning from puzzles in *The Ladies' Diary*, a popular almanac of the time (which her husband is known to have read, and submitted puzzles to when he was at Cambridge)? We will never know, because we don't even know Mary's maiden name.

There's no doubt that Mary Edwards is an enormous aberration in the separate spheres model. So outstanding was her contribution as the key employee in the most important technological organization of the eighteenth century that she seems in all ways to indicate an event that should have caused a significant rethink of the separate spheres model. That, of course, didn't happen and even today few people know her name (although a very minor planet, 12627 Maryedwards, is named in her honour).[5]

There are two things that make models effective. The first is parsimony: a good model should have as few and as simple atoms as is possible. The second is power, or the significance of the output. A powerful model should accurately predict things that really matter. Balancing parsimony and power is what good modelling is all about, in science, and in algorithms. There is always a natural tension between the two, and how one treats observations that don't conform to models is at the heart of that tension.

Box did more than simply say that all models are wrong, and some are useful; he also provided advice on how the scientific process should be affected by observations that don't fit existing models. Box saw these errors as a revelatory part of the scientific process, in that they should make us go back and reconsider the model from first principles. In the same paper as his famous quote, he provided a wonderfully insightful diagram to demonstrate how the modelling process should work, which is updated and amended for the age of algorithms in Figure 7.1. Box captioned his figure thus: 'The experimental design is here shown as a movable window looking onto the true state of nature. Its positioning at each stage is motivated by current beliefs, hopes, and fears.'

Box's movable window is a fantastic metaphor for our inevitably selective perspective and the limited frames we create to model complex problems. To

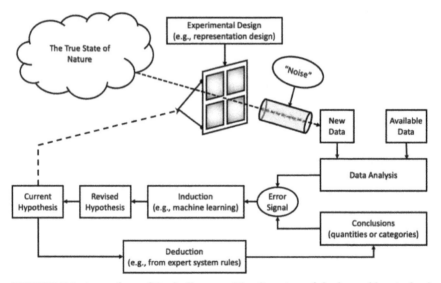

FIGURE 7.1 *An update of Box's diagram. The directing of the 'movable window' is still 'motivated by current beliefs, hopes, and fears', but how we see the 'true state of nature' is now deeply influenced by machine learning and algorithmic deduction, which change representation design, and thus can accelerate and amplify the innate biases in those beliefs, hopes and fears.*

one side of the window is reality, the 'True State of Nature', a fluffy cloud which we cannot fully comprehend or even see; while on the other side of the window, filtered through our 'beliefs, hopes and fears', are our models.

In Box's model, errors drive the modification of hypotheses, which results in steering the movable window (or in the case of humans, the adjustment of opinions and perspectives) that we use to look at the 'true state of nature'. Data that we see through the movable window is always corrupted by 'noise'. The question is whether the errors we see in the observations we make (relative to the models we have) are treated as merely 'noise' in our 'data analysis', or whether they are a meaningful 'Error Signal' that should prompt new steering of the window, to form new models from which we make new conclusions about the world. Are exceptions to our models merely *outliers*, statistical anomalies that are best ignored, or are they reasons to reconsider the models we have? What is the price of mistaking one for the other?

One conclusion is that Mary's low social status and her low visibility role as a rural clergyman's wife meant that her scientific contribution was doomed to remain obscure (despite the fact that the famous Maskelyne knew of her work). In the face of the socially dominant separate spheres model, Mary was clearly considered an outlier. On Maskelyne's death in 1811, the conventional 'beliefs, hopes, and fears' of the new Astronomer Royal John Pond resulted in a reduction in Mary's work until the powerful Board of Longitude intervened and overruled him. But as cottage industry waned and the Almanac's computing work was centralized in London in 1832, Mary's daughter (who took up her mother's work on her death in 1815) was soon to find herself out of work altogether as new Civil Service rules dictated that women weren't permitted to work at the new HM Nautical Almanac Office.

But what if Mary's social standing had been higher, and her work more visible? Would that have helped to shift the movable window and make society re-evaluate the separate spheres model? When contemplating this, a useful comparison is Mary Edwards' contemporary, Mary Wollstonecraft.[6] Unlike Mary Edwards, Mary Wollstonecraft kept her maiden name her whole life, so we know she came from a London family, where her father was a violent drunk who beat her mother and squandered away the family's middle-class status. She left this unhappy home at nineteen and took some of the few forms of employment available to girls of her class at that time. She first became a paid 'companion' to an aristocratic lady, but couldn't get on with her. She then became a governess for the children of a well-off woman, but after a couple of years she apparently tired of caring for another woman's kids and took the extraordinary decision to give up on this relatively reliable, conventional job and try her hand as an author.

This was an exceptionally radical decision, given that virtually no women at that time had succeeded in such an endeavour. But Wollstonecraft forged bravely ahead, supporting herself by translating books from French and German and writing reviews. Meanwhile, she attended intellectual salons in London where she met her future husband, the novelist and political philosopher William Godwin. She managed to publish her first book, *Thoughts on the Education of Daughters*, in 1787. Despite its title, the book was squarely in line with the separate spheres model, an instance of a genre of the time called 'a conduct book'. It was dominated by considerations of morality and etiquette, as well as practical mothering advice. The modest success of this conventional writing fuelled Wollstonecraft's intellectual ambitions, leading her to something far more disruptive. In 1792, she penned the first feminist work in the English language.

That book was *A Vindication of the Rights of Woman*, in which Wollstonecraft argued that women should have an education commensurate to their position in society, and that rather than being social ornaments, women were deserving of the same rights as men. She also argued that women may seem silly and superficial, but that this was due not to any innate deficiency of the mind, but because men had denied them access to education: 'Taught from their infancy that beauty is woman's sceptre, the mind shapes itself to the body, and, roaming around its gilt cage, only seeks to adorn its prison.' She was one of the first people to argue for education as we have it today, nationally provided, with boys and girls attending the same schools daily. She also advocated that both genders should receive domestic training in the home, and argued against the idea of women having excessive 'sensibility'. Despite these radical suggestions, such was the power of the separate spheres model that nowhere does Wollstonecraft state that men and women were actually equal. In fact, she includes the caveat, 'Let it not be concluded that I wish to invert the order of things.'

Wollstonecraft wrote *A Vindication of the Rights of Woman* very much in the public spotlight, at precisely the same time that Mary Edwards was busy working in obscurity. But despite her elevated social position and public profile, in time, like Edwards, Wollstonecraft's attempts to shift the movable window would be dismissed. After her death in 1797 due to complications during the birth of her daughter (also named Mary, who would become Mary Shelley and write *Frankenstein*), her husband Godwin wrote her biography, *Memoirs of the Author of A Vindication of the Rights of Woman*.

By that time, Wollstonecraft was so well known that Godwin didn't have to mention her name in the book's title. True to the pair's progressive, convention-busting philosophies, the book was unflinchingly honest, including details not only of her painful early life, her travels during war and her love affairs, but also her illegitimate first child, her pre-marital pregnancy with their daughter, Mary, and her attempted suicides. Godwin intended the book as a testament to her extraordinary life, but her critics seized on it as proof of how she failed to measure up to the 'moral' standards expected of women of the day. The conservative political periodical *Anti-Jacobin Review and Magazine* dissected the book, using it as an opportunity to discredit both her and her work, saying her *Vindication* lacked 'logic', while accusing her of being a 'concubine' and a 'kept mistress' (though she had been neither).

Condemned utterly as a social and moral aberration, Mary Wollstonecraft was certainly seen as an outlier rather that a reason to reconsider the separate spheres model. While Mary Edwards may have been ignored due to social status and obscurity, Mary Wollstonecraft was forcibly rejected as a reason to re-think models, by public shaming and the de-recommendation of her work, including her early, anodyne conduct book on the education of girls. So complete was her discrediting that her reputation lay in tatters for nearly a century, and was only revived in the 1870s when the Women's Suffrage Movement claimed her as the foremother of the struggle for the vote.

Ironically, after Mary's death Godwin married his neighbour Mary Jane Clairmont and adopted her two children Charles and Claire. Claire Clairmont and Godwin's surviving daughter Mary (later Mary Shelley) were step-sisters and ran away from home together to lead a life of free love and philosophy with Mary's soon-to-be husband, the Romantic poet Percy Bysshe Shelley. In the course of their European wanderings Claire met and fell in love with the celebrated poet and politician Lord Byron. Their brief affair resulted in an illegitimate child, Allegra, who Byron initially ignored, before later adopting her and giving her up for care in a Capuchin Convent in Italy where she died aged five of a fever.

This was far from the only unconventionality in Byron's life, and it's instructive to consider his legacy in contrast to that of Mary Wollstonecraft. Like Wollstonecraft, Byron adventured in war-torn Europe and Turkey, racked up huge debts, had illegitimate children, had affairs (in Byron's case, with both men and women) and espoused radically progressive political and social ideas. Byron's sexual excesses were common knowledge throughout his life, including rumours of one with his half-sister Augusta Leigh, with whom he is said to have fathered a child. Like Wollstonecraft he defied the conventions of the day, in fact far more so, but unlike her, he wasn't vilified for it, at least not to such an extent that he was discarded to the scrap heap of history as an outlier or error to be ignored. Instead, he is considered the first modern-day celebrity, the inspiration for the literary Byronic hero, feted in over forty operas and countless self-promotional portraits. Byron's wife (who he abandoned with child) coined the term 'Byromania' to describe the commotion around him, and Friedrich Nietzsche drew influences from him. Unlike Wollstonecraft, Byron was a game-changing personality who challenged conventions and social mores and opened the door to a new Romantic Age. At least for men.

The casual definition of outlier is 'a person or thing situated away or detached from the main body or system,' but in statistical modelling, it is 'a data point on a graph or in a set of results that is very much bigger or smaller than the next nearest data point.' In terms of algorithms, a statistical model is like the flattened and warped rugby ball, a shape that can be mathematically characterized by a few numbers, which can be in turn manipulated by an algorithm to fit data. In this sense, an outlier is a point that is far from the other points, the fluff on the data cloud which can't easily be fitted inside the warped rugby ball. Since all models are wrong, there will always be points like this that don't fit the model. The question is whether we treat them as anomalies that are fine to ignore, or the exception that should steer the moving window in Box's diagram.

Errors that fall into the latter camp are what are sometimes call *black swans*, thanks to Nassim Nicholas Taleb's popular 2007 book *The Black Swan: The Impact of the Highly Improbable*.[7] Taleb illustrated his titular concept with the one-rule model that simply says, 'All swans are white'. This model is entirely right and useful, up to the point where one sees even a single black swan. At that point, the model's value completely vanishes, because one has to reconsider the entire model (that is to say, the one parsimonious rule). A black swan is the revelatory sort of event that Box was talking about, one that prompts a total re-evaluation of swans – if there are black swans might there be swans of different hues, and what else don't we know about swans now that we've discovered there are black swans? This leads to a shift in the movable window, leading us towards the gathering of more data, followed by new cycles of induction and deduction, to form more useful models.

Unfortunately, steering the window of social models has resisted recognition of black swans, even when they've crashed right into the most important developments in the history of science and technology.

In 1814, Byron married the wealthy heiress Anne Isabella Milbanke, nicknamed Lady Annabelle. She was a highly educated and religious woman and their marriage lasted barely two years as Byron's behaviour grew increasingly erratic, drinking heavily, flying into rages and carrying on affairs. But out of their relationship came one of the era's most extraordinary female black swans, their daughter Ada, Countess of Lovelace, an accomplished mathematician and writer, patron and what many have called the world's first computer programmer.

As the daughter of the most notorious man in England, Ada basked in the legacy of her father's celebrity, but in order to shelter her from her father's excess of poetic sensibility, her mother had her strictly tutored in science and mathematics, at which she excelled. Her wealth, fame, position and intellect gave her access to many of the great scientists, technologists and thinkers of the day, including Michael Faraday, Charles Dickens and Charles Babbage. At the time of their meeting, in 1833, Babbage was forty-two and already one of the most famous inventors in England, while Ada was just eighteen. Still, Babbage was so impressed with Ada's intellect, he showed her the incomplete prototype of his Difference Engine, and so began a long working relationship and friendship.

With the endless complications, costs and delivery delays on the Difference Engine, Babbage found little official scientific interest in England when he launched his new Analytical Engine in 1840, so he presented the work at a meeting of scientists in Turin. Luigi Menabrea, an Italian engineer, attended the lecture, and published detailed notes in French in a Swiss journal. This was the first published account of a non-human computer, but it did Babbage little good at home in England. His proposal for funding the Engine was rejected by Parliament.

By this time, Ada had married, had three children and become an even more elevated member of the aristocracy (first as Lady King, through marriage, and later as Lady Lovelace, through distant inheritance). Given her notable social position, mathematical abilities and skill with languages, Babbage enlisted Ada to translate Menabrea's work into English, as a means of promoting the project. Ada worked diligently at the project for nine months, and finally delivered something more than a translation. Her final work, with notes that quadrupled the paper's original length, was published in the September 1843 edition of Taylor's *Scientific Memoirs* under her initials AAL.

In her notes, Ada set about describing the Analytical Engine's function, which was not clearly understood even by other notable scientists. She also added a section detailing a method for computing a series of values known as Bernoulli Numbers (named for the same mathematician who gave us the first probability distribution), which would have run correctly if the machine had ever been built. It is for this contribution that Ada Lovelace is often described as the world's first computer programmer; however, that description fails to capture the real novelty and insight of her contribution.

While Babbage, Menabrea and others had primarily thought of the Analytical Engine as a number-crunching machine, a reconfigurable version of the Pascaline, or a mechanical version of de Prony's human computer factories, Lovelace realized it could do more, writing that it 'might act upon other things besides numbers, were objects found whose mutual fundamental relations could be expressed by those of the abstract science of operations'.[8]

Lovelace's suggestion is the view forward from calculators like the Pascaline to modern symbol-processing algorithms, with a nod back to the ideas of Llull and Leibniz, that computing could be about symbols rather than numbers. This is a revolutionary shift in perspective. Lovelace was even the first person to engage in speculation about the capabilities of AI, wondering whether computers might be able to compose music, but doubting their ability to create anything new on their own. On these grounds, Lovelace should be recognized not just as a programmer of Babbage's machines, but as a visionary thinker who went far beyond what Babbage was thinking, far beyond the imaginings of her forebears and contemporaries, becoming the first person to really see where computing was headed.

Unlike Mary Edwards, and even Mary Wollstonecraft, Ada Lovelace had every social advantage. She was a rich aristocrat by birth and marriage who had both fortune and fame. She was not denied an education in science and maths, and she made obvious, published contributions under her own name. Despite all this, her contribution did nothing to shift the movable window that was focused on separate spheres, even among contemporary scientists who were sure to have known her. One of those scientists was, of course, Charles Darwin who likely knew of Ada Lovelace's abilities, perhaps even her formal contributions. It's possible that they may have met as they both attended Babbage's popular soirees, but it would have been while Ada was more famous than he as well as being significantly superior to him socially.

Ada Lovelace died of uterine cancer on 27 November 1852. Almost exactly seven years later Darwin rose to become the most famous scientist in history with the publication of *On the Origin of Species* on 24 November 1859.

Journalist Angela Saini's excellent book *Inferior*,[9] which exposes the centuries-old discrimination against women across the scientific spectrum, in biology, psychology, anthropology, philosophy and, more recently, neuroscience, begins by recounting a correspondence between Charles Darwin and Bostonian Caroline Kennard who was an active member in the Massachusetts women's movement. Kennard's letter to Darwin takes issue with the fact that another member at one of her local meetings suggested that women's inferiority to man was based on 'scientific principles', namely those outlined by Darwin in his book *Origin of Species*, but particularly those in his later work *The Descent of Man* (1871), which he published soon after his addition of 'survival of the fittest' to *Origin*, and in which he expanded his evolutionary theory to include a theory of sexual selection.

In *Descent* Darwin explains sexual selection as a combination of 'female choosiness' and 'direct competition between males', concluding that male competitiveness in attracting women for mates had led inevitably to men's physical and mental superiority, so-called 'survival of the fittest' in action. Darwin further writes that women demonstrate sensibilities 'characteristic of the lower races', while commenting that a man can always reach 'a higher eminence, in whatever he takes up' than a woman. He continues that through evolution women were inferior to men in any thinking 'requiring deep thought, reason, or imagination'. These observations were made despite of the manifest evidence to the contrary of women like Mary Wollstonecraft, Ada Lovelace and Caroline Kennard, along with other contemporary female scientists of note, who Darwin's corresponded with, thanked for their contributions to his work and encouraged in their pursuits. Yet Darwin still could not recognize these extraordinary women as anything other than outliers in the separate spheres model. This is particularly ironic, since black swans are the real fuel of evolution, the variants that (if allowed to reproduce) cause lasting change.

In Quetelet's view, the *average* man is the ideal, and variations from that ideal are deviants, but in a Darwinian system, individuals that illustrate extraordinary variation from the average aren't just outliers, they are an existence proof, and if they survive and reproduce, they change the future. Yet Darwin's own attitudes towards women focus firmly on an ideal average, in line with the mainstream conventions of his time, which not only viewed women through the lens of separate spheres, but also restricted them to that narrow, normative definition by opinions precisely like the ones Darwin held. Inflexible opinions like these, fostered by mainstream 'beliefs, hopes, and fears', inevitably retard the progress of science and society. And, as we move to an algorithmic infrastructure, we need to be particularly mindful of the persistence of such error-laden norms.

Despite the indisputable proof of women's ability to contribute intellectually on a par with men, Edwards, Wollstonecraft, Lovelace and thousands of other outstanding female thinkers have struggled to shift the entrenched separate spheres social model over the centuries, even when a change was called for by prominent men. One such influential advocate was John Stuart Mill, who in 1848 (inspired partially by Babbage) published *Principles of Political Economy*, which replaced Adam Smith's influential *The Wealth of Nations* to become the most important political economics text of the late nineteenth century and which was used in economics teaching well into the twentieth century. Mill was a philosophical titan and is considered one of the most influential thinkers in the history of liberalism. He contributed widely to social theory, political theory and economics, and was an accepted authority on social and individual rights. He was also the first member of the British Parliament to call for women's suffrage, arguing that the separate spheres model was simply 'the legal subordination of one sex to the other – [which] is wrong, and now one of the chief hindrances to human improvement'. He made his case for a 'principle of perfect equality' in his 1861 book *The Subjection of Women*, a book that went far beyond Wollstonecraft's *Vindication*. In it, Mill called for the total equality of women, including in education and in the right to vote. He outlined the major hindrances holding women back, including society, gender construction, education and marriage. And he concluded that the continuing oppression of women was a severe impediment to the progress of humanity. The book was considered extremely radical, and despite Mill's high social and intellectual standing none of its suggestions were adopted as social policy.

As an added note on the persistence of prejudiced attitudes about the abilities of women, in Mill's autobiography he makes it clear that not only was his wife, Harriett Taylor Mill, a co-author of *Subjection* (she was the sole author of an essay from which much of the material was drawn), he considered her a full collaborator on his economic text, and many of his other works, as well. Despite this assertion by the author himself, critics continue to question Taylor's contribution to these works and her name remains obscure unlike her prominent husband.

As with many other aspects of social models, it would take a socio-economic black swan of the largest kind – two World Wars – to shift the movable window of public perception, and even then, it moved reluctantly. But with men away at the front during the First World War, women had to fill their factory jobs and they did so with tremendous success. Still, society wasn't prepared to let them keep their jobs after the war, so new laws called Marriage Bars were enacted to bar married women from the workplace. It would take the Second World War and its catastrophic destruction and death toll to forcibly shift the perception of women in the workplace, and finally ensure girls were also included in the rise of mandatory education.

However, the separate spheres model still hasn't been consigned to the dustbin of history. Even when women did earn the right to work during and after the World Wars, they were usually only allowed to perform roles with a different public face to those occupied by men. Since the days of Mary Edwards, the 'back room' nature of computing made it an attractive role for women, being at once intellectually demanding, relatively well paid and out of the public eye. As a result, women continued to compute throughout both World Wars, providing vital calculations that helped break codes, locate targets and drop rescue missions.

Likewise, female human computers made a significant contribution to the space race, with some women of colour playing vital roles, as has recently been revealed in the book and film *Hidden Figures*. As electronic computation replaced human computers, women continued to flock to the field, making it one of the few science subjects with a healthy intake of female graduates. By the mid-1980s, when I was a graduate student, the number of women being granted degrees in computer science in the US was 37 per cent and rising according to the National Center for Education Statistics, while in engineering it was still hovering around 15 per cent.

But then with the advent of the personal computer something strange started to happen. The number of female computer scientists started to drop, and drop dramatically. By current estimates, women now make up just 14–18 per cent of computer science students,[10] a parlous state of affairs when it's been estimated that the number of jobs in computer science will grow by 15–20 per cent between 2012 and 2022.[11]

Why has this happened? How, when the number of computer science jobs is rising exponentially have we managed to drive women away from a field in which they excel? One theory is that personal computers were essentially gaming systems and marketed specifically to men, but a more likely explanation may be that once the role shifted from relative obscurity to a high-profile, highly paid career, then entrenched social bias deemed the role better suited to (mainly white) men, fostering a 'brogrammer' culture, with alienating fringe elements like the 'manosphere', which has probably played a substantial role in moving women out of the field, and implicitly shifting perceptions towards computer science being something women shouldn't (and perhaps *can't*) do. Computer scientists like Bill Gates, Larry Page, Mark Zuckerberg and Elon Musk are now not only enormously rich, but world famous. They have a position in society that far exceeds that of Edwards, Wollstonecraft, Lovelace or Taylor-Mill, and there are no contemporary female equivalents to them.

In opening a 2005 debate on the issue of the relative abilities of men and women in science, then Harvard University President (and former Treasury Secretary under US President Clinton) Larry Summers made comments that were interpreted as endorsing the idea that women may be innately inferior to men in that regard, prompting widespread outrage and condemnation.[12] However, far more interesting was the content of the actual debate, which pitted two Harvard psychologists against one another. One was noted psychologist and author Stephen Pinker (who largely advocated that there is a difference in scientific abilities between genders) and the other was Elizabeth Spelke, a noted psychologist who has focused her experimental work on young children, and advocates that intelligence is complex, and that there is no notable gender difference in those aspects of intelligence related to general scientific ability.[13]

The first Bell Curve appears on slide twelve of Dr Pinker's fifty-eight slide presentation, and he mentions g factor on slide twenty-one. His presentation focused on broad test results of categories of abilities in broad gender-based studies. By contrast Dr Spelke's presentation focused on studies of babies for precursor abilities related to being able to understand the world, as well as evidence of discrimination and social bias, finding few gender-related reasons why these children couldn't go on to achieve in science and mathematics, beyond the obvious effects that demonstrable social forces might have on them.

What does all this have to do with algorithms?

The enduring problem for modelling, and AI, is that all errors are filtered through our 'beliefs, hopes and fears', which don't always lead us to the right conclusions, particularly when we are modelling data about people and society, when preconceived ideas and strong beliefs can sometimes steer the window to a perspective that reinforces a dominant social model or ideology. Add to this the single-minded nature of algorithms and the problem rapidly amplifies. This is because algorithmic models are always going to seek to draw the most powerful conclusions, while looking at the smallest set of simplifying atoms. In modelling people and human society, this has often meant measuring, ranking and categorizing simple features, like finger dexterity, skull size, IQ or the colour of one's skin, or the simplest of all distinguishing human features, gender. Add to this, that for algorithms, the errors are often hidden behind massive data and a fog of mathematics, or in the appendices of papers, like the fashion model error in the jobs study. Black swans are the errors that cause models and thus science and society to evolve. There is reason to be concerned that we won't be able to see these precious black swans when they are obscured by the nature of algorithms, given that in the past we've so often failed to take note of them, and steer Box's window in directions that can reveal more about the true state of nature. The consequences are of increasing importance.

Since the advent of the Internet and the endless torrent of big data it provides, AI systems have proliferated in civic planning, welfare, healthcare, finance, engineering, social media, construction, aviation, defence, policing and now, even, elections and governance. Algorithms now form the basis of our modern socio-technical infrastructure, and are tasked with framing social problems and modelling complex human issues and interactions on a global scale that affects us all. AIs no longer simply recommend books or films you might like on Amazon and Netflix; now they may decide your placement on the wait-list for support from your bank depending on your investment portfolio. Or scan your resumé in an applicant-tracking system for a job; or identify if, as a patient, you should be discharged or might benefit from transitional care. That begs the question: what are the 'beliefs, hopes, and fears' that motivate these algorithmic systems and what steers the movable window in algorithmic models, particularly when so many of them appear to exhibit age-old human biases?

Today's algorithms largely use statistical techniques employing probability theory and Bayesian inference, which result in Bell Curves. These Bell Curves view data around an ideal average and discount any extraordinary black swan variants at the tail ends of the curve – black swans that may hold revelatory information that we very much need to progress our knowledge of the world. We are told that these mathematical tools are unbiased, objective and efficient, but history doesn't provide a convincing record on their unbiased use *by people about people*. Just like when, in 1937, in response to I.Q. tests indicating that women were, on average, a bit more intelligent that men, the test was changed to include more questions, mainly on sport.[14]

The reality is that programmers decide on the parameters of all algorithmic frames, determine what data should be collected or which data sets should be used, and decide on the goals, uses and performance of their algorithmic systems. We should not assume that the data, however 'big', is 'correct' or representative of the 'True State of Nature', for as we have seen time and again data sets are only selective representations of reality and may be dramatically flawed in themselves. Health Canada, for example, didn't explicitly request women to be included in clinical trials until 1997 and, according to Heart and Stroke Foundation's 2018 *Heart Report*, two-thirds of heart disease clinical research still focuses on men.[15] Since women are absent from those trials, it is safe to assume that any system trained on that data will have flawed results, which helps to explain why recent studies are finding that symptoms of heart disease are often overlooked in women. Without appropriate scrutiny of the frames and atoms AIs employ we may never notice their errors and progress to refining our models to something more useful.

Addressing bias, whether sexist, racist or socio-economic, demands not only greater transparency of the science underpinning our AI technology, but requires diversity in programmers, too. Not because people are necessarily ill intentioned, but because people don't necessarily understand what the world looks like from an alternative perspective, and those alternative perspectives are scientifically invaluable to evolving ideas and society.

Alongside Caroline Kennard, another woman with a critical view on Charles Darwin's book *The Descent of Man*, was Antoinette Brown Blackwell, the first woman to be ordained as a mainstream Protestant minister in the United States. But rather than write Darwin a letter, she published her own book, *The Sexes throughout Nature*, as a response in 1875. In it, she critiques not only Darwin, but Herbert Spencer as well, highlighting that balance and cooperation were key features of evolution rather than just struggle and savage rivalry. In particular, she criticized Darwin for basing his theory on the 'time-honored assumption that the male is the normal type of his species'. Blackwell believed both men employed a tainted version of the scientific method, one that embraced a solely masculine viewpoint, adding that while Spencer scientifically 'subtracts from the female', Darwin scientifically 'adds to the male'. Blackwell's radical theories were brought to light over a century later when feminist scientists, such as anthropologist Sarah Blaffer Hrdy, wrote in her 1999 book *Mother Nature*:

For a handful of nineteeth-century women intellectuals, however, evolutionary theory was just too important to ignore. Instead of turning away they stepped forward to tap Darwin and Spencer on the shoulder to express their support for this revolutionary view of human nature, and also to politely remind them that they had left out half the species.

8

What Is Mind, No Matter

I was traveling in the West and I had a ticket with what I think was called
a punch photograph . . . the conductor . . . punched out a description of
the individual, as light hair, dark eyes, large nose, etc.

HERMANN HOLLERITH, inventor, 1889[1]

The ingenious 'punch photographs' that caught Hermann Hollerith's attention are the direct precursor of the punch cards that I had to use when I first learned to program computers nearly a century after the observation that inspired Hollerith to invent the earliest form of those cards. Using a glorified typewriter, my early coding involved banging out punched lines of code on stacks of stiff, pink paper card, one line of code per card. Hollerith, who worked at the US Census, saw the utility of such cards (which were not unlike the cards in Jacquard's looms and Babbage's Engines) for recording statistics. The punch photograph he observed on the train allowed the conductor to identify passengers by typing out a rough description of them against certain categorizing features (gender, hair colour, eye colour, etc.). Hollerith's patented card system took the idea one step further, creating electronic cards where the tiny holes served to make connections between electrodes. As they passed through a machine, electronic connections associated with particular holes incremented counters for the various features that the census surveyed (many standardized tests use a similar statistic-recording technique to this day). Eventually punch cards were standardized by IBM to hold 80 columns of punched holes, which described the lines of computer programs.

After I spent my first year of coding laboriously typing out punch cards, the giant University of Alabama mainframe was boxed up and replaced by PCs, and like all other programmers of that era, I started typing lines of code on green screens, for their eventual storage as bits on floppy discs. Despite the complete disappearance of the pink punch cards by the early 1980s, some concepts of Hollerith's invention remain. When the inputs to algorithms are descriptions of a person, they are much like punch-card photographs, lists of simplified features, shot into machines and summed up statistically. Algorithms are designed to use this statistical big data to create parsimonious and powerful models, categorizing these inputs and, in this case, sorting people accordingly. To have an impact beyond the data they are trained with, these categorizations strive to create effective *generalizations*, categorizing unforeseen, future people (such as students, welfare recipients, criminals, etc.), based on their unforeseen punch-card photos. Unfortunately, categorizing people using simplified features, and then using those categories to generalize, often leads to rather predictably problematic results.

In recent research, Ghanaian-American computer scientist, Rhodes Scholar and Fulbright Fellow Joy Buolamwini found that commercially available facial recognition systems from Microsoft and IBM were unable even to detect her face, much less recognize who she was.[2] This was apparently due to her dark skin tone, since the problem was only rectified by her donning a white mask. Similar stories include the almost comical demonstration of a 'racist' soap dispenser, which refused to squirt cleanser onto dark-skinned hands,[3] and the troubling 2015 *Guardian* report that Google's image classification system had labelled a dark-skinned couple as 'gorillas'.[4]

Google quickly reported that they had taken action to prevent this offensive categorization of people as animals from happening again. It wasn't clear what Google had done to correct it until three years later, when *Wired* magazine tested Google's image classification with pictures of 40,000 animals. They found that while other animals received the correct labels, none of the images of great apes did. *Wired* asked Google what had happened, and they confirmed that they had fixed the racist image classification error by simply removing their algorithm's ability to classify any image as being of an 'ape', 'gorilla', 'chimpanzee', and so on.[5]

Why was the response to this algorithm's error the prevention of *any* image being labelled as being of apes, even when that classification was correct? Why didn't Goggle just add the appropriate atoms to the algorithm's frame, so that it no longer made that apparently racist mistake? Why didn't they give the algorithm the *explicit* ability to tell a black person from an ape? After all, features that distinguish people of colour from apes are surely there in the images?

The reason for this response is that *we can no longer easily correct algorithmic mistakes, because the algorithms involved are too incomprehensibly complex.* Algorithms may start with simplified features, punch-card photos, but they process them in manners that people simply can't fully understand. Sometimes that means their potentially offensive, potentially dangerous outputs are both unpredictable and irreparable.

This is why the award-winning Google AI engineer Ali Rahimi said in 2017 that 'Machine learning has become alchemy'.[6] Machine-learning algorithms are now used in everything from image recognition, to natural language processing, to medical diagnosis, and virtually every other modern AI application. They are the core of big data analysis, and the bedrock of virtually all modern AI, the technology that draws its frames and atoms from big data to overcome the old problems of expert systems design. Yet the implementations of these algorithms, the actual programs doing the classification and generalization, have become so opaque that it is comparable to medieval pre-science. However, that has by no means impeded the growth in its application. Why are we rapidly expanding the use of algorithms that are so complex we can't understand them? The reason is economics.

In an effort to overcome the brittleness and expense of knowledge-based approaches like expert systems, algorithms now search for their own representational atoms, and *self-organize* based on information they glean from big data. That is what has made AI commercially viable, but to give these algorithms sufficient flexibility in finding their own atoms, we have had to give them scale and structure that is intractably complex. Yet we expect them to deliver generalizations that are effective, through *emergence*.

Emergence is a concept that scientists have generally found difficult to define, but in short, an emergent effect of a system is one that can't be derived from the separate, constituent parts of that system, but requires their combination or interaction into the system as a whole. Modern algorithms are so complex that we certainly can't derive their ultimate behaviour from their constituent parts, so we count on their emergent behaviours to be the things we intended. In particular, we count on their emergent ability to generalize from the data we give them, to conclusions on data in the uncertain future, data that they haven't yet seen (e.g. generalizing from millions of online photos of animals, including people, to labels saying what sorts of animals they are).

The old, commercially unviable AI that existed before the AI winter was sometimes called *symbolic AI*, because it worked like the ideas of Llull, Leibniz, Lovelace and others, operating on abstract symbols rather than just numbers. That AI has largely given way to more economic AI that is driven by big data and statistics. By contrast, these approaches are often called *sub-symbolic* AI, because while they focus on number crunching on a massive scale, the intention is that effective symbolic processing will emerge from their operation. Faith in this emergence of symbols (for instance, photograph labels) from complex networks of numbers and functions is largely based on metaphors to the brain's complex network of neurons and synapses. However, this metaphor of algorithms and brains has to be examined carefully. Does the processing of high-level, symbolic categories of things, like people that emerges from big-data-digesting AI bear any relationship to the way people think symbolically?

I first saw *The Hallucinogenic Toreador* in 1991, hanging in the Salvador Dali Museum in St. Petersburg, Florida, not far from where my parents retired. At the time, I was in my first year as a professor at the University of Alabama, and I'd come down to visit my folks during the Christmas break. I've always been a great fan of the famous Spanish surrealist, so I'd travelled up to St. Pete to go on a tour of the museum. Dali's masterpiece, the symbolist rendering of the bullfighter, was the tour's culmination. I had seen small reproductions of the painting in books, but I was really captivated seeing Dali's enormous canvas (nearly four metres by three metres) in person. It is spectacularly filled with merging, melting images, at the heart of which is the figure of a shadowy toreador emerging from the negative space between repeated renditions of that famous classical sculpture, the Venus de Milo.

The genius of the painting is Dali's ability to warp reality into dreamlike forms and conjure a complex network of cultural symbols which reverberate within the mind of the viewer. Tucked amid the folds of drapery shrouding the Venus are a whole panoply of images which tell the story of Dali's life: in the bottom left is the bay of Port Lligat, Dali's childhood home; a small boy stands on the shore with a hoop, simultaneously depicting Dali and his dead brother; the classical depiction of Venus speaks to Dali's art-school experiences of drawing plaster casts; the toreador embodies Manolete, Spain's most famous bullfighter gored to death by Islero, the bull; a dense cloud of flies swarm over the dying bull, indicative of its molecular decomposition and Dali's interest in atomic science; and, finally, in the top left, is a portrait of Dali's stern-looking wife, Gala, who views the whole scene with distaste, framed by the arc of a bullring. But the painting is not a simple autobiography. Museum-goers and art fans knowledgeable about Western Christian traditions will find further, deeper, thematic suggestions: the Venus represents an idealized and immortal version of beauty; the tearful toreador evokes the passion of adolescence; the small child in his sailor suit speaks to the innocence of youth; and, the slain bull and swarming flies signify sacrifice and the resurrection. Dali was right when he said: 'My painting is like an iceberg, where only a tenth of its volume is visible.'[7]

While I was taking in the painting for the first time back in 1991, the tour guide asked our group if anyone could spot something very odd and particular amongst the dense symbolism of the painting. I was surprised that it jumped right out at me, so I raised my hand. It took a second for me to realize, but the reason I saw what he was referring to was because I had used the image a few days earlier in teaching my class on the AI technique known as neural networks (see Figure 8.1).

FIGURE 8.1 *If you look carefully at any of the ubiquitous reproductions of Dali's Hallucinogenic Toreador, you can see that he rendered this photograph at the bottom of the canvas, near the centre. The photo has been widely used to illustrate the strange nature of human visual understanding. How easily can you see its subject?*

Source: Ronald C. James, 1965, Dalmatian Dog. Originally appeared in *Life* magazine 58(7): 120. Reproduced with permission from the Ron James Photography Collection, University of California Santa Clara Special Collections and Archives.

The image appeared in the neural networks textbook I was using, and I had picked it out as a part of my lecture, projected it onto a screen in my classroom, and asked if the students could tell me what it was a picture of. About half of the students instantly raised their hands. Then I gestured a bit at details of the picture to give some focus, and most of the remaining students brought their hands up as well. I told the class it was a picture of a dog, and then the rest of them saw the Dalmatian, wearing a collar, with its nose to the ground, as it walks towards the shade of a narrow tree.

I then asked the students (who were all experienced programmers, working on Master's degrees) how they would write a program to do what they had just done, and recognize this image. Better yet, how would they get a computer to not only recognize this image, not only recognize Dalmatians, or even dogs, but recognize a wide variety of objects in such visually limiting conditions? They all struggled to find an answer, because this problem is seriously hard for conventional computer programming. Yet humans do it instantly, or nearly instantly given some vague prompting clues. This exercise was intended to demonstrate how the human visual recognition system does something very difficult from a computational perspective. It's meant to point out that there must be something special about the brain, something very different from conventional computers, that gives it these amazing abilities.

The Dalmatian image has been widely used to illustrate this point, but that doesn't explain why and how it is also in Dali's painting. In researching the image, I discovered that it originally appeared in Life Magazine in 1965, as one of the miscellany items that the photography magazine would often put on their last page. It was taken by Ron James, a photographer who was particularly interested in the psychology of human perception. I imagine that Dali, who himself appeared in Life several times, and likely subscribed to the popular magazine, saw this photo there, and incorporated it into the double-image laden *Hallucinogenic Toreador* as a commentary on how people perceive images. But Dali's images were about *symbolism* in a far more human way than the abstract symbols of pure computation.

Why are brains able to do some things easily that conventional computers find hard to do? The theory that is emphasized in neural networks is that people are able to see images like the toreador and the Dalmatian because of a difference in the *architecture* of computers and the architecture of brains, and that therefore this architecture should deliver the special properties of human thinking if it is used in computation. The term 'architecture' is used here in much the same sense as in buildings, but to understand this argument by analogy it's useful to start with the foundations, the *substrates* upon which computers are built.

Babbage couldn't get his Engines to work, largely because they were built on a nineteenth-century mechanical *substrate*. In short, brass gears and levers had too much mass and friction for practical computing. Given their lack of practical success, one could argue that the most important contribution of Babbage's Engines was getting people to think seriously about the range of things that computing could do. Ada Lovelace was one of the first people to speculate about computers manipulating not just numbers, but symbols, and how similar such manipulations could be to human thought. Less abstract evaluations of what computing could do came from mathematicians decades later. In 1900 the German mathematician David Hilbert posed twenty-three open problems in mathematics, one of which was critical to testing the limits of what computers could do. Hilbert asked whether any formal system of logic can be made *complete*. That is, whether within such a system, there always exists a *mechanical* procedure (an algorithm) for validating all statements you can make in that system.[8] It turns out there doesn't, though it took until 1931 for another German mathematician, Kurt Gödel, to prove it, by showing that every formal system of logic must contain statements that are inherently paradoxical to that system, and therefore can't be validated.

While philosophically fascinating,[9] it was spin-off questions from the problem Gödel solved that really impacted on computing. Specifically, what exactly was the nature of Hilbert's 'mechanical procedures'? What was the complete range of possible 'mechanical procedures' that could be created with systems of logical rules? In other words, what defined all the things that algorithms could possible do?

In 1936, British mathematician (and later war hero) Alan Turing designed a theoretical mechanical device, and a mathematical proof that it could do *any* mechanical procedure, that could be implemented on any computer, ever. This device, which we now call a Turing Machine, involved configurations of mechanical 'states', and the ability to write to and read from memory (in the form of symbols written on an infinitely long roll of tape). In every way, the Turing Machine is like Babbage's Engine, if that Engine had infinite memory in its 'store'. In fact, the whole point of Turing's proof was that this machine was equivalent to *any* general-purpose computer, and therefore any general-purpose computer is just like any other. That is to say, Turing proved that regardless of whether it was built on a substrate of brass gears and levers, vacuum tubes, as-yet-uninvented semiconductor chips, or even biological cells, the Turing Machine could implement any algorithm[10] that could be implemented on any other computer. It defined the range of what could be computed by algorithms.

This is known as the theory of *universal computation*, and is a basis upon which many believers in AI feel that the brain is just a kind of computer. After all, they theorize, everything that can possibly be built must follow the mechanical rules of physics. Thus everything that can be built is a mechanical device. Turing showed that all such devices that compute, regardless of the substrate they are built on, have the same ultimate algorithmic capabilities. The theory concludes that the brain is just another mechanical device, a built 'machine' that must follow the rules of physics. Therefore, the brain can't do anything that a Turing machine, and thus any other computer, can't do. By this argument, the brain is just a computer.

Of course, the ultimate 'capabilities' assumed in this line of reasoning are the execution of Hilbert's 'mechanical procedures' (algorithms). Whether this is all brains do is a debatable question that is philosophically central to AI. Regardless, many believe that universal computation indicates that the *substrate* of computing is irrelevant. That is to say, whether computing is done with brass gears, electrons or neurons in the brain, it's all the same thing. It's all algorithms.

So, given that the substrate apparently doesn't matter, why would the architecture built upon those foundations make any difference, make it possible for the brain to see that Dalmatian quickly, while conventional computer programs have to chug along at a witless crawl to solve similar image recognition problems? The argument is that the brain is more efficient at such problems not because of its different substrate, but because it exploits a different *architecture*. Specifically, it uses *networks* to perform computation.

How we *see* and, therefore, *represent* the world is tied to what symbols mean to us. This is critically important to AI, if intelligence is defined as an ability to reason, comprehend or understand 'truths', facts or meaning. For human-like AI, computers need to deal with human concepts, which we convey through symbolic representation, the most common of which is language (others include art, music, dance etc.). Therefore, in order for computers to 'reason' a robust symbol-processing system is required. In computers, numbers rather than words or pictures are used for this purpose, because numbers have an objective, static meaning, whereas words and images can have internal and social meanings which are subjective and fluid and are hard (if not impossible) to codify. For computers to have "intelligence", they have to have a way to understand meaning, and in order to do that they need a means of interpreting what symbols mean and why.

As we've already seen, in the early days of AI, Herb Simon pioneered what was known as symbolic AI, a method based on the assumption that computational "intelligence" could be achieved through the manipulation of human-readable symbols (i.e. words) via a formal system of logic. However, like Llull, Simon needed a way to overcome the combinatorial complexity of real-world decision-making if he was to get his computers to "think" robustly. To do this, he borrowed the idea of heuristics (mental shortcuts) from his economics work and surmised that just as people use heuristics to make calculations about the unfathomably complex marketplace, so computers could proceed to an *optimal solution* by trial and error *within a framework of rules.*

The symbolic AI approach quickly generated expert systems, which used a framework of rules in the form of "IF this THEN that" statements. An expert system starts with rules and some base facts, then logically processes the rules to make deductions and determine what additional information is needed (i.e. what further questions to ask) to progress, near-optimally, to a solution. Figuring out the "this" and "that" is the job of the knowledge engineer and the resulting framework they designed is known as the symbolic knowledge representation.

The brain's architecture, however, is very different from those rule-based algorithms, and very different from conventional computers. Every conventional computer is largely like Babbage's Difference Engine, though implemented on an electronic substrate rather than a mechanical one. Conventional computers have a central processing unit (the CPU, which Babbage, in a reference the industrial machines of his time, called "the mill") sequentially executing rules against memory (which Babbage called "the store"). By contrast, the brain has no CPU, no "central" place where computation goes on, and it has no central store either. The argument that the Dalmatian picture is often used to illustrate is that the brain operates *sub-symbolically*, not through rule-based processing symbols like words, but through the activation of what appear to be simple on/off switches (the synapses between neuron cells). In the brain, synapses "fire" by releasing a stored-up burst of chemicals and energy generated by the cell's metabolism of sugars, so in effect a synapse has two states: firing and not firing. Rather than a single mill of symbolic word-based rules plodding against a central store of memory, industrially, one after the other, synapses fire in massive parallel waves of activity that sweep around the brain. The theory is that it is this difference in architecture that gives the brain its ability to perform things like image recognition (although we're not sure exactly how).

That's the argument, but look again at the painting. When people look at Dali's *Hallucinogenic Toreador* they aren't just registering the shapes and colours in the painting, they're making complex connections in their minds, to memories, experiences and cultural symbols, which are so deeply embedded that they're often not aware of them. That's the nature of *symbolism*. In fact, Dali first conceived of his masterpiece while looking at a pencil box, when the image of a man's face emerged from the shoulder, breast, and abdomen of the Venus Di Milo branding of the pencil's manufacturers that appeared on the box's cover. Dali's mind associated the man with a bullfighter, and this led to the cascade of associated, personal symbols that are rendered in the painting, including not just the Venus and the toreador, but the bullfighting arena, the dying bull, the boy in a sailor suit and even the Dalmatian. Is all of this association of symbols merely from a substrate of algorithms like those in a computer that are running on a neural architecture? Why did people start thinking that while the substrate doesn't matter, the architecture does? In particular, when did people begin to think that massive networks of simple computations held such vital power?

I imagine that it is not a coincidence that the painting connects the idea of symbol association to the brain's startling ability to decipher optical illusions like the Dalmatian. *Associationism* was a theory of mind that Dali was familiar with. Although associationism is a line of thought that descends from antiquity, it was eighteenth-century philosopher and psychologist David Hartley who developed it into a modern school of thought by founding the associationist school of psychology. This school posited that all human thought was triggered by sensations, which caused 'vibrations' in the brain. Each 'vibration' was the activation of a concept which led to progressive sympathetic 'vibrations' that were associated to related concepts. For instance, a thought about a Dalmatian might trigger a thought about leopards, which might cause one to recall the novel *The Leopard* by Lampedusa, then thoughts of Sicily, where the book is set, and so on. According to associationism, the 'vibrations' are the fabric from which the mind's thoughts emerge, the idea being that the mind is a network of individual, idiosyncratic associations.

Hartley developed these ideas long before neurons were discovered by the Spanish physician Santiago Ramón y Cajal s around the close of the eighteenth century. Many technical details of neural network algorithms, the AI subfield called *connectionism*,[11] follow from the most basic details of Cajal's discoveries, and the discoveries of other early neuroanatomists. However, the faith that all the associations of human thought arise from massive networks of the simplest possible devices, mere on/off switches, comes from more than early theories of how neurons work. Like other developments in AI, this faith has connections to theories of economics.

Ever since the invention of the wheel, technological invention and development has been closely interlinked with economics, including our conception of the architectures of computers and AI. In fact, Babbage's Difference Engine (with its 'mill' and 'store' architecture) was inspired by the factory network of eighteenth-century England. It in turn informed his economic treatise on the division of labour and the efficiency of specialization in work flow. But the problem with economics is that, unlike the universes of physics and mechanics, filled with unthinking particles and machine parts, economies are filled with people. Economics is a *social*, rather than a hard, science. It deals with more than mere physics; it deals with people's thoughts, hopes, fears and dreams. That's why Adam Smith, Herbert Spencer and John Stuart Mill (who, by the way, was a strong proponent of the associationist school of mind) and other early economists were considered to be philosophers and social theorists as well.

But as the eighteenth century gathered pace with the fabulous new proofs, calculations and machines that sprung up in the wake of Newton and Leibnitz, economists began to suffer a severe case of physics envy. In France, a new school of economists called physiocrats emerged and developed the idea of the economy as a circular flow of income and output, based on the excess generated from agricultural production. In reaction to late Renaissance mercantilists who had supported the proliferation of trade regulations to protect guild workers, the physiocrats advocated a laissez-faire policy of minimal government intervention in the economy. Adam Smith described the physiocratic system 'with all its imperfections' as 'perhaps the purest approximation to the truth that has yet been published'.

Envious of Newton and Leibniz's neat mathematics that enabled physicists to describe the world from the scale of an atom to the movement of the planets, these economists thought to extend this modelling revolution into their own field, replacing philosophical theories of the mind with precise calculations. But in order for economics to work in the same way as physics it needed a robust model of how those people made decisions. That model was created by French engineer-turned-economist Leon Walras who believed 'the pure theory of economics. . .is a science which resembles the physio-mathematical sciences in every respect'. Inspired by Adam Smith's self-interested butcher and baker, as well as his engineering background, Walras devised a mathematical model in 1874 that appeared to demonstrate economic systems driven by self-interested individuals, like systems in physics, fell into a stable *equilibrium*.

Equilibrium means balance, and equilibria are stable states of balance that systems naturally fall into. In physics, the easiest example of equilibrium is a small ball in a much larger, smooth, round bowl. If the bowl is still, the ball settles to the bottom. Any perturbations of the ball will lead it eventually back to lying still at the bottom of the bowl, which is its *stable equilibrium*. A more complicated example would be structure of wooden beams, each with their own springiness and strength. Under the action of loads and gravity this structure will stretch and bend, but if it's strong enough, it will settle into a natural shape. A knock or two might cause the structure to shudder, but it should eventually settle back into its stable equilibrium shape. An even more complicated example of an equilibrium would be a machine comprised of springs, levers and motors which provide a fixed or variable torque. If you look at the entire motion of the machine over time, it should settle into a comfortable cycle of operation. Looked at as a cycle, the repetitions of this motion are as stable as the ball bearing at the bottom of the bowl. This is a *dynamic* equilibrium, but an equilibrium none the less. One could knock the machine this way and that, but if its equilibrium is stable, it should return to correct operation. Stable equilibria are exactly what a physiocratic economist or politician would want from an economy: a state of stable effectiveness that can take perturbations and return to smooth operation.

Walras found a way to describe economic systems as if they were physical systems that settled into equilibria. He did this by imagining that the people in his economic model were as simple as levers and springs. He *assumed* individuals simply sought to maximize *utility* (a concept that he likened to energy in physics). That is, individual economic actors were always seeking the greatest benefit by trading things they had and didn't need for things they wanted and didn't have. He also assumed that they did this with perfect logical rationale, foresight and a free market. In that free market, each actor traded the surplus of things that they had for things that they wanted, while constantly trying to maximize the net utility returned by each trade. Reducing the thinking of people to a single drive to satisfy their own needs not only made economic modelling possible, it also turned acquisitive self-interest into a prime atom of economic good.

With the addition of a centralized auctioneer to enact the trades, Walras's economic trading network settled into a *predictable* equilibrium, which priced every good in terms of every other good, like a smoothly running machine. This is the origin of economic modelling, and it wasn't only mathematically convenient, it was morally convenient, too. Other economists, notably Jevons in England and Pareto in Italy, contributed to the theory, refining it to show that not only did the machine fall into the smooth motion of an equilibrium, it was an equilibrium that generated the most social benefit to the economic participants overall, given the constraints on production and consumption in the economy. This revolution in thinking made social policy a lot simpler: less interference in the markets lubricated them, allowing them to move more efficiently towards their socially beneficial equilibria.[12]

It's important to note that this is a model, not a real economic system. There are no real participants, markets or auctioneers in the theories of Walras, Jevons, Pareto and similar economists. There are mathematical equations, built on assumptions, that *model* those realities. There work was not observing the conditions of real economics, but deriving proofs that the equations in those models have equilibrium solutions. The assumptions involved about people are significant: that they are certain about everything in the world around them, stable in their perceptions of utility (preferences), logically rational with regard to the actions they take in their trades, and always pursuing gain for themselves relative to their preferences. These assumptions treat the participants in the model as if they were simple levers and springs of a physical structure, resulting in straightforward mathematical equations, which can be solved for equilibria.

It was the economist Frederick Hayek who connected this evolution in economic thinking back to AI, and particularly to our faith in networks. Hayek is one of the most famous proponents of laissez-faire economics. He was a hero of computer scientist Herb Simon, progenitor of expert systems AI heuristics, and the only person to win the Nobel Prize in Economics and the Turing Award for Achievements in Computing. While Hayek never explicitly worked in AI like Simon, the faith in networks that Hayek promoted (both in economics and in the brain) is at the core of connectionism.[13]

In economics, Hayek held that due to the vast complexity of economic networks, it was impossible to gather the information necessary to determine a strategy for making those networks deliver the best social benefit. From his perspective, that complexity ruled out even trying to control economies. In the way that complexity doomed expert systems, Hayek thought economic complexity doomed all attempts at economic regulation. Therefore, he suggested that markets should be largely left alone by government, so that they could freely organize and evolve, emerging into a state of stable equilibrium, which he called *spontaneous order*.

Both *spontaneous order* and *self-organization* are terms for *emergence* – that is, a resulting effect that can't be derived from separate, constituent parts, but requires the interaction of those parts to generate the emergent effect. However, spontaneous order is a term used primarily in economics and other sociological systems, while self-organization is a term used primarily to describe physical systems and simple biological systems. While the terms appear to describe the same thing, the words carry very different connotations. The word 'organization' is from fifteenth-century Middle French, and is based on the Latin word *organum*, meaning organ or instrument. In the eighteenth century, it took on the meaning of a system, or establishment. Thus, self-organization implies a structure, organic or collective, where the constituent parts act together, without oversight or planning, to form 'a system'.

Order, however, implies something much more than organization. It originates from the ancient Latin *ordinem*, meaning row, rank, series, arrangement or pattern, in particular, the arrangement of rows of thread in a loom. Thus, the word implies a precise sequence that generates a desirable, complex pattern, just like the fabric patterns determined by the ordered sequence of Jacquard cards, and their descendant rules in computer programs. In the thirteenth century, 'order' took on the meaning of a disciplined group, such as a religious order, from the French *ordre*, which implies position, rule, regulation. Then, in the fifteenth century, the sense of a community under a directive or rule of law (as in 'law and order') was incorporated and, finally, in the eighteenth century the idea of classification, as in the pre-Darwinian sense of categorizing species, was added.

Thus, Hayek's spontaneous *order* implies that the operation of the free market will result in the emergence of a *correct* sequence of events and categorization of things that give the socially best possible arrangement of goods/prices, resulting in a desired state of equilibrium without any deliberate thinking, planning or social policy (particularly by governments). Like Spencer's notion of 'survival of the fittest', spontaneous order is a faith that what naturally emerges is for the best.

Hayek did more than apply the idea of spontaneous order to economics. Hayek was perhaps the last economist-philosopher and, like Spencer, he wrote about the application of his theories across sociology, even venturing into psychology. In his *The Sensory Order: An Inquiry into the Foundations of Theoretical Psychology* (1952), he was the first person to discuss a theory of the mind that would overtake associationism, and become a permanent part of the scientific and social zeitgeist. Hayek speculated that cognition simply arises as a spontaneous effect of the synaptic activities of neurons, operating under simple computational rules, as a massively connected parallel distributed system of synapses. He further speculated that learning is through simple adjustment of the propensities of synapses to fire, and the consequent emergent effects on the brain's operation. Like the order that arises from the interactions of self-interested economic actors, the order of the brain is simply driven by sensory inputs and a few simple computational actions of neurons, playing out as an emergent behaviour, a spontaneous order, in a massive evolving network.

The engineers of connectionist algorithms are less likely to know of Hayek's *Sensory Order* than the work of Warren McCulloch and Walter Pitts (1943),[14] who showed that networks of simple on/off switches, intended to represent neuron synapses, could compute mathematical functions, or the work of Donald O. Hebb (1949),[15] who outlined principles that led to simple equations for adjusting parameters in those functions, and the most common and basic form of machine 'learning'. But while these researchers provided the technical details of the basic algorithms in connectionism, it is Hayek's philosophical belief in emergence from complex networks that are a part of the zeitgeist that encourages our belief in spontaneous order from such networks.

Another part of this zeitgeist is just an accident of context, an artefact of the substrate and architecture details of early electronic computers. The first working computers of the 1940s were largely big boxes filled with on/off switches, the bits of computer memory which implemented Babbage's 'store'. There were no 'programming languages' for these machines, and to create an algorithm you had to plumb the switches together using patch codes, and spin a few knobs to set the machine into the desired configuration.[16] The following is an image of ENIAC, the Electronic Numerical Integrator and Calculator, the first general-purpose electronic computer, which was created for the US Army to replace two female human computers who did all the calculations that allowed soldiers to correctly aim massive Second World War artillery guns. Note the wall of patch cords and the panels of knobs (see Figure 8.2).

The rat's nests of wires connecting the switches was suggestive of a network not dissimilar to the brain's complex web of neurons and synapses. This conception of the brain was probably widely held as it is apparent in one of the earliest generalized papers about AI, written by Alan Turing in 1948, and entitled 'Intelligent Machinery'. Although the paper wasn't published until 1968, it contained an early ground-breaking description of computing devices that are very like connectionist algorithms.[17] Furthermore, the paper illustrates some striking similarities with ideas in Hayek's later work, which emphasized the brain-like mess of patch cords in ENIAC and other early computers. In line

FIGURE 8.2 *ENIAC: the world's first general-purpose electronic computer, a mass of wires and knobs.*
Source: US Army photo.

with the zeitgeist, Turing called his supposed brain-like computers 'unorganized machines', positing that infants' brains were similarly largely unorganized until implicit biological algorithms shaped them towards a more structured (educated) spontaneous order..

These ideas are apparent in the first real connectionist computers. The Mark 1 Perceptron was a connectionist computer developed by Frank Rosenblatt, an American psychologist at the Cornell Aeronautical Laboratory in 1957. The Mark 1 was an ungainly giant device by modern standards, consisting of an array of 400 photocells, a massive cabinet of actuator-driven potentiometers (what we would recognize as old radio volume knobs) and a grid of electric lights. But its most impressive feature was a mass of *randomly* connected wires between these components. Given that programming computers with patch cords was in recent memory at the time, the idea of being able to connect cords

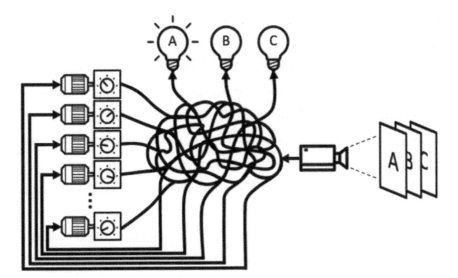

FIGURE 8.3 *The metaphors and realities of early connectionist computers. The wires and knobs of early computers like ENIAC were thought to be like the initially "unorganized" neurons in the brain, which reached "spontaneous order" through the tuning of synapses. In the earliest connectionist computer, the Mark I Perceptron, these metaphors were made real, with random connections of wires, banks of motors algorithmically turning volume knobs, and "learning" shown through the emergent matching of simple image inputs (like the signals from cameras pointed at letter cards) to categories represented by lights.*

at random, and have correct computer behaviour simply emerge, apparently imitating the biological actions of neurons in the brain, made the Mark 1 particularly compelling.

The Mark 1 did work, by apparently 'learning'. Rosenblatt created the Perceptron Learning Algorithm (PLA), the first machine-learning algorithm, as a mechanical rule for turning the knobs in the Mark 1 so that the correct 'associative memory' emerged from the machine after sessions of 'training'. Rosenblatt also wrote a simple mathematical proof that showed that, under the PLA, the Mark 1 would converge to the right answer for any given set of training data. One example of training data inputs was illuminated shapes, for instance the shapes of letters of the alphabet, that were 'seen' by the Mark 1's photoreceptors. In the case of letter shapes, the output was the categorization of the shape as the correct associated letter. Learning amounted to 'showing' the Mark I the training data, and running the PLA. After learning, the Mark 1 was tested to see how well it had learned, by showing it the same inputs, and observing whether the right light in the grid came on. This was a great demonstration of apparent spontaneous organization of associative memory from very simple, autonomous mechanical actions, and a randomly configured machine, and it was a practical realization of suggestions made by both Hayek and Hebb, that learning in the brain was simply an adjustment of the firing propensity of neuron synapses. Rosenblatt interpreted this as adjustments of the 'strengths' of connections between 'artificial neurons'. Of course, this is all a metaphor. The PLA is, in fact, terribly simple: it literally moves each knob a larger amount the larger the error in the answer, with the direction of movement determined by the sign of the error.

Let's consider an economic example, where we're trying to model the preferences of one of Walras's economic actors, a shopper in a market. Imagine that the actor sees a set of different kinds of goods in a shopping trolley each day, and rates it with a 'like' (indicating it's fully stocked or overstocked with what that actor wants) or 'dislike' (indicating that it is unsatisfactory for the actor's preferences). Let's also assume we have been gathering big data on the shopper's opinions of many trolleys, for many days. What we want the perceptron to do is to 'learn' the shopper's preferences and be able to 'like' or 'dislike' any trolley of goods (or less metaphorically, any set of numbers that represent the quantities of goods in that trolley) in the same way the shopper would. To do this, we use example trolley from the big data gathered on the actor, along with the actor's 'likes' and 'dislikes'. At a minimum, we want the perceptron to get the same answers as the actor on all the example data we have but, moreover, we want the perceptron to correctly *generalize* from those trolleys to any possible trolley of goods, such that the machine duplicates the preferences of the economic actor perfectly.

Under the PLA, you start by randomly wiring the perceptron, and randomly spinning all the volume knobs. Then you input the numbers representing a trolley of goods (this much cereal, that much washing liquid, this much milk, that much beer, etc.), and check whether a light bulb at the end of the perceptron lights up (representing a 'like') or stays dark (representing a 'dislike'). If the output matches the shopper's known response, you do nothing. If it is lit, and the shopper said 'dislike', you adjust all the knobs down that were set to make the light go 'on', and all the knobs up that were set to make the light go 'off'. You do the opposite if the light is dark, but the shopper said 'like'. In either case, you adjust each knob in proportion to the quantity of each good in the current trolley (if you had lots of beer in that trolley, you adjust beer knob lots, if you had very little cereal, you adjust that knob only a little). You do this over and over again, for different trolleys of goods, until the knobs stop turning.

That's all there is to the perceptron learning algorithm. The interesting thing is that this simple algorithm is guaranteed by a mathematical proof (which Rosenblatt derived) to stop at a set of knob settings that duplicate the 'like/dislike' behaviour of the economic actor *in the example data, if such a set of settings exists*. Generalization to unforeseen trolleys full of goods is not guaranteed. But the proof of convergence of the perceptron learning algorithm seemed a phenomenal accomplishment at the time, and the hype for Rosenblatt's learning computers was significant. There was much talk in the press of computers being able to program themselves in the future. Then, as now, AI seemed right around the corner.

That was, until 1969, when two researchers at MIT, Marvin Minsky and Seymour Papert, published a book called *Perceptrons*,[18] which proved that there was a vast category of problems for which no settings of the perceptron knobs existed which could deliver the correct results. For these commonplace problems, there was no desirable equilibrium into which the perceptron learning algorithm could settle, so the knobs would just spin uselessly forever. Minsky and Papert's book sunk the Perceptron research programme, which died almost completely with Rosenblatt in 1971.

If one removes the random tangles of wires, and the motorized volume knobs, it isn't hard in retrospect to see why perceptrons proved quite incapable. All they really are is a weighted combination of numbers (like the orientation of axes in PCA), with a relatively simple rule for adjusting the weights ('learning'), and an on/off interpretation of the output number as a category for the inputs. In short, the problem with early perceptrons was the simplicity of their connections. More complicated connections were needed to overcome their limitations.

It would take the redevelopment of connectionist AI (after the AI winter brought the failure of Herb Simon's symbol-processing expert systems) to overcome this problem. But by the 1980s connectionism had lost all the hardware trappings that suggested real networks, all their random tangles of wires and volume knob synapses. Computers were no longer programmed with patch cords, relay or vacuum tube switches were replaced with microscopic bits of storage in semiconductor chips, and all the knobs were simply numbers stored in silicon memory. So connectionism stopped being vaguely brain-like hardware, and became software programs, running on the conventional architecture of a CPU. While the 'neural' architecture remained in the software description of connectionist AI, the actual execution was (in all but a smattering of research experiments) that of a conventional computer algorithm.

When one examines these redeveloped 'neural' programs, the metaphor to 'neurons' become even more strained. In reality, almost all modern connectionist algorithms are really just collections of nested mathematical functions, running in conventional computer programs.

Discarding metaphorical language, a typical connectionist algorithm of the 1980s vintage looks like this:

$$\vec{y} = W_2 \vec{f}\left(W_1 \vec{x}\right)$$

The inputs are a vector (list) of numbers $\vec{x}$, and the layers of 'neuron synapses' (which were once volume knobs, but are now just numbers in computer memory) are the multiplication of matrices (tables) W_1 and W_2 (called 'weight'

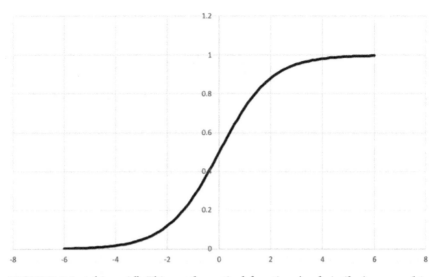

FIGURE 8.4 *A 'sigmoid'. This mathematical function (and similar) are used in the core of connectionist algorithms.*

matrices) against this list, in two big multiplication steps of the algorithm, generating output numbers in another vector (list) $\vec{y}$. The one critical additional element is the function f, which is applied to the list of numbers in between the two multiplication steps. This step is the key to making connectionist algorithms overcome the limitations of perceptrons pointed out by Minsky and Papert. But with a little examination, they are doing something that is mathematically familiar.

The typical function f (metaphorically called the 'neuron activation function') has a shape like the one shown in Figure 8.4. That is, as the weighted input numbers ($W_1\vec{x}$) go up, the output of the function rises smoothly from zero to one. However, what that second round of multiplications in a connectionist algorithm does is combine a whole bunch of these functions together.

Consider that two such functions can be slightly offset from one another, by adjusting particular W values that are called 'biases'. The algorithm can effectively subtract the two offset functions from one another, and come up with a resulting function that looks like Figure 8.5.

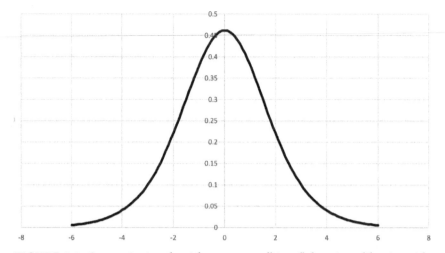

FIGURE 8.5 *Connectionist algorithms sum up 'biased' functions like sigmoids, and this is the result of such a sum. It has a similar shape to a Bell Curve. In fact, Bell Curves are sometimes used (as an alternative to sigmoids) in connectionist algorithms to model data.*

It has a shape that is very reminiscent of a Bell Curve (which is ironic, given that function's historic association is with real-world *human* biases). So what is really going on in those nested, complex equations is something very similar to the Gaussian Process Classifier in the job-computerizability model. The algorithm is picking out ranges of numbers to place under a warped Bell Curve shape. Just like in that example, connectionist algorithms are warping and fitting simple shapes, that are mathematically easy to specify and manipulate, to cover data in big data sets, and then dividing that data into categories, the way that Goddard's categories divided IQ tests into categories ranging from imbecile to gifted. This warping and fitting is usually done using the calculus of Leibniz, to turn the problem of finding the numbers in W_1 and W_2 into a mathematical optimization problem. The algorithms that solve that problem usually have very little to do with anything that is known to go on in the brain, but unlike Rosenblatt's early perceptrons, the resulting algorithms do have mathematical proofs behind them to say they can 'learn' a complete range of mathematical functions.

Does this new algorithm generalize, such that, for instance, it produces the correct answers on future trolleys of products that our actor hasn't seen before? In general, no. The problem of effective generalization remains unsolved, and that's unsurprising, since all this maths has nothing to do with the way that a *human* actor is liable to generalize. In fact, the optimization techniques of modern connectionist algorithms have little in common with the operation of real, biological neurons, other than metaphor. Where there are commonalities at all, they are superficial. By and large, the theories of modern connectionism are taken from mathematical optimization, probability theory and statistics, not the biology of the brain, or even theories of human psychology. While the theories from Hayek, Rosenblatt and other connectionist pioneers drew on highly simplified models of biological neurons, most latter-day connectionist algorithms are better described as highly complex mathematical optimization problems that have only the scantest similarity to the brain.

With the added complexity of an additional 'layer' (that is, the function f and the weights W_2) the connectionism of the 1980s, if properly configured, worked, in as much as it could replicate the patterns in big data, and provide a shallow, not-terribly predictable or human form of generalization. However, they were hard to engineer, and they scaled poorly, making them unreliable and impractical for big problems. As the era of really big data dawned, more automatic and scalable connectionist algorithms were needed. The solution was to make the networks *even more* complex, by adding even more 'layers'; that is, more nested functions, more multiplications and more numbers for the algorithms to manipulate. Avoiding the stretched metaphors of neural networks, the mathematical functions represented now look like this:

$$\vec{y} = W_n \vec{f}_n \cdots \left(W_4 \vec{f}_4 \left(W_3 \vec{f}_3 \left(W_2 \vec{f}_2 (W_1 \vec{x}) \right) \right) \right)$$

The typical word used to describe these networks is 'deep' and the weight-tuning algorithms employed are now called 'deep learning'. That term is certainly justified in terms of the layers of mathematics being utilized in these deeply nested functions. In deep learning networks, layers upon layers of numerical functions (often Bell Curves, or functions that combine into other, similar, simple shapes) are being moved around fields of numbers, to produce intricately linked mathematical 'atoms' of emergent representations. The depth and complexity of these links is the key to being able to flexibly and easily model any big data. That is to say, such networks are very good at mapping numbers (like the O*NET ratings in the jobs study) to other numbers in really complicated ways. These networks can wildly warp shapes over big data in ways that are impossible to visualize, but can categorize that data in exceedingly complicated ways. Those categories are 'hidden' atoms within the data. There is no need for a human expert to find these atoms, as they are dictated by the selected numbers (features) fed into the network, the data itself and emergent effects of complicated mathematics.

However, this flexibility is also the reason that those networks become incomprehensible complex systems. It's why we find it impossible to understand how they will generalize from what they've learned, and why some researchers see them as a new kind of alchemy. A complex system was required to allow connectionist algorithms the capacity to work well, because more layers of mathematical functions are needed to provide the flexibility of warping shapes around the data. But it is precisely this complexity that make their generalizations unpredictable, opaque and well-nigh irreparable when mistakes are made.

The main thing that brains and connectionist algorithms share in common is opacity, but it would be a huge mistake to think that the algorithms have reached the complexity of brains. The largest known deep learning networks have something like 10^{10} parameters (the numerical weights in those matrices).[19] Most have far fewer, but to get a feel for their maximum size, consider that the length of a year is around 10^{10} milliseconds. To imagine how much larger and more complex the human brain is than the largest deep learning neural network, imagine stretching each of the milliseconds in that year to be the length of a year themselves. That's the comparable size of the brain (10^{20}), if we just compare the number of real neural synapses to the number of numbers in the biggest ever deep learning connectionist algorithm. However, that's only a gross, *quantitative* difference. Far more differences exist between connectionist algorithms and brains.

While the connectionist model of the mind is focused on synapses as switches, the networks of neurons in human beings are far more complex in their behaviour. Neuron behaviour is influenced not only by synaptic activations between neurons, but also by interactions with the body's hormonal system, its immune system,[20] the peripheral nervous system and the so-called 'second brain' of neurons that operate largely autonomously in the human gut. While the neurons within the brain itself are insulated by myelin, making them act much like patch cords, such that the neurons on either side of a synapse only communicate with one another through that synapse, the interconnected systems of the nerves in the muscles, spine and gut are not insulated in the same manner. These additional neural systems may use ephaptic communication, through cross induction that is not like a synaptic 'switch'. The purely synaptic model of Hayek and others is a vast simplification of how neurons interact and function as a system in a real, embodied human being.[21]

The non-synaptic interactions of human systems that contribute to thinking, those in the body and the gut, are usually thought of as being a part of 'feelings' rather than rationale.[22] However, that is predicated on the idea that human thinking is all 'rational' computation, in the sense of Hilbert's mechanical procedures, and their legacy of algorithmic models of human intelligence. It assumes that the brain is just flipping computational bits, in the form of firing synapses, to implement algorithms just like those of conventional computers, but played out on the different architecture of a massive interconnected network of simple switches. Modern theories from neuroscience and psychology tell us that this is not a correct model of how humans actually think, and that the non-synaptic systems play a significant role in human cognition.

Universal computation tells us that the substrate of computation is irrelevant, but the argument for connectionist algorithms ability to do brain-like things tells us the curious corollary that the architecture built on that substrate is vital. However, the only aspect that is roughly copied from the brain to connectionist algorithms is masses of interconnected on/off switches in networks. The mathematical functions of a connectionist algorithm are very different from real neurons, and real neurons interact in ways that are very different from the raw, connectionist algorithmic paradigm. Moreover, there is even more to the architecture of human cognition than the details of neurons, and their interaction with the other complex interacting systems in the human body.

Consider the deep associations in Dali's painting, how they sprung from his unique cognition, and how they impact each and every viewer differently, causing a series of unique associations to vibrate through that viewer's thoughts and feelings. Further consider how each of those people is a part of a larger social network that interprets cultural symbols, stretching over space and back in time to the earliest human communities. The painting depicts numerous symbols that hold profound meaning both for Dali and for the viewer, and those meanings will continue to evolve as people and art change. The broken Venus de Milo is one of the most famous classical artworks in the world, visited by almost ten million tourists a year. The tilted head of the toreador, standing in the arena as the bull dies, conveys both a mythology and a recognizable sadness. If one looks carefully at the dying bull, its shapes, dappled like the spots of the Dalmatian, warp into a landscape, which is the shape of Cap de Creus, the region where Dali lived. Regardless of interpretation of these symbols, the painting is infused with feeling, passion even, as its glowing reddish/yellow hue suggests, and must have invoked in Dali much more than simple synaptic firings, implementing one of Hilbert's 'mechanical procedures'. Likewise, the feelings and thoughts it evokes in viewers like me, and millions of others from different backgrounds, cultures and even times (the painting is now forty-eight years old), are no more reducible to an algorithm.

While it is certain that the brain, and in fact all the other systems of the body that affect human cognition, must be rooted in the laws of physics, the argument that all they do is compute algorithms like a computer is actually ignoring a larger point about the architecture of human thought: it is an emergent phenomena of the most complex systems anyone knows of. Emergent behaviour from complex systems is specifically about the irreducibility of such systems into constituent parts. Therefore it's hard to think that just one aspect of the architecture of human thought, embedded as it is in continuously adapting architectures of society, culture and history, along with individual, intricately interconnected architectures of feelings and thoughts, could be separated from the others. Assuming that the synaptic connections of the brain are like a computer algorithm running on a network architecture is focusing on a single aspect of an architecture that can't be torn apart, even from its substrate, without reducing it.

Yet there is a larger sense in which our algorithmic architecture is now relying on emergence from networks. Simplifying models that rely on emergence from complex networks are commonplace in economics, politics, and now in algorithms that affect everyone's day-to-day lives. The binary switches of 'likes' and 'dislikes', along with many other simplified measures of people online, have become the commodities that are traded, where profiling of economic actors and profit-via-clickthrough have created the most frictionless free market possible. Based on the same faith that supports 'spontaneous order' from free markets, many think it will lead to a desirable spontaneous order for society. While economic actors who relentlessly and unconsciously seek gain are questionable models of people, those models do accurately encompass the relentless and simple-minded drives of algorithms. Those algorithms are now not only actors in our economies, but actors in our society, through their actions as information providers and curators, the arrangers of social interactions and the assigners of work to people. They are profoundly changing the communications we have with one another, and what that means to our lives. The systems they create are certainly complex enough to demonstrate emergent behaviours, outcomes of complex networks that cannot be predicted from their individual parts. However, the emergent, spontaneous order these agents help to create may not be the one many people would desire.

9

Defining Terms

Human communication cannot be reduced to information.
Science-fiction author URSULA K. LE GUIN, 2004[1]

Just like image recognition, natural language processing (NLP) is at the vanguard of AI today, and is exploding in its use, employing deep networks, machine-learning algorithms and the explosion of big data on the Internet (in the form of documents, websites, blogs, posts, tweets, etc., estimated to be enough text to fill 10^{11} A4 pages, with a large fraction of that text changing daily).[2] NLP researchers and algorithm engineers face the daily challenge of getting computers to process, analyse and 'comprehend' some fraction of this text, as well as the challenges of recognizing human speech (audio and video content are also exploding online), and even generating some natural-sounding language in print and audio form. NLP is being applied to online question answering, news-gathering, automated journalism, text categorization, chatbots and voice activation, but also archiving, through large-scale content analysis and the ability to summarize large documents (particularly in the financial and medical sectors).

Still, despite the limitless promises, really *understanding* human language isn't something algorithms do, because for a person to really understand, they have to integrate new knowledge into the larger body of the unique things that they already know. On the back of understanding, human *communication* is a deeply complex and nuanced interaction. Such matters remain subtle, and therefore extremely difficult to model with mere mathematics. Yet *communications* is an established, completely practical subfield of engineering, and has been since the 1950s.

When engineers talk about 'communications', they don't mean the vital, human exchange to which Le Guin is referring; they mean the transmission of data in coded form, through the airwaves or down a wire. Moreover, for the algorithms in engineering communication, *meaning doesn't exist*, only information does. I'll pause for a minute here, just to let you get your head around that statement. *For algorithms, meaning doesn't exist, only information does.* What does this apparently contradictory statement even mean? Most of us would find it hard to separate information from meaning; in fact, the very word 'information' seems to imply the conveyance of meaning. So, if information conveys no meaning, is it really information?

But this isn't a contradiction for algorithms, because the word 'information' has a *technical* definition that *explicitly* disregards meaning. Like many of the other words in AI – 'neuron', 'synapse', 'knowledge', 'intelligence' and 'truth' – the meaning of the word 'information' has been warped in order to describe a computational technology that is, in fact, very different in nature from the meaning of the original word. Since the beginning of computation, the meanings of words have been blurred by the tendency of engineers to give numbers, procedures and algorithmic outputs the name of human phenomena. The blurring and confusion between these words and our common understanding of them causes us to unjustly anthropomorphize algorithms, particularly when the words involved have a deep significance to the human experience.

In 1981, the AI researcher and Yale University professor Drew McDermott called this practice of naming computational phenomena with words denoting human characteristics and capabilities *wishful mnemonics*.[3] He suggested that technologists' use of such words reflected a deep-seated desire for the computational objects in question to magically assume the human-like qualities being described. For instance, one of the most powerful examples of wishful mnemonics in AI is the word 'learning', as in machine learning. In every machine-learning algorithm, 'learning' describes the adjustment of parameters in nested mathematical functions. In contrast, *human* learning (except for the most rote memorization) is the incorporation of new sensations and ideas into an individualized context of existing knowledge. It is far from clear that this deeper meaning of human learning can be accounted for by mere 'parameter adjustment' in the brain.

Likewise, 'uncertainty' in algorithms is represented by probabilities, while human uncertainty is a mental and, possibly, emotional phenomenon that isn't consistent with the laws of probability. This is clearly demonstrated by the fact that when people are tested on probabilistic problems in a laboratory, they seldom return answers that are consistent with algorithmic, probabilistic reasoning. Ironically, when such experiments return this troubling result, researchers have taken to viewing the human response as a deviation based on 'biases', implying *flawed reasoning* on the part of people being tested. But it's not at all clear that the test subjects' answers are flawed, because it's not clear that human uncertainty and algorithmic uncertainty are the same thing. Probability calculations are only valid in the case of truth uncertainties (i.e. uncertainty in the answer to technically well-posed problems), while human beings have to continually cope with semantic uncertainty (i.e. being unsure of the meaning of symbols) and ontological uncertainty (i.e. uncertainty about the unforeseen range of things that you might run into).

So there are two things going on here. One is that algorithms don't really understand language: they only process it, using precisely the sorts of simplifying algorithmic tricks previously discussed. The other is that our language is changing, incorporating wishful mnemonics, which conform more to algorithmic definitions of words than the subtler meanings that humans understand. Now that algorithms are penetrating every corner of the human experience, we have to consider how those two effects might interact, and even feedback on one another. Words are powerful things and they shape the way we see ourselves, our place in the world and our technology, including algorithms. If algorithms are '*super*-intelligent', then that may imply that they are more than and people are less than; equally, if algorithms are 'rational' and 'objective', then the implication is that people are innately 'irrational' and 'biased'. Algorithms are now becoming participants in the cultural conversation themselves as they try to parse, understand and create language that is, in return, sent out into the world for people to consume. Because of this, it is critically important to renew our awareness of what words mean, not just with regard to algorithms, but in the human context, where changes in words and meanings can have effects that span history and society.

I enrolled for my first summer term at the University of Alabama with the intention of shortening the time and expense of my education but found there was little on offer that fitted my tightly sequenced engineering curriculum besides Early American Literature. While discussions of Cotton Mather and Walt Whitman weren't the way I wanted to spend what should have been my vacation, the course conveniently fulfilled one of the small number of humanities requirements for my degree, so I signed up. The opening class didn't seem promising, as I discovered the course was to be held at midday in an un-air-conditioned classroom, presided over by an intimidatingly rugged professor. Dr Tensom no doubt sensed his students' sweaty summer dissatisfaction, so he opened his first lecture by saying in a booming voice, 'So, let me tell you about my time in Nam'.

He explained that while Vietnam was no war of words for him, it had been a war *about* words. At the start of his first tour as a commander, his unit had been tasked to 'search and destroy'. Those words made their mission clear. They were to find places that were or might become bases for the Viet Cong (he called them 'Charlie'), and destroy everything they found there.

Halfway through his second tour the name of his mission changed. Though the everyday operations of what he did stayed exactly the same, his team was now commanded to 'search and clear'. This was in response to the American people's growing dissatisfaction with the deadly conflict and endless hours of death and destruction they were seeing on TV. As stateside opposition to the war grew even more intense, the name of his mission changed again, to 'reconnaissance in force', a term that suggested very little about destroying places where an enemy might be hiding, while also fighting, capturing or killing any enemy soldiers encountered along the way.

Dr. Tensom told us that after the war, he spent some time in hospital recovering from the awful things he had experienced, and explained that even there his condition was the subject of shape-shifting words that seemed to disguise the realities of the war's impact on people. He told us how during the American Civil War, soldiers traumatized by battle were described rather poetically as having 'soldier's heart', which was suggestive of the sadness and sickness of a deep trauma. During the First World War, the condition was renamed first 'shell shock', and then 'war neurosis', suggesting the anxiety and nervousness typically observed. After the dawn of Freud's psychiatry, it became 'combat hysteria', then 'battle fatigue' during the Second World War. It wasn't until the Vietnam War that it was given the name of Dr Tensom's own diagnosis, 'post-traumatic stress disorder', a scientific term that suggests nothing of the cause of the problem, or the direct effect it had on the men involved with their broken hearts, neuroses, hysteria and fatigue. In recent years, this disassociation has become even greater, with the now preferred use of the acronym 'PTSD', which sounds more like a code used by a computer than a human condition.

Dr Tensom explained that the dehumanization of the words had disturbed him profoundly, because he had been raised by Jesuits in New Orleans. The Jesuits, or the brothers of the Society of Jesus (also known as 'God's Soldiers'), were dedicated scholars, known for their rational bent as well as their devotion.

As a result, when speaking in class, if he uttered any word that was even remotely vague, his Jesuit teachers would demand, 'define your term', and hold him and all the other children to a rigorous standard of meaning in their discourse. He explained that this formative context from his youth combined with the changing landscape of meanings that he saw in the war and, after his recovery, motivated him to take an English degree on the G.I. Bill, then continue on to become a professor of English. In light of all this, our task that summer term, he explained, was to examine the meanings of the word 'nature' in early American literature, exploring the tension between nature as the wellspring of human beauty and virtue (e.g. the ideas that descend from Emerson and Thoreau) and the idea of nature as the source of human sin and savagery (e.g. the ideas that descend from Mather to Hawthorne). This tension, he concluded, exemplified the entire American literary tradition.

Dr Tensom was right: it is important to define your terms. In this post-truth era, it is becoming ever more apparent that words matter and have consequences for how we interact with the world, and even how we perceive it. Words and phrases are embedded in the human cultural narrative in myriad complex ways. What words we use for which things shapes our perception of those things, and perceptions change meaning, and meaning determines actions which, in turn, may change perception. This is a vital feedback loop that affects social and cultural evolution and it's a loop that now involves algorithms. So, it is now imperative that we understand the meaning of words applied to algorithms and how algorithms generate words about and for us.

Alan Turing's contributions to the world are on a nearly unimaginable scale. Due to the deeply rooted societal bias against homosexuals, he was, until recently, the greatest unsung hero of the Second World War, perhaps the greatest of all time. He was instrumental in the creation of a computer that deciphered the coded messages of the German's Enigma machine, a feat that is thought to have shortened the war by at least four years and thus saved millions of lives. His invention of the thought-experiment computer the Turing machine literally created the field of computer science, the bedrock field for an immeasurable fraction of today's global society. And he created another thought experiment that has forever altered the cultural zeitgeist about man and machines: the so-called Turing test.

The test was first described in the 1950 paper entitled 'Computing Machinery and Intelligence',[4] in which Turing acknowledges the difficulty of defining 'thinking', such that one could answer the question, 'Do computers think?' He posed instead the alternative question: 'Are there imaginable digital computers which would do well in the imitation game?' The imitation game (Turing never used his own name for the test) is a thought experiment about communication, which he saw as a way of determining progress in AI. Curiously, in a now largely forgotten detail, the original game was concerned with the ability of a computer to imitate a woman, as well as a man could imitate a woman. In his paper, Turing started his game with a man imitating a woman, being judged by another person. To prevent this judge from guessing the gender of the imitator based on appearance or the sound of their voice, Turing placed a wall between the judge and contestant, through which they could only pass pieces of paper through a small slot in order to communicate. He then suggested swapping the male imitator for a computer and judging the quality of the computer's intelligence based on how well it did, compared to a man, in imitating a woman. To further challenge the computer, he later expanded the puzzle so the machine simply had to convince the judge it was a person, rather than someone/thing playing a role in a gender game. But the restriction of passing notes through a wall remained, as it was important for the judge not to consider anything except written symbols as communication. The problem is, Turing's wall changes what we call 'communication' particularly in the human sense of the word, which involves a great deal more than a disembodied, mute exchange of abstract symbols.

While Turing was writing about his famous test, Claude Shannon, an American code-breaker and electrical engineer, was theorizing on purely symbolic communications. At Bell Laboratories Shannon developed *information theory*, a set of ideas that are vital to every modern electronic communication and computation device, because they make reliable data transmission possible, not just between one smartphone and another, or a media provider and a smart TV, but between memory, CPU, hard drive and every other part of a computer, in every computer on Earth.[5]

Both early computers and telecommunication devices had to send signals (we'll call them messages for now) down wires, or through the air on radio waves. All such messages are subject to random errors, caused by everything from nearby, poorly insulated toasters to cosmic particles zipping through space. Shannon reckoned that one could fix these inevitable errors by sending extra data with every message and using that extra data as a check on the original data. This is easiest to explain with messages that are just numbers. For instance, if you sent the message '321', Shannon figured you could, for instance, send one more number, the sum of those three numbers (6), and help overcome some of the problems of interference. When the message is received, if the numbers don't add up (for instance, you received '322' and '6'), and you figure errors of more than 1 in any given number were unlikely, you know something was probably wrong (one of the numbers must be one too high). Of course, you don't know which one, but you could then ask for the message to be sent again. However, you could make your error detection a bit better by sending two extra numbers, the sum of the first two numbers (3 + 2 = 5) and the sum of the second two (2 + 1 = 3). Then, if you received 322 and 53, you not only know you've had an error, you can figure out what that error was (the last bit should be 1), and you don't even have to ask for a resend: you can correct the error yourself. The interesting thing is that with a bit of clever maths to extend these ideas, Shannon determined schemes for sending extra data that allowed this sort of error detective work to be effective, while sending the minimum amount of extra data. Shannon's methods proved surprisingly practical. It turns out that in situations where the interference of toasters, the cosmos and so on isn't too bad, you can fix corrupted messages with high probability by adding only a modest amount of extra data. The resulting error correcting codes are being used right now, all the time, in all your devices, to fix innumerable errors in the data transmission that is constantly going on within and between all our devices all the time. Without Shannon's theories, real-world *electronic* communication (and computation) would be virtually impossible.

However, Shannon's electronic communication is very different from human communication, in several important ways. The maths in Shannon's theories requires the assumption that messages being sent occur with definite probabilities, which are independent of the probabilities of any other messages. It is as if each message passed through the slot in the Turing test is generated by a roll of dice, with no consideration of its context in amongst other messages. Once you've made that assumption, you can start to make some conclusions about the most efficient ways to send messages. For instance, you can logically conclude that common (high probability) messages should be short. If you're going to text your spouse 'I'm in the taxi right now' every time you get off your train home from work, in time you will probably just send the word 'taxi' (or maybe just its emoji). Rarer messages should be the only ones that require lots of words. Under the assumption of randomly generated messages, Shannon figured out that in the most efficient *coding* of messages, the amount of data needed for a message that occurs with probability P is proportional to:

$$I = - \log_2 P$$

For a message you are going to send half the times that you send a message at all, the amount of data you need is $1 = - \log_2 0.5$, which Shannon called one *bit*. In this case, sending a '1' means 'I'm sending that message I send about half the time', and sending a zero means 'I'm not sending that message I send about half the time' (which you might then follow with another message). For a message that occurs a quarter of the time, two bits are needed ($2 = -\log_2 0.25$), and so on. As the probabilities of messages get smaller, the number of bits needed swells towards infinity, but it does so slowly, which is part of why Shannon's theories remain so practical. When you add in the error correcting data, under Shannon's efficient (probability based) coding ideas, you end up sending far fewer bits than you might have figured.

However, the confusion between human communication and Shannon's information theories really begins with Shannon's use of *metaphors* to describe his theory. He sometimes called the equation *I* the amount of 'surprise' associated with a given word appearing, given that as the word's probability dropped, the surprise of seeing it rose, along with the number of necessary bits. He also called *I* the amount of *information* in the message. It seemed natural that the amount of information in a message was related to how surprising it was. Telling your spouse you are out of the train and in the taxi isn't really telling that much. However, saying you just talked to the queen on the train is really informative, and really surprising (and certainly requires more emojis). But in human language, surprise means 'an unexpected or astonishing event, fact, or thing'. In Shannon's theory, it means *I*, the number of bits that are needed for a message in an efficient coding, and nothing more about human expectations and astonishment. The disconnection of 'surprise' from human feelings is questionable, but it turned out to be far less impactful than changes in the meaning of the word *information*.

Shannon's theories also required another calculation, the *average* number of bits needed to represent a *set* of messages:

$$H = \sum_i P_i(-\log_2 P_i)$$

This equation might seem complicated, but upon further examination it's pretty straightforward. The term in the parenthesis is *I*, the number of bits needed in Shannon's efficient coding of messages (assuming the messages are generated at random). This term is being summed up over all possible messages (the space of messages is assumed to be fully enumerable, just like in Cardano's games) weighted by the probability of each message, so this is just an average over all messages.

The metaphor Shannon used for describing the equation H was physics based. He called H the *entropy* of the set of messages. In physics, entropy is the amount of disorder in a system. For instance, a rock crystal has molecules that are very ordered into mathematically easy-to-describe shapes. Thus, crystals have low entropy. By contrast, a gas is a collection of randomly moving molecules, and has very high disorder, high entropy. In physics, differences in the disorder of systems (say, between a crystal and a gas) are measured by a formula that is remarkably similar to H. This seems more than a mathematical coincidence, which made the metaphor appealing, in much the same way that physics analogies appeal to economists: it implied that the information in communications behaves like physics.

However, consider that to make H as high as is possible, the messages should be *as random as possible*. High H comes from messages that are sent by rolling dice. Now consider Turing's slot. It seems odd that passing messages completely at random is somehow most informative about what's on the other side of the wall. Shannon's theory says that maximum 'information' comes from a random message generator. This is because, due to Shannon's use of metaphor, the word 'information' has changed from its conventional human meaning, to a technical meaning that doesn't relate to human intuition about that word.

When Shannon presented his theories in a paper at the 1950 Conference on Cybernetics,[6] he must have known of how jarring inconsistencies between his theory and common sense seemed, because he was careful to point out his precise technical meaning for the word *information*, and how that meaning was completely disconnected from the human meaning of the word. He wrote: 'Information here, although related to the everyday meaning of the word, should not be confused with it.' Shannon of course knew that messages being sent down electronic wires and processed by computer algorithms had to, at some point, be read and understood by people, so he went on to point out that his information was disconnected from meaning, as well: 'Frequently the messages have meaning. That is they refer to or are correlated according to some system with certain physical or conceptual entities. The semantic elements of communication are irrelevant to the engineering problem.' Note how strange this sentence is. Messages *frequently* have meaning? It makes one wonder what use a meaningless message would actually be.

Shannon went on to make a new technical definition for communication itself by stating: *'The fundamental problem of* communication *is that of reproducing at one point either exactly or approximately a message selected at another point.'* That is to say, he saw communication as mere transmission of information, like the message '321', such that messages could be sent from a transmitter and accurately duplicated by a receiver. With these metaphors dictating the technical meaning of human terms, the words 'communication' and 'information' became explicitly divorced from *meaning*.

Even attendees of the cybernetics conference had doubts about this profound shift in the meaning of these powerful words, and the simultaneous abandonment of the concept of meaning itself. One attendee, the physicist, philosopher and AI pioneer Heinz von Foerster, commented:

> I wanted to call the whole of what they called information theory signal theory, because information was not yet there. There were 'beep beeps' but that was all, no information. The moment one transforms that set of signals into other signals our brains can make an understanding of, then information is born—it's not in the beeps.

Yet information theory is now ubiquitous not only in engineering communication theory, and every single aspect of computing and telecommunications, but in 'deep' AI, where algorithms derived from this theory are often used as a means of deriving representations from data, based on probabilistic assumptions.

People have been thinking about meaning for a very long time. The field of semiotics (the study of meaning-making) is as old as Aristotle, but it was nineteenth-century logician Charles Sanders Peirce who first attempted to connect semiotics and modern symbolic logic. Throughout this career, Peirce sought formal philosophical ways to articulate thought processes through the logical study of language and symbols (aka 'signs'). He postulated that each symbol must consist of three parts: the object/person/phenomena being symbolized, the symbol itself and the thing that connects the two together. To Peirce this last element was not a set of immutable features, but a condition of the habits of the mind of the individual, or an implicit consensus that emerged in social communities. He saw the human mind as integral *to* meaning, rather than as a separate, passive observer.

While semiotics deals with the philosophical meaning of symbols, semantics is the study of meaning in linguistics. Though Shannon said that the messages he was sending down wires and through the air only 'frequently' had meaning, at some point all of them had to be conveyed to people through human language. It was inevitable that someone had to look at what was technical about that language, and what was not. This connection took place through the work of American linguist Noam Chomsky,[7] who undertook pioneering work in the 1950s to derive a technical representation of human communication. In his PhD dissertation at Harvard University, Chomsky created the key idea of *formal languages*. Like the formal operations in logic, formal languages have precise rules, which are called the *formal grammar* of that language. These language rules are commonly referred to as *syntax*.

Chomsky's theories divide formal languages into a hierarchy of four increasingly sophisticated types. Each type of language in this hierarchy is a set of rules that can generate ('write') or parse ('understand') sentences in the language (though those human-meaning-laden words are only used metaphorically here). Like an expert system, one can run the rules of a formal language from a starting point, chaining through rule-after-rule, until one reaches a final rule, a destination, which is the completion of the sentence. One can also run the rules over sentences, to determine whether they are valid in that language.

Chomsky's theories about language hierarchies created the entire field of computational linguistics, and the study of human language in terms of computational syntax. It also created the area of computer science concerned with the power of programming languages (code). Like languages, computer codes require a formal system of rules on which to operate. However, unlike human languages, computers can come up with nonsensical outcomes because the code doesn't contain a representation of meaning. Chomsky's theories defined what was syntactic about human language, but not what was semantic (related to meaning).

To elaborate, at the bottom of Chomsky's hierarchy, as the least complex and capable form of language, is the *regular language*. Regular languages just generate patterns of words, based on patterns they are given as inputs. They have no internal 'states', and in some sense that makes them like expert systems that have no rule chaining: they merely take the input and spit out an immediate, related output. A famous example of a regular language generator is the AI therapist called *ELIZA*, which was created by MIT professor Joseph Weizenbaum in the early 1960s. You can still find implementations of it online, if you'd like to have a little regular-language-generated therapy. Here's a typical ELIZA session, to give you a flavour for how regular languages hold up to a few minutes of the Turing test:

> Hello, I am Eliza.

* Are you a computer, or a person?

> Would you prefer if I were not a computer, or a person?

* I'd prefer you to be a computer that successfully imitates a person.

> We were discussing you, not me.

Despite Eliza's therapist-like deflection of direct questions with other questions, interactions of any length quickly reveal that ELIZA is just reconstructing sentences with rote rules. Yet the program is a precursor of online chat 'bots' that are ubiquitous today, and was an early, primitive example of AI NLP.

Next up in Chomsky's hierarchy are context-free grammars. These sets of rules advance a bit on ELIZA, and can include internal references to parts of their own sentences, thus making for more interesting sentence blocks. These grammars are behind many of the catchphrase generators that you can find online today. For instance, online generators of political soundbites created these random sentences:

I want an America where drug dealers and rich oil companies can't take away our Christian values.

Unlike my opponent, I support our glorious future, our precious schools and our medical dramas.

As Mother Teresa always said: it's the economy, stupid!

While an improvement on the rote recitations of regular grammars, these context-free generators also have no sense of the meanings of the words they are using; they simply string sentence elements together in ways that are referentially and grammatically correct. Because of this, even simple generators can generate sentences that have completely unintended implications, like an online meme generator I found recently that created the sentence 'Yesterday I happily ate into a few white people'. The apparent racial tinge of this random sentence isn't surprising when one realizes that there is no real understanding of the words involved, only a stringing together of those words according to grammatical rules. Context free grammars contain no definitions at all of the words they are stringing together.

The next two steps up Chomsky's hierarchy, the context-sensitive grammars and the recursively enumerable grammars, are similar to one another. They are both Turing machines, the former with finite memory and the latter with infinite memory. In other words, they are the set of languages that can be rendered by full, general computers. They describe the complete range of computer programs that might be created to try to generate or understand language.

Chomsky's hierarchy jumps quickly from primitive bots to any program anyone might ever write, but its categorization has proved useful in separating what's mechanical about language, the part that we can easily describe in computers, from the part that is subtle and human. In fact, the Chomsky hierarchy is more utilized in fundamental computer science than in linguistics or even AI. This is because, like expert systems, rule-based systems never quite managed to deliver real natural language generation or understanding for computers. That was never Chomsky's goal, and he has always been straightforward about the limitations of both formal languages, and the implied capabilities of computers to understand human communication. The intent of Chomsky's work was not its prescriptive use for algorithms to create talking computers, but drawing a dividing line between the purely formal structure in human language and what language actually *means*. To illustrate this point, Chomsky offered the sentence: 'Colourless green ideas sleep furiously.' This sentence is *syntactically* correct according to a formal grammar. However, *semantically* it is utter nonsense. There have been attempts at poetical interpretations and, it is true, that there are sentences that may seem nonsensical but, in the context of a particular moment, may make sense to human interpreters. But it is precisely the vast potential of this unpredictable context that gives human language a semantics that cannot be bound solely by syntax and some enumerated range of features in an algorithm. For this reason, Chomsky has always been careful to insist that syntax is divorced from meaning (semantics), because as Peirce posited before him, meaning can only reside in a human mind.

This brings us back to Hayek and the theory of *emergence*. If one has faith in Hayek's theories of spontaneous order, the question for AI is whether computer semantics can *emerge* from a sufficiently complex network of formal rules or calculations. That question has been a subject of rigorous debates between linguists and computer scientists for years, one of the most famous being in 1978 between Noam Chomsky and his contemporary Roger Schank, an AI. researcher at Yale University.[8]

Schank rejected the distinction between syntax and semantics and thought that Chomsky denied the *inherent* role of meaning in language. Furthermore, Schank believed it was possible to encode sufficient rules (syntax, along with data structures, including Schank's work on structures that described stories) in a computer that semantics (meaning) would emerge. In the debate, Chomsky disagreed with Schank's theories vigorously, saying that if they were right, human psychology itself would turn out to be uninteresting. The only two interesting avenues, according to Chomsky's statements at the debate, were a psychology that was 'like physics', or one that was only examinable through novels.[9] With this statement, Marvin Minsky, the AI pioneer who derailed perceptron research, chimed into the debate from the audience, saying of Chomsky, his fellow professor at MIT: 'I think only a humanities professor at MIT could be so oblivious to the third interesting possibility: psychology could turn out to be like engineering.' There remains an open debate over whether it is possible to engineer meaning into computer algorithms, but the basic progression of AI history has largely rendered that debate moot. Just like with other applications of AI, NLP experienced a dramatic shift with the onslaught of the AI winter, and the arrival of the Internet. Intentionally designed grammars and natural language knowledge representations (story structures, etc.) were relegated in favour of systems that were based on big-data analysis.

Today, all of us constantly interact with computers that seem to have some 'understanding' of human language, and some ability to generate that language. Virtually all of these systems are based on statistics drawn from big data. With a little experimental probing, the fact that the language computers generate is coming from statistics of the language we human beings are using in our electronic communications becomes obvious. A familiar example is the autocorrect function of your smartphone, which is operating when you type anything into the device. The following experiment, which you can conduct with your own smartphone, is revealing. Type in a few words, then select the next suggested word that autocorrect[10] offers you (it is usually in the centre of the area just above your keyboard). For instance, when I type in 'Are women' into my iPhone, the next word suggested is 'in', and if I click that, and continue clicking in the same place, I get the following: 'Are women in a meeting with the other girls and they have to go home to get a coffee or a coffee drink and drink it and drink a drink and then go home and then get home and get to work on a coffee drink.'

What's happening under the bonnet is that the word combinations in the evolving text are being transformed into numerical values. These values are then being used to determine the probability of next words, and the word with the highest probability is the one suggested in the middle area above the keyboard. A hidden algorithm is at work combining some simple grammar rules with probabilities that have been sourced from the statistics of texts I've sent in the past, and texts that many, many other people have sent as well. For example, in predicting the first occurrence of the word 'coffee', the algorithm must have had a high probability value for $P('coffee'|'to\ go\ home\ to\ get\ a')$. Recalling that conditional probabilities are just rules, another, clearer way to look at the same construct is as the rule:

If 'to go home to get a' *then* 'coffee'

Each successive word is selected because it has the highest probability in relation to the former word, according to the big data that was used to generate such rules.

This is how rules-based NLP has transformed into statistics-based NLP, creating systems that are ubiquitously used today. However, viewing language through this probabilistic lens is, unsurprisingly, fraught with problems, which are becoming increasingly apparent. In 2016, researchers from Boston University and Microsoft Research fed an algorithm a data set of three million English words from Google News text, focused on the ones that were most frequently used, and then prompted it to fill in the blanks.[11] 'Man', they asked, 'is to computer programmer as woman is to ... what?' The machine returned the answer, 'homemaker'. In the same way, the word 'cooking' is most often associated with images of women and its why research has shown that Google ads on the Internet are six times more likely to show high-paying jobs (with salaries in excess of US$200,000) to men than to women.

The power of these probabilistic algorithmic systems is their ability to find correlations between words, in this case genders and professions. The algorithms have no understanding of the complex human issues of gender equality or systemic racism; they simply identify the patterns and return them to us due to their high historic correlations. Ironically, the result is that some of our most cutting-edge technology is re-discovering deeply problematic historic biases, re-surfacing it in the present and possibly prolonging it into the future. More complex language algorithms, like those that attempt to understand news articles, write legal opinions, even generate movie scripts, use a few more computational tricks, but they are all reflecting our own words back at us, through a lens of big data statistics and probability.

Algorithms combine a simplified, syntactic view of human language with a probabilistic view of big data, which is both incomplete and heavily biased by the past. The great body of human text from the past contains biases about things like gender, race and religion. Since many of those ideas are about simplified features of people leading to their categorization, it seems natural that algorithms that explicitly search for simplifying features by which to categorize things are liable to tune into these biases. Moreover, just like today's advanced image classification algorithms, most advanced algorithms for understanding and generating human language are based on incomprehensible, deep-learning neural networks, such that biases are lost in a sea of parameters and maths.

As with image processing, these algorithms have no understanding of what they are doing; they are merely processing numerical features, in a manner that has little to do with the way humans think or communicate. Their next-word predictions, their measures of the similarity between words, their reasoning about the role of words in sentences and documents, and all the other computations they perform on words are all strictly structural, like Chomsky's hierarchy, just supplemented by statistics of big data analysis. None of these algorithms comprehend meaning in any real sense of the word; instead they simply assume that the statistics of past human communications in their big data sets predict the propensities of human words, sentences and documents in the future. Thus, they simply feed back to us our own words, *replicating* things we have said in the past, and echoing them into the future. The question is: how might such feedback effect the evolution of human culture?

The biologist, author and former Oxford Chair for Public Understanding of Science Richard Dawkins introduced the word 'meme' in his 1976 book *The Selfish Gene*, to suggest an analogy between genes (the atomic encoding elements in evolutionary biology) and the theorized existence of similar atomic elements of human cultures. Dawkins' notion was uniquely focused on culture as an evolving entity, but his idea has similarities to earlier concepts like sememes and mythemes.

Sememes are the theoretical structural units of meaning in language, a concept introduced by American linguist Leonard Bloomfield in 1933, whose theories dominated structural linguistics before Chomsky invented formal grammars. Like Chomsky's contrast of the structure of formal language to meaning, Bloomfield contrasted sememes to morphemes, structural units of language syntax. Bloomfield was theorizing that morphemes, like putting 's' at the end of a word in English, carried the meanings of sememes (like the idea of 'plural'). Mythemes dealt with larger ideas of meaning, not unlike the story structures that Schank suggested. Mythemes are a concept invented in 1958 by Claude Lévi-Strauss, a French anthropologist who looked at common cultural myths, and theorized that they shared a similar structure. For instance, myths that have role relationships between dominating fathers and sons who challenge them is one mytheme, while another is the story of jealous siblings conspiring against each other to gain favour with their parents. The exact details of the fathers, sons and siblings are variations on those mythemes, but the fundamental story structure is the same. Each of these ideas, sememes, mythemes and memes, are trying to describe the atomic units of meaning in language.

Not much came of these ideas outside of academic theory, because it proved difficult to find clear examples of sememes, mythemes or plain old memes replicating in human cultures. That was until the advent of the phenomenally successful Hollywood blockbuster *Star Wars*. George Lucas's 1977 space opera was directly based on the work of mythologist Joseph Campbell, whose book *Hero with a Thousand Faces* was influenced by Lévi-Strauss's mythemes, and suggested that all human myths have a common structure, which arises from our common experiences of birth, childhood, adolescence, adulthood and death.

Campbell's main mytheme, which Lucas used as the basis for *Star Wars*, was the classic hero's story: a tale of a boy, who has been raised by a family he feels is not his own, meets a mysterious stranger, goes on an epic quest and finally encounters his true father in a fight to the death to gain his own power in life. The monomyth theory is convincing since so many stories can be seen as following this pattern. In his 1949 book, Campbell described dozens from every human culture. Even Mary Shelley's classic sci-fi tale *Frankenstein* could be described very precisely as a tragic version of the hero's journey. And, in the same way, the story of Ada Lovelace would make a fine Hollywood hero's journey with Ada as Luke Skywalker, Charles Babbage as Obi-Wan Kenobi and Byron's Romantic image as a sort of psychological Darth Vader.

The unprecedented success of the film series led to an explosion of similar stories that draw directly on the Campbell/Lucas mytheme, including *Spider-Man, Harry Potter*, even *Rain Man*. Consciously or unconsciously, people began writing more stories that were clearly based on the Campbell structure and now there is a whole industry that turns out scripts using this theory as a rote formula. The script formula was so successful that (in something of a nod to Schank's story AI approach) computer programs were marketed that claimed to take any author's story and character ideas and algorithmically mould them into a Hero's Journey script.

When Dawkins posed his meme theory, everyone understood that culture evolves and propagates, but no one could point confidently to an *atomic* encoding unit for culture that could mutate and recombine like a gene. The Joseph Campbell monomyth certainly qualifies as popular cultural artefact that has been mutated and replicated, but it is also a product *of* culture. Perhaps we see so many stories this way, because that is what we now *expect*. Nevertheless, Campbell's hero's journey does illustrate how commercial fitness can drive a concept's replication and survival.

More compact, atomic elements of culture, along the lines Dawkins suggested, have remained elusive. In some sense the Internet meme is a first viable candidate for a real-life, gene-like meme. However, Dawkins has said that they are not what he intended, because they are not subject to simple replication and random mutation like genes; they are consciously changed by people, in an explicit cultural dialogue that itself must contain memes. That's because humans don't simply replicate old ideas based on their apparent 'fitness', with occasional alterations based on probabilistic effects; they process them with deliberate intent and understanding of their meaning.

However, algorithms, which are increasingly participating in the human cultural dialogue, are not human. In human culture, memes might be theoretical, but in algorithms – which replicate simple concepts with random, probabilistic variations – they can be seen as real, and their real effects can be observed.

Consider studies that suggested flu epidemics could be predicted by the number of Google searches investigating flu symptoms and treatments in a given local area. When people asked questions that seemed to be about flu, Google took that as a sign of a possible flu outbreak.[12] While initial results appeared promising, it was later found that feedback loops created by autocomplete were confounding the results. Autocomplete started suggesting searches related to flu symptoms, which made people think about whether they might have flu, so they clicked autocomplete's flu-related suggestion, increasing the probability that autocomplete would make similar suggestions to others. This not only corrupts the idea of Google Flu Trends, it also shows how feedback loops between algorithms and people take place. In the same way, the *Guardian* story about the Google search suggestion 'are Jews evil' and 'are women evil' promoted and propagated the story and the phrase across social media, intensifying the feedback loops.[13] Without the intervention of Google, there's no doubt this feedback loop would have promoted anti-Semitic and misogynist material to huge numbers of people. Feedback loops between algorithms' simple NLP and people's actions are having real effects on what people are reading, talking about, learning, and then reflecting back to one another, and to the algorithms themselves, creating further feedback loops.

It is precisely their simplified and statistical nature that makes algorithms intense cultural meme generators, and it is why they will always prefer simplified ideas, words and phrases to more complex ideas. Consider works of literature held in high regard and the often complex, multi-phrased, nuanced sentences that accomplished writers fashion. It is this skilful wordsmithing that conveys real nuance in human communication and thought. But, for statistical word-processing algorithms, every added word makes a phrase less probable, and therefore less likely to be noticed as a statistic.

At some level, people are already aware of this, and it is shaping how they communicate, through the popular business practice of writing copy in an effort to achieve search engine optimization (SEO). Nearly all marketeers are familiar with this practice, where text is written using words that are *most likely* to show up in Internet searches, due to their high probability. This practice is becoming more widespread. For instance, my wife is a freelance travel writer and editor. In one of her recent jobs, instead of the usual brief to write inspiring copy full of interesting insights and recommendations, she was presented with a detailed spreadsheet of words, which she was asked to include in the copy in particular combinations and with a particular frequency. Unsurprisingly, the resulting text was less than inspiring, full of repetition and devoid of any flair or personality. However, this was the type of text the client, an online travel content provider, wanted, not because it would make people inspired or more informed about destinations, but because algorithms would be more likely to propagate the copy across the Internet delivering it towards the top of searches.

Linguistic trends associated with algorithms, from simplifying language to fit algorithmic search engines, to creating text using algorithmically pre-selected language and phrases, point to a worrying loss of sophistication and nuance in human communication and culture. While there's no doubt that concision is to be cherished among writers, complex and subtle ideas and arguments require sophisticated and subtle language of a sort that algorithms are incapable of parsing or generating. Plus, through wishful mnemonics, we're describing elements of algorithms with ambitious metaphors because we only wish they were capable of those sophisticated human abilities.

Intuition is a word that has been used to describe one of the most popularly lauded AI triumphs of recent years, Google's AlphaGo. Created by the Google subsidiary DeepMind, AlphaGo is a program that was designed to play the 2500-year-old Chinese board game Go, in which two players alternate placing white and black stones on the intersections of a nineteen by nineteen grid. The winner of the game is the player who captures the largest territory of the board, based on various scoring rules that evaluate the territories occupied by the stones.[14]

Although it has simple elements and rules, Go is considered one of the most intellectually challenging games ever devised, with a complexity that dwarfs Chess. Thus, it was a great surprise when, in 2016, AlphaGo beat South Korean Go grandmaster Lee Sedol four-out-of-five times and was declared the winner in that five-game match.[15] It was a victory that no one thought possible for an algorithm, prompting Geoffrey Hinton, professor and senior Google AI researcher, to rather ambitiously explain the victory's significance to a questioning reporter thus:[16]

> It relies on a lot of intuition. The really skilled players just sort of see where a good place to put a stone would be. They do a lot of reasoning as well, which they call reading, but they also have very good intuition about where a good place to go would be, and that's the kind of thing that people just thought computers couldn't do. But with these neural networks, computers can do that too. They can *think*[17] about all the possible moves and think that one particular move seems a bit better than the others, just *intuitively*. That's what the feed point neural network is doing: it's giving the system intuitions about what might be a good move. It then goes off and tries all sorts of alternatives. The neural networks provide you with good intuitions, and that's what the other programs were lacking, and that's what people didn't really understand computers could do.

If you think that sounds quite incredible, it is, in the true meaning of that word. The implication is that AlphaGo is a computer program that can *think* about all the possible alternatives and then *intuitively* decide on the most strategic move in one of the most challenging human games. But given what we know of wishful mnemonics, it's important to consider how AlphaGo actually works in order to discover whether it is thinking and intuiting.

AlphaGo's system consists of two deep-learning neural networks (of the type discussed in the previous chapter); that is to say, two deeply layered sets of massive, nested mathematical functions. Each network takes in twelve types of human-designed numerical features (each of which is a list of numbers) that represent the positions of all the stones on a Go board at some point in the game. The first network is called *the policy network*, and its output is a set of numbers that are used as probabilities for every possible next move (every legitimate placement of the next stone). The other network is called *the value network*, and its output is a numerical rating of the quality of any board position: a number that is intended to say how good that board position is, relative to an eventual win.

To begin with, AlphaGo's policy network was first trained (in much the same fashion that a perceptron was trained) to replicate next moves of real human players, based on the big data of 30 million moves gathered from the games of expert players. After this training, the policy network was used to make AlphaGo play against itself, adjusting its parameters to emphasize the moves it made that resulted in wins. In this process the current champion, winning version of the policy network was played against randomly selected, previous versions of itself for many, many games. Finally, the policy network was played against itself without updating its parameters, while the value network was trained to return a numerical value for each board configuration that reflected how likely AlphaGo was to win the game from that position.

Given these two networks, AlphaGo selects its moves in Go matches in the following fashion. In every turn, it *looks ahead* at thousands of possible moves that could occur based on the configuration of the board, selecting its moves (and its opponent's likely moves) based on the probabilities given by the policy network. While *looking ahead* in this way, it also accumulates an estimate of each next move's long-term value, drawing on the numbers generated by the value network. After performing this massive, semi-random *lookahead*, AlphaGo takes the move that seems to have the highest predicted value. In summary, after all is said and done, AlphaGo is a complicated function that rates every Go board configuration possible, looks ahead massively at things that might happen in the game's future, and places every stone to maximize the accumulated value function based on those lookaheads.

With AlphaGo's algorithmic details revealed, it seems highly wishful to imply that this complicated value-seeking algorithm is somehow like human 'intuition'. Concentrating on the meaning of words, 'intuition' is the ability to understand something *based on a feeling* rather than conscious reasoning. Not only is this subtle, human word warped by its wishfully mnemonic application to this program, it even seems wishful to say that AlphaGo *plays* Go at all, if one considers the human definition of the word 'play': 'to engage in activity for enjoyment and recreation rather than a serious or practical purpose'. In that sense, AlphaGo does not *play* Go so much as it reduces the game to the maximization of a value function. There is no psychological evidence to suggest that any human being plays Go in this way, or that human intuition has anything in common with any given aspect of AlphaGo's processing. In fact, given that AlphaGo has reduced the game to a mathematical optimization problem, examining more moves in its training and search than any human master is ever likely to play, and utilizing up to 1378 computer CPUs in that process, the dramatic triumph is that a human is able to win even one round against AlphaGo. Bravo, Mr Sedol, and whatever human characteristics (intuition?) allowed you to accomplish this astounding feat!

Since we're concerned about these events changing the meaning of the word 'intuition', it's useful to consider what intuition in human beings really is. The word originates from the Latin *intueri* (to consider) and the late Middle English *intuit* (to contemplate), and has a multitude of complex meanings including: unconscious cognition, inner sensing, insight, sensibility, the ability to understand something without conscious reasoning, unconscious pattern recognition and even illumination (in the spiritual sense).

Intuition as a phenomenon hasn't been formally studied much in psychology. However, in 2016, a team of Indonesian and Australian psychologists made intuition the subject of a carefully considered experiment.[18] One of the researchers, Joel Pearson from the University of New South Wales, described their initial interpretation of intuition this way:

> Many people use the phrase 'intuition' to describe a sensation or feeling they have when making decisions, but these are only descriptions, they don't provide strong evidence that we can use unconscious information in our brain or body to guide our behaviour.[19]

To test the theory that people can use unconscious information in decision-making in a way that ties to 'sensations' or 'feelings', the team conducted the following experiment. Human subjects were shown fields of moving dots on a computer screen. While the dots were moving in random directions, they had a subtle tendency to the right or left, and the subjects were tasked with saying which. Unbeknownst to the subjects, images were flashed into their eyes while they performed the task. In one eye, if the dots moved in one direction, a random, emotionally positive image (for instance, of a cute baby or puppy) was flashed. If the dots moved in the other direction, a random, emotionally negative image (for instance, of a striking snake or a gun pointed at the subject) was flashed. In the other eye, a random collection of shapes was flashed, in just such a way that the subject couldn't consciously register the emotional image being shown in their other eye. The images in one eye interfere with the images in the other eye, so the subject doesn't consciously 'see' the emotional image.

Although the subjects were not consciously aware of the emotional image they were being shown, the researchers, by examining skin conduction, could tell that the emotional images caused arousal in the subjects. While the brain in their heads couldn't see the images, they registered feelings about the images. Moreover, this emotional arousal affected the decision-making of the subjects. If the images, which were imperceptible, and only reliably distinguishable due to their positive or negative emotional character, were shown, the subjects could more quickly state the right-or-left movement of the dots. From this study, it appears that advanced, complex, human capabilities like intuition are directly tied to emotions, and more specifically to feelings.

It is precisely those characteristics of human decision-making that are not considered in the algorithmic model of thinking. These characteristics also aren't considered in algorithmic models of communication.

Just as aspects of how individuals really understand words aren't in algorithms, social aspects of meaning are ignored as well. Ursula K. Le Guin highlights this in her essay on communication, describing how that limited, mechanical conception of language, which conceives of human minds like transmitters and receivers sending signals back and forth, fails to realize that human communication is socially complex:

> The message not only involves, it is, a relationship between speaker and hearer. The medium in which the message is embedded is immensely complex, infinitely more than a code: it is a language, a function of a society, a culture, in which the language, the speaker, and the hearer are all embedded.

The social context that words are embedded in matters, particularly when those words apply to people. As Dr Tensom's war experience revealed, words can downgrade the profound to the merely technical, turning a fundamental human experience (like the tragedy of war) or a fundamental human capacity (like intuition) into no more than a coded diagnosis, or a programmatic detail. The fluid and context-based social nature of meaning can even be illustrated in the communities of the Internet, through the continually evolving and community-based meanings of emoji.

Emoji are the little ideograms that now litter electronic communications, which have evolved from expressive faces to all manner of cartoons that enhance text. Take for instance the image of a vomiting face. For most of us, this emoji just conveys disgust on the part of the sender, but a recent study[20] showed that the Belgian far-right party Vlaams Belang has adopted it as a coded hate symbol aimed at Muslims. Similarly, the online misogynist "incel" (involuntary celibate) community has adopted the cowboy-hat wearing emoji (that is sometimes frowning or angry) as their symbol.[21]

For worse and for better, humans communicate with one another in freewheeling ways that occupy the highest level of Chomsky's syntactic hierarchy of languages that are riddled with complex social references, individual idiosyncrasies, omissions, assumptions and out-of-order thoughts, which remain intractable for computers to parse. Moreover, when people communicate, we share our experiences, not just by passing word messages through a slot in a wall, but by communicating in the context of our societies and culture, using facial and physical expressions, vocal intonations, and other senses such as touch and smell, of which we are hardly aware. Our communication involves proximity, and it isn't just one person to another; it's often addressed to groups, and might even be (purposely) loud enough that passers-by can overhear. Natural communication is open, multi-modal, social and full of complex context and meaning.

By contrast, the natural language algorithms of today communicate in the manner of the Turing test, in coded messages of binary bits or pixels. And they work based on probabilistic distributions of words drawn from big data devoid of meaning, as per Shannon's theories. Even systems like Siri, Alexa and IBM's Watson are not really semantic, and rely on computational tricks, simple pattern matching and a big-data statistics-based understanding of natural language. Yet these algorithms are now creating cultural memes and viral ideas and soundbites that can be spread and emphasized at the speed of light, impacting on real people.

Consider the upshot of Hinton's comments on intuition in AlphaGo. The use of 'intuition' to describe an AI program was picked up by the media, appearing in dozens of venues. As a result, it has become widely accepted that not only does AlphaGo possess the elusive quality of intuition, computers can now mimic abilities that were heretofore considered the most prized aspects of humanity. *The Atlantic* enthusiastically reported that the important thing to take away from the match between AlphaGo and Sedol was:

> not that DeepMind's AI can learn to conquer Go, but that by extension it can learn to conquer anything easier than Go—which amounts to a lot of things. The ways in which we might apply these revolutionary advances in machine learning—in machines' ability to mimic human creativity and intuition—are virtually endless.[22]

Emphatic memes like this, which tie algorithms to words like 'intuition', are tailor-made to be picked up by other algorithms and spread in popular consciousness. The dissemination of the idea that computers now have similar capabilities to human beings plays no small part in the assumption that computers can do the same things people can do, in the workplace, in the collection, management and distribution of the news we receive, in the arbitration of justice, and in myriad other ways.

Wishful mnemonics change words that describe human characteristics into technical descriptions. Even the words 'information' and 'communication' themselves have been changed into words that describe numbers and algorithms. Algorithms have a simplified view of human language, which combines syntactic rules with statistical patterns gleaned from big data. Due to their simplified focus on short, frequent phrases, algorithms can act as powerful meme generators. Human beings collaborate with their actions, warping human communication, sometimes because of the feedback between wishful mnemonics and simplifying algorithms, and sometimes under the sway of commercial imperatives like SEO. My intuition is that the combinations of these effects could lead to profound changes in the way we communicate about everything, including even the subtlest characteristics of ourselves.

10

It's a Lot More Complicated than We Think

Thinking is a human feature. Will AI someday really think?
That's like asking if submarines swim. If you call it swimming
then robots will think, yes.

NOAM CHOMSKY

Chomsky's quote shows how not just challenging words like 'think' but even simple ones like 'swim' convey something that is more than merely mechanical. That semantic weight in words is what makes human communication not only the fuel for real individual insight, but an engine of advancement for society, perhaps the thing that made society possible in the first place. This is why not just the sending of signals in a syntax but the conveyance of meaning in nuanced and patient conversations with one another matters. Thinking is a human feature, and so is communication.

Yet today, humans are communicating in ways that are more and more like algorithms, and more and more to algorithms' liking. We increasingly talk to one another through binary 'likes', or through on/off decisions about whether or not to 'share' preconfigured content, most of which is algorithmically offered to us in the first place, and some of which is even algorithmically generated. Even when human beings actually write, they conform to algorithmic desires, like SEO and the restrained length of tweets. While Chomsky's quote crams a lot into less than 140 characters, that constraint doesn't allow for much more than a quip. Furthermore, our communications are now ordered into 'feeds', where what we see first to last is algorithmically controlled, despite the fact that algorithms only have a simplified and statistical understanding of the things we say. And while social networks are promoted as a medium through which we can all become multicast publishers, in reality they are wired together in relative static networks that preclude other people from overhearing and joining in, yet make algorithms decisions about what to show us far easier. Where community building is allowed in these technologically mediated communities, it is controlled by the 'friend' recommendations of algorithms.

How does this computerization of human communication affect the evolution of society and the interaction of people? Does it have anything to do with the ugly divisiveness and polarization that is beginning to *emerge* online? Recent research suggests that it does. In May 2016, a few months prior to the American presidential election, the Pew Research Centre reported that 62 per cent of all Americans received their news via social media sites such as Reddit, Facebook, Twitter, Instagram, YouTube, Tumblr and LinkedIn, and so on, with a whopping 44 per cent of the US population finding their daily news on a single platform, Facebook, where algorithms promote varied news stories to different users according to their algorithmically assessed likes and interests.[1]

You might wonder, what's wrong with that when Facebook's mission statement is to 'give people the power to share and make the world more open and connected'. Although this noble goal is Facebook's stated intention, the reality is that Facebook's algorithms are actually servicing an older and more familiar goal, the maximization of value in pursuit of economic self-interest, first proposed by Adam Smith in the eighteenth century, refined by utilitarian philosophers such as John Stuart Mill, and transformed into an apparently reliable science by Thomas Walras's theory of equilibrium and Frederick Hayek's theories of connectionism and spontaneous order.

Hayek's neoliberal theories, which gained widespread acceptance in the 1980s and 1990s, were based on the idea that the pursuit of individual, economic self-interest leads to the creation of greater value, which inevitably benefits society and results in the improvement of humankind and their general lot in life. The individual self-interest being pursued in this case is that of Facebook, a legal person (thanks to the notion of 'corporate personhood'), whose board and directors are mandated to deliver the maximum value to the company's shareholders. Facebook's algorithms are the virtual limbs of this corporate body, tasked with reaching out into the marketplace and finding the best financial returns. In such a situation, where only a single agenda is present, the optimization algorithms involved are the ultimate realization of the rational agents at the centre of two centuries of economic theory. They are allowed to act on their profit-maximizing agendas autonomously, and the particulars of their 'actions' are not controlled (or even tractable) by human beings.

In fact, the massive growth in AI speculation and development that we've seen over the last decade would not be occurring if these self-organizing algorithms did not link so seamlessly with self-organizing free-market theories. This combination of algorithms and networks is, in fact, the world's first perfect economy, at least in the sense of economic theory. It relies only on non-physical resources (views, clicks and likes) to generate economic activity. People create most of the content online, free of charge, which provides the data which algorithms need to create demographic 'packages of people' that are then automatically sold to advertising customers. In addition, the data provided enables these algorithms to make decisions about how to stimulate people into generating and sharing more content, creating a never-ending cycle of supply and demand.

Algorithms do most of the economic work as well. Advertisers' algorithms can subscribe to demographic packages of consumers that are put together algorithmically. What content is delivered to which people is decided algorithmically. Which adverts are placed where is also algorithmically decided, and all payments, from both advertisers and content consumers, are taken algorithmically. Prices respond instantly in a market made up largely of machines, forming a near frictionless marketplace, the ideal of self-organizing free-market economics, married to self-organizing social networks and self-organizing algorithms.

As perfect economic agents in the online media economy, algorithms are *single-minded* in achieving their profit-driven goal by ensuring the maximum frequency of human interaction. To that end, election cycles like the Brexit referendum and the American presidential election are gold rushes where AIs can mine people's heightened attention for lucrative click-throughs. What no one foresaw was that in order to keep us clicking and sharing, headlines had to work ever harder to grab our attention amid the sea of online content, shouting ever more sensational and titillating news stories. Aaron Banks, the British millionaire businessman and principal donor to the Leave.eu campaign body, summed it up neatly: 'The more outrageous we are, the more attention we'll get. The more attention we get, the more outrageous we'll be.'[2] There is nothing new about media moguls using outrageous headlines to garner attention and sell newspapers (and associated advertising). In 1898, Hearst and Pulitzer fanned the flames of war by promoting the phrase 'Remember the Maine!', thereby increasing the circulation of their newspapers. While one can disapprove of profit-driven newspaper owners, they were after all human beings, as were their editors and writers. And, as such they had complex motivations and operated within a complex web of human relationships.

By contrast, the algorithms that now promote inflammatory headlines are *actually* only concerned with profit. Their single-mindedness favours headlines that illicit anger, fear and outrage, as this is the emotional fuel that prompts click-through and sharing, which generates profits. Today, beneath and within each CNN article, every one of which is offered with a tempting headline, there appears copious paid content. This is part of an algorithmically driven revenue generation strategy called 'smart ad placement' by Turner Broadcasting, the subsidiary of Time-Warner that owns CNN. Turner's site even boasts of how optimizing algorithms generate ad placement 'in the style of CNN editorial content, with the ability to be placed directly in editorial streams of content and alongside relevant CNN editorial videos and articles'.[3]

Some are concerned that this has created a whole genre of 'fake news'. While Wikipedia defines 'fake news' as a synonym for news satire, more recently it has become at worst a condemnation of real human journalism, and at best an umbrella term for the uncontrolled explosion of misleading information dispersed on social media. Mark Zuckerberg has pledged to make Facebook impede fake news. But it's unclear how, as in the past his company has eliminated human editors and curators in favour of algorithms, ironically to ensure *less bias* in their presentation of news. As we've seen before, being able to determine what is true and what is fake is not a goal that algorithms can achieve easily. Furthermore, the war on fake news misses the point. Regardless of whether algorithms present 'true' or 'fake' news, they will still be working towards their primary directive: the maximization of value.

Another unforeseen emergent phenomena of coupling neoliberal economic values to highly efficient, optimizing algorithms is the segregation of people into more closed communities (so-called 'filter bubbles' and 'echo chambers'). While selective organization of the online social network is something that is done by human beings, their 'unfriending' actions can't be disconnected from the emotional states generated by the news stories algorithms deliver and the comment wars that ensue. This escalation is in itself profitable, as the segregation of people into effective market segments commands more premium advertising rates. Constant contact with misinformation may also result in another emergent phenomenon, which Aviv Ovadya, Chief Technologist at the Center for Social Media Responsibility, calls 'reality apathy' or trust decay, whereby people stop believing anything they see and hear, including the truth.[4]

The truth is that people are no more simply Republican or Democrat, Leaver or Remainer, than news is simply true or fake. Segregation of real people into crisp, saleable demographic packages serves only to simplify a complex human picture made up of difficult social and political issues. But the vast algorithmic network that now disseminates much of the information we receive is not concerned with this complexity, only with its stated goal of value maximization. And it's doing a great job. Through the US election cycle Facebook's stock rose 924 per cent faster than the US S&P 500 stock-market index.[5]

Since the eighteenth century, when Erasmus Darwin, Godwin and Shelley first formulated theories of evolutionary utopianism, we have thought of evolution as optimizing. If we think of natural selection along the lines of Spencer's 'survival of the fittest', then evolution is optimizing fitness, where fitness is perceived as a quality metric. If evolution optimizes that quality metric, then optimization must be a desirable feature. This metaphor has the added advantage of not requiring the mathematical effort of complicated calculus-based models, because if one just focuses on populations, reproduction and variance, 'survival of the fittest' is assumed to happen inevitably as an emergent effect, a spontaneous order.

There have always been two metaphors for optimization algorithms, computer programs that try to find 'the best' of something. One is 'hill climbing'. It you imagine that a mathematical function is like the surface of the Earth, and that higher points are better than lower ones, the hill-climbing metaphor becomes clear. We all instinctively know that the fastest way to get to the top of a hill (if you have the bravery and the skills) is to climb the steepest, shortest route possible. This is why optimization algorithms have an inevitable relationship to the calculus of Leibnitz and Newton, because calculus is all about rates of change, steepness is a rate of change and calculus provides a mathematical means to point to the direction of steepest, fastest accent. Thus, calculus-based algorithms are implicitly based on a hill-climbing metaphor, and they are the algorithms used in the nested mathematical functions of deep-learning networks of programs like AlphaGo.

The other metaphor for optimization is evolution, and this metaphor has been an inspiration for optimization algorithms since the dawn of electronic computation. In Turing's posthumously published paper, *Intelligent Machinery*, which included ideas about neural networks, the father of computer science speculated that some form of "genetical search" could play a role in transforming and organising the random connections of his "unorganized machines."

While Turing was working on breaking WWII codes, John Von Neumann was working on the Manhattan Project. Von Neumann was an American-Hungarian genius and polymath, and his work designing nuclear weapons was only one of the ways in which he changed the world forever. The others include devising a way to make ENIAC (arguably the world's first real computer) programmable; making substantial contributions to quantum physics and equilibrium theories in economics; and, inventing game theory, an area of mathematical research which shaped cold war politics for a generation through his descriptions of a game-theoretic construct he called "mutually assured destruction." Inspired by Turing's papers on computation, von Neumann also came up with the modern conception of Babbage's 'store' and 'mill' computer structure, in what is now called the 'von Neumann architecture', the architecture at the heart of almost all modern computers.

Amongst this world-changing productivity, von Neumann also speculated about how computer programs, like genetic organisms, might be able to self-replicate. His 'cellular automata' theory closely parallels the actual replication methods of biological DNA, despite the fact that von Neumann's work was done in advance of the actual structure of DNA being discovered by Watson and Crick in 1953.[7]

At the same time, statistician George Box suggested 'evolutionary operations'[8] as a methodology for optimizing industrial processes in the late

1950s, though he never implemented the procedure as a computer algorithm, and there are a number of other scientists who also struck close to the ideas that would eventually emerge as evolutionary computation.

So the evolutionary metaphor for computational algorithms was a firmly set context from the very start of computation, but it wasn't until the late 1960s that the foundational idea of evolutionary algorithms really began to gain traction in various research centres around the world.[9] In Germany, a group led by Ingo Rechenberg developed a kind of optimization algorithm called 'evolutionsstrategies'.[10] On the West Coast of the US, a group led by Lawrence Fogel developed another called 'evolutionary programming'.[11] And, at the University of Michigan, John Holland pioneered another form called 'genetic algorithms'.[12] Of all of these researchers, it is John Holland who has the most direct connection with Von Neumann's early theories, since his PhD supervisor was Arthur Burks,[13] who worked on the ENIAC engineering team and extended von Neumann's work on 'cellular automata'.[14] Furthermore, Holland was granted the first PhD in computer science and went on to teach at the University of Michigan where he advised many students on PhDs that involved evolutionary computation, including my own PhD supervisor, David Goldberg.

Goldberg wrote the first textbook on genetic algorithms while I was a part of his research group in 1989. Lots of work from Dave's research group was in the text, including some of my own, and I helped edit the book's first draft (by making red ink marks on a ream of dot matrix paper). So at the time, as a know-it-all, young researcher in an exciting 'new' field, I thought I knew pretty much all there was to know about optimizing algorithms that were based on the theory of 'survival of the fittest'. Most GAs at the time were being used in optimization problems, trying to find the best version of something, usually an engineered artefact, like an aircraft wing, a laminated composite beam, or the parameters of a robotic control algorithm. This was natural, as Goldberg's group was in an engineering department, and his text was entitled *Genetic Algorithms in Search, Optimization, and Machine Learning.*[15]

As a student of Dave's, I was lucky enough to receive an invitation to attend the world's first workshop focusing on emergence at the Santa Fe Institute in the New Mexican desert. Since 1984, SFI has functioned as a not-for-profit think tank that gathers together economists, physicists, computer scientists, biologists and many others from the broadest possible spectrum, to study Complex Systems. Fellows include physics Nobel laureates Murray Gell-Man and Philip Anderson, economics Nobel laureate Kenneth Arrow and Dave's PhD supervisor, the now deceased MacArthur Genius Award Fellow John Holland. The focus of the institute's multidisciplinary research is to better understand the principles of complex adaptive systems (systems characterized by interconnected elements and the ability to perpetually change and learn), including physical, computational, biological, environmental and social systems. Examples of such systems include the stock market, the weather, social insect colonies, the biosphere, the brain, political parties and every human community. These capital-C Complex Systems are the real-world phenomena that defy conventional scientific understanding, demonstrating truly unpredictable emergent behaviours.

One of the organizers of the SFI conference was Stephanie Forrest, another PhD student of John Holland's, and an external professor at SFI to this day. If anyone qualifies as an extraordinary outlier, a black swan, it's Stephanie. She has been a downhill skier, a stevedore and a breeder of Bernese Mountain Dogs, but when I met her in 1991 she was beginning to make her mark as one of the most interesting computer scientists in America. At the time, SFI was housed in a building that was once the Cristo Rey Convent, and its lecture hall was in the deconsecrated chapel, so when I first heard Steph lecture, she was partially lit by the southwest sunlight through an old stained-glass window, which was fitting as the experience was something of a conversion for me.

In her talk, Steph described how her algorithmic simulations were giving informative results about the behaviour of biological immune networks, which were one of the hottest topics in Complexity Science at that time. In 1991, deaths from the AIDS virus were approaching their peak, and academic interest in understanding the complex dynamics of immune systems couldn't have been higher. Stephanie (along with Alan Perelson, an SFI theoretical immunologist) had obtained interesting results with an evolutionary algorithm, and while they admitted that their algorithm was an incredibly simplified model of immune system evolution, they felt it was showing results that could lead to new and valuable insights.

At the pulpit in the chapel, Stephanie was standing before a projected chart that showed these exciting results to a rapt group of scientists, all of them far more prestigious and experienced than me, when I spoke up from the audience.

'That can't be right,' I said.

In my limited defence, I was still fairly young and rather over-confident in my opinions. With my background in evolutionary optimization, I found their results hard to believe. That's because Stephanie's and Alan's work was pretty unique, and radically different from what I was used to. They were using GAs not to optimize an engineered system, but to find out about a real-world evolutionary system. Blinkered by my own belief in 'survival of the fittest' reasoning, I was challenged by the radical change in perspective that their results demanded.

Along with the hormonal, peripheral nervous and gut nerve systems, the immune system is sometimes described as one of the body's 'other brains'. It is a particularly unique 'brain' because it is mostly fluid, with no static connections between its network of elements, which are constantly circulating in the blood stream and lymphatic vessels. Despite their constant motion and only sporadic contact with each other, immune cells function as an integrated adaptive system, which behaves in complex autonomous ways, and even talks directly to the body's 'first' brain. Immune cells generate chemicals that prompt the stress response, which in turn combines with brain signals to regulate immunity. This interaction is one of a vital set of feedback loops that ties together the state of our body, our feelings and our decision-making, into an integrated state of our various 'brains' that results in how we think, what we do and who we are.

Like the head-bound brain, the immune system matches patterns, stores them for future use and generates innovative new patterns to cope with unforeseen future events. For immune cells, the patterns are the molecular shapes on the surface of *antigens*, the external molecules that invade our bodies. The mechanism of pattern matching for immune cells (which are called *antibodies*) is to stick to the surface molecules of antigens, shape-to-shape, like a key in a lock. Through this focused and particular sticking mechanism, antibodies surround and isolate antigens, impeding any pathological function they might have, and allowing other body systems to eventually flush them out. Many other mechanisms are triggered by antibodies binding to antigens, including those of antibody reproduction, which (in effect) store the shapes of successful, matching 'keys' in the distributed memory of the immune system, as copies of the key-matching antibodies. Like in other evolutionary systems, the copies aren't identical, so there is variance, which acts as a means of generating innovative new antibodies that could fight similar (but not identical) antigens in the future. In this way, the immune system is evolutionary, combining a form of natural selection with variance, just like in Darwin's theory.

Steph's algorithm was superficially just like the genetic algorithms that I was studying under the guidance of David Goldberg and using to optimize engineering problems. These Holland-style evolutionary algorithms consisted of a population (typically of hundreds or thousands) of bit strings, with each string representing a different solution to a problem. There was a computer routine that would translate the bits of each particular population member into a solution to a problem (for instance, the shape parameters of an aircraft wing). Different bit strings gave different solutions (different shaped wings). Critically, there was another routine that translated these solutions into a numerical *fitness*. For instance, this *fitness function* might simulate the aerodynamics of the wing and translate that into a net efficiency of the wing lifting an aircraft. That fitness was used as a rating that determined how many copies of that particular population member got made, and whether the population member lived on into new populations or was deleted. Bit flipping operations ensured variance, and the algorithms ran on, keeping up with the best solution found, until a computational limit was reached. The ultimate best solution was declared the 'optimal' solution.

What made Steph's algorithm different was that the population of bit strings were treated as a model of a population antibodies, and there was another population of (fixed) antigens as well. To simulate the immune response, a single antigen was selected at random, to represent one half of the encounter between antibodies and antigens in the bloodstream. A random sample of a few antibodies was selected from their population, to represent those immune cells that just happened to be floating close to the antigen in the bloodstream. From those nearby antibodies, the one whose bit string (representing its surface shape) best matched the antigen (ones match zeros and zeros ones, like a key in a lock) was given a match score based on how many bits matched. That quantity was added to the antibody's fitness, and the process was repeated, with GA reproduction and variance going on in parallel, to evolve the antibody population. What Steph's results showed was that this procedure led to antibodies that nearly perfectly matched the set of antigens, such that there was a good key for every lock.

This is why I found it so hard to believe Steph's results could be right. There was no optimal, 'fittest' antibody. Instead, her final set of antibodies had all the various antibodies it needed to tackle the diverse (fixed) set of antigen invaders.

I just didn't think GAs worked that way. Partially, that's because during my editing of Goldberg's text, I'd repeatedly read the work of friend and fellow PhD student Kalyan Deb,[16] whose work showed that genetic algorithms don't stay diverse on their own, at least not without some additional algorithmic effort. In GAs, survival of the fittest should always take over, and drive out diversity. Even if you had two entirely different solutions that returned equal values from a fitness function, that didn't matter. In such cases, something called 'random genetic drift'[17] would take over. In 'drift', the inevitable random errors in reproduction would give one individual more copies than an equally fit competitor. Then, in an algorithmic optimization battle to the death (or fittest), those copies would get more copies, and more and more, until, by sheer random effect, one solution type would take over the population, and drive out all diversity. By that effect, a single solution would come to dominate and force out all alternatives, becoming the fittest not by real superiority, but by an effective fitness that was based on a dominance of numbers. Thus, Steph's results shouldn't have found a diverse, effective final solution. That wasn't how evolution worked, at least not in the simple form I thought Steph was using.

From Kalyan's work, I also knew you could prevent this diversity elimination in evolutionary algorithms, by using a computational trick that Holland described in his 1973 book that provide the foundation for GAs, *Adaptation in Natural and Artificial Systems*.[18] This trick was a procedure called *fitness sharing*. Simply stated, if you divided the fitness number of each population member by a factor that reflected how commonplace its bit combinations were, you could reduce the number of copies it would receive, and overcome random genetic drift. You literally *reduced* the fitness of the individuals who were drifting towards taking over the population. With this mathematical fitness degradation you could get a population that had diverse, 'fit' solutions, balancing diverse fitness across the population. This algorithmic intervention was entirely necessary if one were to overcome inevitable drive and drift towards a single, 'survival of the fittest' solution. Steph's simulations appeared to show no such mathematical trick, so I assumed her simulations must be wrong. Survival of the fittest must inevitably win out, or so I thought. From my perspective her simulations *must* converge to a single, dominant solution type.

'But they don't,' Steph said, hardly hesitating at my interjection after I'd gone on a bit about my point. 'These are real simulation results,' she said, 'and it always stays diverse, at steady state.' She was professional in her response, and when she moved on to other questions, I couldn't help but feel embarrassed at my outburst, but confused by her results.

As the meeting was ending and we were all filing out, Stephanie made an effort to catch up with me. Perhaps because of my background in the male-dominated field of engineering, or in the dogmatic religious culture of Alabama, I expected further argument, or perhaps a stern rebuke for speaking out in church. Instead I got one of the most interesting invitations I've ever received. Steph asked if I'd like to come and spend some time with her, at SFI, working on figuring out why her algorithms did something I thought wasn't possible.

I spent two summers working with Steph and Alan, and I used some ideas from probability theory to model her complex immune network models. All models are wrong, but some are useful, and the models we developed together showed something I never expected: that the natural behaviour of an immune network was not predicated on survival of the fittest. An effect very much like fitness sharing was intrinsic and natural in Steph's algorithms, as intrinsic as any 'survival of the fittest', and this effect revealed something extraordinary about many, if not all, natural evolutionary systems.

In real-world terms, the critical detail I'd overlooked is the 'stickiness' of antibodies. Once an antibody binds with an antigen, it is as if it has jammed its key into the lock, ensuring no other antibody can stick to the same antigen. In Stephanie's simulations, the key detail was that only the *best matching* antibody got any score at all: all other antibodies got no score, because they were in effect locked out. This unique lock-and-key system meant that each antigen was like a resource, and once it was consumed, no other antibody could have it. There were a finite number of each antigen type in the antigen population; in effect, each of them was a finite food resource for antibodies. Because of this, once a particular antigen shape was consumed by the best-matching antibodies for that shape, those antibodies began to be selected as the best-matchers less because, in effect, their food supply was gone. Thus, because there were no antigens left for these good matchers to consume, their fitness declined, slowing their tendency to drift towards dominance of the antibody population. In the end, this made things balance towards diversity of the antibody population, making Steph's results precisely correct, and quite amazing. This is exactly what Kalyan's more literal fitness-sharing algorithm was doing, except in the immune model there was no fitness-sharing function acting numerically on a numerical fitness. Instead, what the simulation showed was that natural resource sharing in the immune system had the *emergent effect* of maintaining diversity.[19]

If we recall the theory of eighteenth-century curate Thomas Malthus, limited resources are supposed to assure a sub-optimal social equilibrium, making evolutionary utopianism impossible. Darwin and Wallace transformed that idea into the mechanism of natural selection, which was eventually re-branded 'survival of the fittest'. In their view, limited resource availability drove evolution because the less 'fit' didn't survive and reproduce, ensuring the population became more and more fit over time. But contrary to both of these theories, what Stephanie's simulations showed (and scores of other diversity-preserving genetic algorithms have shown since) is that resource limitations can have another, vital emergent effect: they can *preserve diversity*. In fact, since the notion of 'the fittest' is largely tautological, one could argue that a better interpretation of the real-world action of natural selection is not 'survival of the fittest', but 'adaptive diversity preservation'. That is what natural selection does in the real world: it adapts, and preserves diversity, in response to the ever-shifting resources available in the environment.

Nearly a decade after my work at SFI, when I took a post in computer science at University College London, I was introduced to a scientist who had been exploring the complex system of the financial markets in the wake of the 2008 financial crash, and how the human actors navigated within it. David Tuckett is a psychoanalyst and economist who, when I met him in 2011, was just finishing a book called *Minding the Markets: An Emotional Finance View of Financial Instability*.[20] The book had been funded by the Institute of New Economic Thinking, a not-for-profit institution funded by George Soros. Like most people, I knew of Soros as a famous rich guy, but from David I learned that he had been a student of the philosopher Karl Popper, and he himself had extended Popper's theories into the realms of economics.

Soros' philosophical contribution is a theory known as *reflexivity*,[21] which he applied in his financial trading, but also wrote about as a general phenomenon in evolving human social systems. Reflexivity theorizes that human social systems are intrinsically different from physical scientific systems, in that actions taken within a social system change fundamental things about the system itself. Taking a measurement of the position of a star does not change that star's position, nor does it change the astronomer. However, in a financial market, participants' views and opinions may change the perception of an asset's value, as well as the value of the asset itself, which in turn might alter the participants' views of that asset.

Reflexivity goes far beyond this simple, single, monetary transaction. The theory posits that there is a circular relationship between cause and effect in human belief systems. In economics, Soros pointed out that prices influence preferences for goods in ways that are inconsistent with the general equilibrium theories that underpin mainstream economic thinking. For instance, people can believe that something is of value because its price *rises* (e.g. house prices, vintage wines or artworks), which can, through the normal mechanisms of supply and demand, cause the price to rise further. This self-reinforcing cycle can eventually break when costs exceed some socially acceptable (or tolerable) threshold, causing cycles of boom and bust. In economics, reflexivity builds in the effect of people's beliefs about value and their social aspirations, and Soros has said that his instincts about the actions of reflexivity in the market is what gave him the edge in many of his great investment successes.

As a psychoanalyst of the Freudian school, David Tuckett was advancing economic theories that could relate to reflexivity theory through an investigation of how people dealt with radical uncertainty in the real world, specially the financial markets. Tuckett's theory proposed that people, both as individuals and groups, formulated their beliefs by constructing stories about what might happen in the future. They might, for instance, tell themselves that the value of mortgage-backed securities was going to continue to rise for the foreseeable future, or that their beautiful painting by Dali will maintain its value due to its eternal desirability. Key to Tuckett's theory is that people become emotionally invested and committed to these stories, which he calls *conviction narratives*. This is where a person's emotions (probably modulated by the 'other brains' in the body) impact on and inform their decision-making. In Tuckett's theory this emotional investment is not treated as some mal-adapted sideshow, as emotions are in many theories of 'rational' action. Instead emotion is a critical part of dealing with real-world uncertainty.

The reason for this new consideration of emotions in decision-making is clear when we consider the nature of complex systems and the radical uncertainty their dynamic and constantly adapting nature engenders. If the world is radically uncertain, filled with information that is conflicting, overwhelming and frequently inaccurate, and systems are reflexive, chaotic and irreducible to simple models, presenting people with decisions where all the elements are unknowable and the significance of phenomena isn't always clear or easily decipherable, then *there is no rational method of decision-making* that does not involve some assumptions (e.g. story-telling) about the future. Conviction narratives are these assumptions, and they allow people to convince themselves to take necessary actions in a complex and uncertain world, rather than becoming paralysed by uncertainty. Conviction narratives may involve models, but they have to involve a narrative, a story, as they are projections of known events into the unknowable future.

As new information comes in, narratives should be appropriately adjusted to adapt to new situations, in what David calls a healthy *integrated state* of mind. Through integrating new information while maintaining conviction narratives, individuals are able to cope with reflexivity and radical uncertainty. But Tuckett's theory recognizes that this process can go awry, resulting in harmful emergent effects. According to Tuckett, if a person (or an entire society) commits to a narrative too strongly so that they begin to eschew incoming information that runs counter to their narrative, they enter a *divided state* of mind. In this divided state, a person may hear information that should cause them to become uncertain about their narrative, but they hold it separate from the part of their mind that is convicted towards action, they do not integrate the new information into their narrative. Often, reality eventually catches up with a divided state, and the conviction narrative eventually becomes impossible to sustain in the face of real-world events. Then the internal narrative collapses (sometimes resulting in emotional instability and collapse, as well).

In his research for *Minding the Markets*, Tuckett conducted a series of interviews with hedge fund managers to see how they coped with the radically uncertain world of the financial markets. What he found was that managers seldom predicted anything reliably. This begged the question, 'How could they convince themselves to invest the huge sums of money involved?' The answer was that rather than constructing elaborate probabilistic models in their minds, they imagined scenarios and stories (conviction narratives) about the value of stocks and securities, which enabled them to emotionally invest in their decisions in order to act. Tuckett's research clearly showed that economic actors, even those with superior training and information, used their emotional attachment to conviction narratives as a way of coping with uncertainty. David was lucky, and his research for the book spanned the 2008 crisis, allowing him to observe that some fund managers entered into a severely divided state during those events, continuing to invest in increasingly unreliable financial products, despite widely available information about the increasing risks and eventual catastrophic consequences.

What I brought to David's research was knowledge of algorithms for analysing big data sets, particularly methods of looking at textual data. In order to demonstrate David's theory in new real-world scenarios, David and I (along with our student and colleague Rickard Nyman) examined huge data sets of textual data, including emails, newspaper articles and financial reports that spanned the crisis. We focused our attention on news stories that mentioned 'Fannie Mae', the Federal National Mortgage Association, a quasi-governmental US company that backs mortgages. We looked at the balance of words that indicated excitement to words indicating anxiety (based on David's theories) in these stories. What we saw was that the relative number of excitement words swelled in parallel with indicators that the property market was a good place to put money. But as the housing market peaked, and significantly fell away from its best, the excitement just continued to grow, ignoring information from the market that everyone had, saying that it was time to be anxious about investing in mortgage-backed securities. This indicated a divided state, where people were ignoring information in favour of the conviction narrative that housing was going to make them rich. This untethered excitement continued until there was an utter collapse in the housing market, which finally destroyed the widespread faith in the investment potential of housing-backed securities.[22]

The results appeared to confirm that people separated what they were hearing from colleagues, reading in the newspaper and seeing on the news

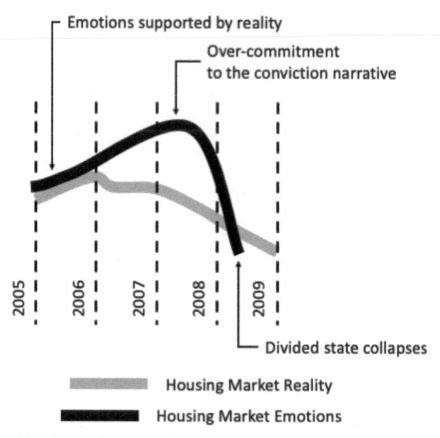

FIGURE 10.1 *The pattern of results we found by looking at emotive words surrounding Fannie Mae: the paralleling of excitement emotions to a market rise extended far beyond the point supported by market realities. This apparent divided state in a conviction narrative eventually resolved itself in a dramatic collapse of excitement relative to anxiety. An integrated state would have allowed more realistic tracking of reality, and better adaptation.*

from what they believed, and became even more motivated to cling to their conviction narratives until the bubble collapsed, finally destroying their narrative (as well as their balance sheets).

In 2016, Orowa Sikder became interested in how David Tuckett's conviction narrative theories might play out in social networks. He had a novel idea for a PhD project, in which he proposed looking at how signal dynamics in networks might evolve in response to simple models of 'motivated reasoners', much like the hedge-fund managers who refused to relinquish their carefully constructed narratives. So, he sought out me and David as PhD supervisors for his project.[23]

Interestingly, the project had echoes of the work I did with Stephanie at SFI in the 1990s, but with some very different emergent effects. Like the immune system, social networks consist of 'agents' (in this case, not antibodies and antigens, but people) connected in a network by their 'friend' links, like in the picture shown in Figure 10.2.

In Sikder's model,[24] every actor in a social network is modelled as a simple algorithmic agent, which receives 'information' in binary signals (zeros and ones), where each signal represents one side of a binary argument (say, support for one or the other political candidates in a two-party system). While this model, like Stephanie Forrest's model of the immune system, is clearly simplified and metaphorical, it too yielded interesting insights.

As an example, let's say some signals in the network, represented by 1s, support the 'positive' side of an argument (say, the belief that a political decision will be good for a country), while others, represented by 0s, support the 'negative' side of the same argument (that the same decision will damage the country). Most agents in the model are intended to show some conventional form of rational reasoning based on evidence. They take in new signals from the agents immediately surrounding them, and use this information to adjust what they 'believe'. In particular, the preponderance of evidence they gather determines what they re-broadcast to the other nearby agents they are connected to in the social network (in a manner similar to a 'like' or a 'share'). If the majority of signals such an agent receives are positive, they broadcast positive signals (1s) to other nearby agents. If the majority of signals they receive are negative, they send out negative signals (0s).

While this is what most agents in Sikder's model do, some agents (precisely a fraction f of all agents) behave differently. They are *motivated* to send out

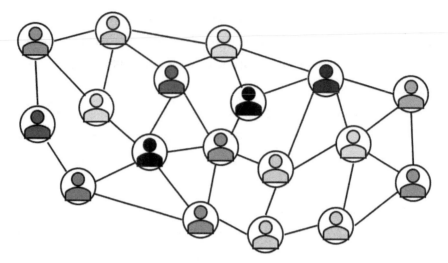

FIGURE 10.2 *Imagine this is a social network, which we're going to treat as a technical model of simple 'agents'.*

signals that represent a particular, pre-defined bias. So, when they receive a signal that differs from their pre-determined 'point of view', with probability q they flip the signal to match their current 'belief', sending out a signal that is opposite to what they receive, reinforcing their 'point of view' on those nearby. The simulation included biased agents on either side of the 'argument', who were motivated to enforce both points of view. Of the fraction f of motivated agents, a further fraction $y_B^+(0)$ have a positive bias.

Consider the starting point of a network, as shown in a small a simplified form in Figure 10.3. Solid black circles represent motivated reasoners in the network that have a 'negative' point of view, while solid white circles represent actors motivated to have a 'positive' point of view. These agents send out signals that conform to their perspective, regardless of the signals they are receiving from other actors. Grey circles represent normal agents, who base their outputs on the majority of what they hear from those nearby.

Some actors in the network are naturally 'surrounded' by motivated agents, meaning that the majority of signals they receive come from those agents, so they quickly make the 'rational' decision that what those agents are saying is

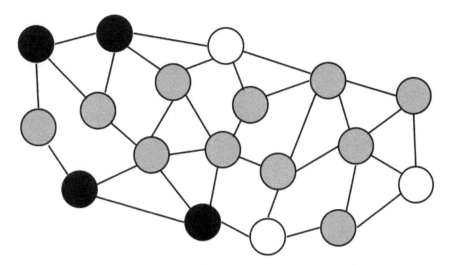

FIGURE 10.3 *The social network model shown before, but with colours indicating the 'opinions' of the 'agents', which they broadcast to one another. Pure black and white agents are motivated reasoners that broadcast their respective, polarized signals regardless of what they receive, but grey agents decide what to send based on the majority of what they receive.*

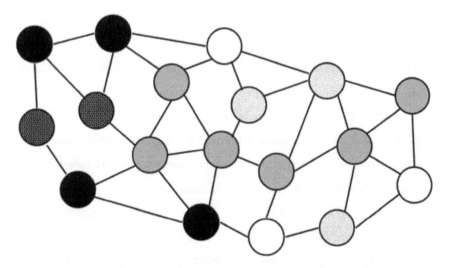

FIGURE 10.4 *Agents who happen to have a majority of black or white motivated reasoning agents around them are 'recruited' to become effective motivated reasoners themselves.*

correct, and they echo their signals. These agents are shown as shaded black and white circles in Figure 10.4.

Once these surrounded agents are recruited, they start to behave like motivated reasoners themselves, sending out a single signal that they have decided is the 'truth', based on the majority of signals they're receiving. They, in turn, surround other agents and in a process very much like genetic drift, an equilibrium emerges for every agent where their signals are fixed by those of the majority of agents around them. This creates a virtual divide between agents that have a majority of 'positive' agents around them, and those that have a majority of 'negative' agents around them, as shown in Figure 10.5. Once this equilibrium is reached, the actors won't ever change the 'opinions' they've taken on.

The interesting thing about Orowa's model is that you can calculate the equilibrium ratio of 'white' and 'black' oriented actors into which the social network will settle, as a function of the probability q of motivated agents flipping signals to match their own point of view, and the fraction of motivated agents in the network. Figure 10.6 illustrates the results.

In this figure, the shade of the graph indicates the balance of white agents to black agents in the final network. The shade represents the binary opinions across all agents at equilibrium, after everyone has 'made up their minds', and fixed into an uncompromising state. Pure white means everyone has decided on the positive point of view, pure black means everyone has decided on the negative point of view and shades in between represent the relative number of actors on each side of the argument in an equilibrium where no single decision has overtaken the entire network. The two solid, quarter-circle-shaped coloured segments show that if there are more positive motivated reasoners than negative ones (or vice versa), and both kinds of motivated reasoners aren't completely dogmatic (their probability of inverting signals to match their own, motivated opinion isn't too high), then the dominant motivated

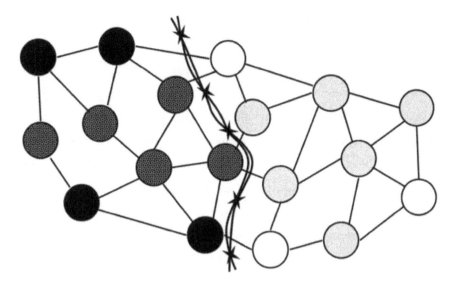

FIGURE 10.5 *The 'recruitment' effect propagates, until all agents are polarized and divided.*

FIGURE 10.6 *A symbolic representation of Orowa's analytical result. With highly determined motivated agents (the far right of the graph), the percentage of such agents (black or white) completely determines the balance of opinions in the final polarized social network. With motivated agents that can eventually be swayed (the left of the graph) some possibility exists for consensus to form.*

reasoners (the ones with a higher percentage in the network) take over the entire network, and drive opposite opinions out completely.

Perhaps even more interesting is what happens outside these two solid coloured areas, where there is a shaded gradation, representing the sustained existence of two different, and completely divided, points of view in the social network. In these situations, all the agents in the network have decided on one position or the other, it's just that fewer or more agents are on one side or the other, depending on how white or black the graph is. The colour represents the percentage of agents who have fixed on one point of view versus the other. The interesting thing is that in every case, the number of actors with each point of view is entirely determined by the relative percentage of biased, motivated reasoning agents. The motivated agents control the final distribution of signals sent in the network, without exception. Either the dominant, biased point of view of motivated agents becomes the point of view of everyone, regardless of their rationality, or there remains a balance of two opinions, but precisely in proportion to the relative dominance of biased agents. In either case, it is the biased agents who completely control the distribution of opinions in the final, completely divided network.

Despite starting off from a complex networked system similar to the immune system, what Sikder's model demonstrates is that in social networks, rather than preserving and maintaining a diversity of views in the system, a handful of biased agents maintain complete control, by recruiting otherwise rational agents into polarized echo chambers, where all they hear are opinions of one particular polarity. Sikder's work demonstrates how the presence of motivated agents in a network can have the effect of dividing agents into isolated groups who all maintain the same viewpoint, much like the echo chambers people have observed online. In this way, the effect of motivated reasoners in a network results in a sort of informational segregation.

Of course, this is only a model, and all models are wrong (but some are useful). In our real-life social networks, most of the actors are real people embedded not only in online communities, but real-world communities, too, and they have their own complex reasons for believing the things they do. Under Tuckett's conviction narrative theory, each person in our human network is constructing their own unique narrative about the world and the events they experience. These stories are shared in human communities via complex human communication, entirely unlike the propagation of on/off signals in Sikder's algorithmic simulation.

Except that, online, many of the actors are algorithms, and their method of communication is precisely like Sikder's binary 1s and 0s. We behave more like algorithms in online social networks as well, posting and sharing and retweeting views and opinions that in turn shape the views and opinions of those in our own friend networks, propagating these simplified communication effects. In this setting, online content-placing and ordering algorithms play the role of the ultimate motivated reasoners, reinforcing 'points of view' that satisfy their programmatic goals in the most simplified and dogmatic ways possible. Most of these algorithms are optimized for profit or are utilized for political gain.

Consider the techniques of the now defunct marketing, political consulting and data brokerage firm Cambridge Analytica, who utilized big-data statistics to segment target audiences. By turning data into efficient statistical distributions, they were able to segment those distributions into atomic categories of people, who could then be targeted precisely with persuasive personalized adverts and editorial. During the American presidential election, they were reported to be using 40–50,000 different variants of adverts every day. Responses to those variants were continually measured, and the content was evolved based on those responses. The big-data-based categories used by Cambridge Analytica facilitated the segmenting of the social network audiences they attempted to influence.[25] This segmenting, like the nature of social network communication, facilitates the effectiveness of this approach, through effects similar to those observed in Sikder's model. While the actors in that model were persuaded only by the majority of evidence, one can imagine that playing on their hopes and fears would only make it easier to persuade them to lock their opinions, and become agents in the propagation of polarizing walls across social networks. As the model shows, algorithms can control the conversation, and the polarization. While that polarization is only binary in the model, algorithms could promote similar effects across a statistically segmented audience, for both commercial purposes, like the placement of advertising, and for pitting people against one another, and dividing their potential as a common voice, in a sort of digital gerrymandering.

If even a fraction of the effect that Sikder has revealed exists in real human networks, individuals and communities can be easily led by motivated agents to segregate themselves into opinion echo chambers. If that happens, it could in turn reinforce the effects of each group's conviction narrative and, though comprising otherwise rational people, society could come to exist in a truly divided state, eschewing information that doesn't conform to the dominant beliefs of each group.

To illustrate the effect of such motivated reasoners, in 2016 the *Observer* newspaper published a 3D map of the right-wing news ecosystem in the US around the time of the election. The diagram, produced by Jonathan Albright, assistant professor of communications at Elon University, North Carolina, shows the shadowy presence of 306 fake news sites as dark blobs surrounding the mainstream news media. Like Sikder's motivated reasoners, these sites connect to the news ecosystem via 1.3 million hyperlinks, through which they bombard those who get their news online with monotonous, single-point-of-view stories (signals) in an effort to colonize areas of network with their divisive views.[26] The *Columbia Journalism Review*[27] published a distinct but similar analysis of the media ecosystem by researchers from Harvard University.[28] If algorithmic selection of news stories does have an innate biasing effect, it may play a significant role in the recent extreme polarization of public discourse.

Regardless of whether it shows what *does* happen, Sikder's models, like Forrest's, show what *could* happen in real-world complex systems. Both models revealed complex emergent phenomena in evolving systems, which don't fit the 'survival of the fittest' trope. In the case of Forrest's immune-system model, the positive effect was the preservation of diversity in a stable adaptive system. On the other hand, Sikder's model settles into a divided state of isolated, segregated communities, cut off from the wider network in self-reinforcing echo chambers. This illustrates that emergence in complex networks is not always towards a desirable spontaneous order. Emergence is not always for the good, and care has to be taken in the design, implementation and implications of algorithms in the field to encourage positive emergent effects.

Armed with this information, it's up to us to decide how we shape the Internet and society of the future: are we happy to settle into a perpetually divided state, always at odds with each other, unable to come together and thrash out complex problems and find a compromise; or, do we want to preserve a diversity of opinions, cultures and perspectives, in a stable and resilient society where our differences enrich us and help us to adapt in the face of the intractable uncertainty we face? If the latter, can we change algorithms to help this happen, and if so, how?

One additional observation from Orowa's work is that if it is desirable for the social network to come to a consensus, to decide that one or the other point of view is preferable, the presence of a few motivated reasoners (in both directions) actually helps the process of coming to a consensus, rather than entering a state of complete, sustained, but divided equilibrium. It seems that motivated reasoners (who could represent people or algorithms) can help encourage productive debate, as long as they don't hold too much sway over the entire network. While this is a model, it is a useful one, indicating that algorithms could help in promoting diversity that leads towards eventual consensus, rather than division that leads nowhere. The question is whether we can tune algorithms to achieve these desirable, emergent effects.

11

Strength in Diversity

The system is its own best model.

BRUCE DIKE, circa 2000

The need to balance diversity and optimization in order to innovate effectively is something that has become increasingly clear to me throughout my career in AI. The first inkling I had of the fundamental relationship between diversity and creativity was in the early 1990s. At the time, I had just started my first job as a professor at the University of Alabama, filling the role vacated by David Goldberg, who had taken up a position at the University of Illinois. What Dave was doing with genetic algorithms in engineering at the time was pretty rare, and I was one of the few people that fit the bill to even attempt filling his shoes, so they hired me to continue running the lab that Dave set up.

Most of the work I undertook in the GA lab applied evolutionary computation to optimization problems. I worked in research projects with students and industry, optimizing the weight and stiffness of laminated composites, optimally allocating tasks to parallel computers, optimally controlling spacecraft, optimizing petroleum exploration and production, and routing cables optimally in nuclear power plants. My research life was entirely dominated by optimization, so much so that I was completely taken aback when I received a phone call, out of the blue, from an engineer called Bruce Dike at the aerospace and defence company McDonnell Douglas.

On the phone, Bruce was nearly breathless with excitement telling me about the difficult, real-world problem he was working on, and how he thought some of my GA work might offer a solution. Bruce headed a research group at McDonnell Douglas that was tasked with helping the corporation create cutting-edge fighter jets. The goal of each new jet that McDonnell Douglas designed and built was to give fighter pilots new capabilities that would give them an edge in aerial combat. The problem was that no one really understood how top-gun pilots actually achieved the amazing things they did with aircraft. Engineers could design new *aerodynamic* capabilities into planes, but how those capabilities turned into combat advantage was a real mystery. The *expertise* of a top-gun pilot was an indecipherable human skill that was proving incredibly hard to capture.

Knowing the mapping from aerodynamic performance to dogfight success was important to companies like McDonnell Douglas, because it provided guidance for the most expensive and critical business decisions they made, determining what kind of planes they needed to design and build. Bruce explained that up until that point, they had just winged it a bit. They'd build an actual, one-off plane (they might go so far as to build two), and then they'd let the pilots play with these stunningly expensive prototypes. The resulting unique aircraft were part of the famous 'X' (for experimental) series of planes that started with the X-1, in which Chuck Yeager first broke the sound barrier in 1947. The X planes were operated by NASA in conjunction with the US Air Force, but they were manufactured by all the great aerospace companies.

Starting with supersonic flight, the X planes pioneered every great aircraft innovation, from increased agility to greater altitude to reconfigurable wings to advanced guidance systems to vertical take-off and landing. After their construction, pilots would throw X planes around in top-gun simulated combat, flying out from NASA's Dryden Research Center at the edge of Edwards Air Force Base, in the California high desert. NASA and the USAF owned and operated the aircraft, but regardless, the corporations that manufactured the X planes were in a critical competition for contracts to produce the best future products. Based on academic papers of mine, Bruce seemed convinced that he and I could solve the problem of mapping aircraft capabilities to real dogfight performance, giving McDonnell Douglas a real edge.

Bruce explained that his research group had first tried addressing the problem with von Neumann's game theory, but that those ideas had proved too constricting. While Bruce's team could construct game-theory models of fighter combat, with parameters for turn rates, climb angles, and so on, no fixed-frame set of atoms like these seemed to account for the really creative things that a top gun could do with a plane, the innovative manoeuvres that would often give them the critical advantage in real-world combat.

With game theory getting them nowhere, the team had turned instead to simulation, setting up the most advanced simulators in the world at the time. Far more than mere video games, these simulators were real cockpits mounted on massive actuators that tossed and turned to simulate both angles and g forces, while within them pilots saw realistically simulated images roll by on a screen, as they flew models of as-of-yet unbuilt planes, based on detailed aerodynamic simulation models that Bruce's team could construct. But this approach wasn't working either. Top-gun pilots are the most expensive and in-demand personnel in the military and it was hard to drag them out to St. Louis to spend time in a dark warehouse on what they saw as a glorified funfair machine. On top of that, they hated the simulators, complaining that they lacked realism. As they saw it, their valuable time would be better spent throwing real fighter aircraft around the sunny skies over the Mojave.

So Bruce's team had no effective way to understand how their promising pen-and-paper designs could be made into effective turns and dives of a top-gun pilot. This was where I came in, Bruce told me, as he was sure we could use ideas that he had (rather wildly) extrapolated from academic articles of mine that he had somehow found online. The papers in question covered some genetics-based rule learning I'd done on simple and abstracted problems in my

PhD thesis. Bruce was convinced we could take these ideas and use them as a basis to get computers to do his test piloting for him. We'd get the machines to *learn* rules that described fighter combat manoeuvres, by flying simulated dogfights between computers.

This was 1991, and his idea sounded insanely ambitious to me. When I managed to get a word in edge wise, I tried to push Bruce back to reality, back to real technical details, back to breaking things down to a simple problem I knew how to solve, an optimization problem.

'What metric are you trying to optimize?' I asked Bruce, several times.

'It's not really an optimization problem,' he kept responding, continuing to elaborate on his grand vision.

We must have gone round and round like this for an hour, before Bruce finally got through to me, with a magic word:

'What we're really looking for is *novelty*. Manoeuvres that no one has ever seen before.'

The word *novelty* got my attention. When I finally hung up, I found myself a recruit in Bruce's dream.

I booked a flight and went up to St. Louis. When Bruce met me at the airport, he didn't look crazy, he looked like the most stereotypical aerospace engineer I had ever seen: briefcase, dark pants, white shirt, tie, pocket protector (with pens) and horn-rimmed glasses. Despite having invested in his scheme, it still took me a while to be sure that, despite looking exactly like Michael Douglas in *Falling Down*, Bruce had not, in fact, cracked under the tension of his job. I found him to be brilliant, a man with an infectious enthusiasm for his work, a stunning breadth of knowledge, unusual insight and that greatest of all qualities in a technologist, true creativity. We would become close friends and collaborators for nearly two decades, through our work on computational creativity for fighter-aircraft applications.

At the time of our first meeting, the hottest X plane was the X-31, an aircraft with two prototypes flying at Dryden. What made the X-31 so exciting was that it was a 'post-stall' fighter. In normal planes, if you tip the nose up over 15 degrees, relative to the direction of travel, the plane will stall, losing all lift and controllability. In a normal plane, alarms go off when you approach that 15 degree boundary, because it takes a great pilot and great deal of luck to avoid a crash once you go post-stall. But the X-31 was no normal plane. It had demonstrated controlled flight at a mind-boggling 70-degree angle of attack. I remember being stunned the first time I saw it: a plane pointed skyward but flying on a line parallel to the Earth. The X-31 performed this, and many other related feats, by using computerized control of 'canards' (little tiltable wings at the front of the plane) and 'thrust vectoring' actuators (paddles that steered into the jet of air from the plane's engine, to point that thrust in directions other than along the plane's axis). This advanced technology yielded precisely the sorts of aerodynamic capabilities that *might* result in amazing dogfight performance. But that required hours of top-gun flying to figure out.

Working with Bruce and his team, our project started by running simulations of an X-31 in a dogfight with a more conventional fighter, McDonnell Douglas's own F/A-18 Hornet. Our simulated Hornet flew using an expert system model of 'standard combat logic' for a guns-only dogfight. This AI system was basically a few rules that always tried to turn the plane as fast as possible, such that its nose pointed at the opponent, so that it could train its machine guns on the enemy aircraft. By contrast, our AI system for the X-31 had a set of rules that was being evolved by a *diversity-preserving* genetic algorithm, to see if it could evolve interesting and novel ways of using the plane's capabilities. Feedback was given to our evolving rule sets based on how well the X-31 could avoid the Hornet's guns, balanced with training its own guns on the Hornet.

Our idea worked, rather spectacularly. Without any human intervention, using only feedback on how well it did in each randomized dogfight, the evolutionary algorithm found unique moves from every theorized and practised class of real-life post-stall manoeuvre. It found all the truly innovative moves that top-gun pilots had so far demonstrated while playing with expensive prototypes. For example, it found the phenomenal 'helicopter gun attack', where the X-31 would rotate around its own vertical axis, inside the tight turning radius dictated by the Hornet's expert system, keeping its firing guns continuously trained on the spiralling opponent, while falling out of the sky in a flat spin. In a normal plane, this would be an insane and irrecoverable manoeuvre, but the X-31's thrust vectoring made it controllable and brilliant (as is shown in Figure 11.1).

Our machine-learning system also discovered moves that were like the 'Cobra manoeuvre', first discovered by Russian fighter pilots (in a non-post-stall MIG that made the trick much more dangerous than in the X-31). In this infamous move, the plane would tilt its nose way up, reducing forward speed dramatically, such that any trailing opponent 'on your 6' would rocket past, and

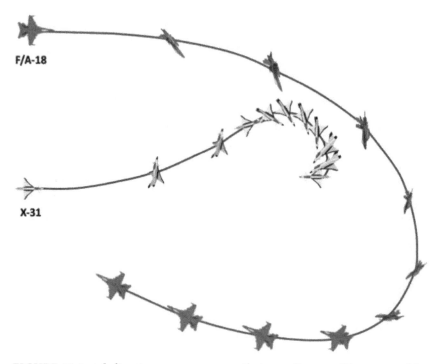

F/A-18

X-31

FIGURE 11.1 *A helicopter gun manoeuvre that was discovered by our machine learning system.*

you could drop your nose like a striking snake and shoot the passing enemy from behind. Our simulated X-31 modulated speed in its manoeuvres with precisely these sorts of nose-raising, drag-manipulating tricks.

Even more amazingly, our program found the vaunted 'Herbst manoeuvre', first theorized by aerospace engineer Dr Wolfgang Herbst, one of the originators of the technologies in the X-31. The manoeuvre involved throwing the plane's nose towards the sky like in a Cobra move, but then spinning the plane around the direction of travel, as much as 180 degrees, and then diving in the opposite direction, in effect turning the plane on a dime in mid-air, as shown in Figure 11.2.

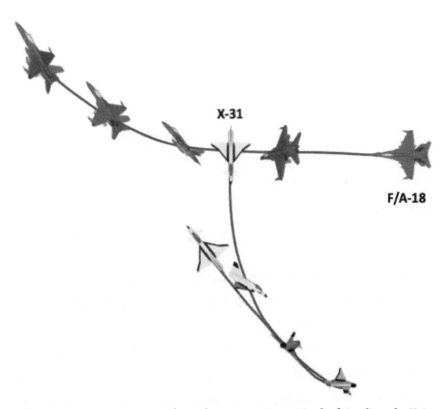

FIGURE 11.2 *A manoeuvre where, despite starting out in the firing line, the X-31 quickly gained the advantage, demonstrating the dogfight edge a rapid Herbst turn could give.*

Not long after the work Bruce and I did with his team, the X-31 prototype became the first plane to execute this manoeuvre in real life, on 29 April 1993. The X-31 was completely innovative then, and it changed how fighter planes work today. The computer-controlled, post-stall capabilities of the X-31 are now an accepted part of the design repertoire of 'super-manoeuvrable' fighter planes.

The computational creativity that Bruce and I realized in the early 1990s is not some dinosaur ancestor of the autonomous combat drones people are discussing today. Our goal was never to control real planes or replace top-gun pilots, and that was a good thing, because our program often found promising proto-manoeuvres and then crashed the (simulated) aircraft into the ground on the next run. This complete lack of stability was okay for us, because setbacks in progress and outright failures were often followed by unusual but interesting twists and turns of the aircraft, *black swan ideas*, that were just the sort of revealing phenomena the engineering design team (and top-gun pilots) wanted to see.

The program allowed us to see how these ideas recombined with other parts of what the computer had learned and turned those combinations into fully functional manoeuvres. This capability could allow McDonnell Douglas's engineers to explore the raw aeronautical capabilities of an aircraft that no one had ever built and see how they might be useful in a real-world dogfight. We showed aircraft engineers and top-gun pilots what the machine had learned, to check whether they should, in their designs and flights, emulate, tweak or invest further. The machine-bound creativity of the algorithm became really interesting when set in the context of human designers, engineers and pilots who all brought their own, unbounded, human creativity to the project.[1]

Bruce was right. While evolutionary algorithms were really good for optimization, they proved far more interesting and useful when utilized as a creative tool, which, in retrospect, was always what GA pioneer John Holland had in mind. In Holland's 1975 book *Adaptation in Artificial and Natural Systems*, he showed why diversity and mixing were key to adaptation.[2] While

Charles Darwin realized that variety (diversity) was the grist of the mill for the evolutionary engine, Holland showed that it was variety *plus* recombination (mixing) that enabled powerful adaptation.

In genetic evolution, recombination of different gene subsets takes place in a number of ways, but the most obvious and well known is in sexual reproduction. When two individuals reproduce, they have some genes that are the same (at least enough to make reproduction possible) and some that are different. The genes they have in common have existed and survived in two different contexts; that is, the context of the genes that they don't share. In addition, the individuals involved will have had completely different life experiences, ensuring the genes they have in common have implicitly demonstrated their value in the context of two differing life stories. Across many different couples, there are even more contexts (both at a genetic and environmental level) that demonstrate the usefulness of any common gene, and common combinations of genes, shared by subgroups of people.

The fact that populations evaluate genes in many different contexts is what makes recombination different from mutation. To see why, imagine you reproduced in isolation, not only without a partner, but without any social context, as if isolated on a desert island, where you are required to produce a child as your replacement. Now imagine all people reproducing this way, on separate, isolated islands. There would be natural selection, because some of those islanders would never live long enough to construct their replacement, and there would be variance, because every reproduction would have inevitable mutations, 'errors' in replicating the parent. So, there would be Darwinian evolution, particularly if we allow extra children from the survivors to replace the unlucky ones on their abandoned islands as the process goes on.

This is very different from sexual reproduction. If you are able to bring a mate to your island, you know that your mate (and that mate's genes) have already survived in a different context, the island they came from. Through the process of recombination, your child will have a randomly selected mix of both yours and your partner's genes, resulting in something unique and *new*. The genes from your partner that you didn't share with them can be seen as random mutations of the genes you passed to your child. But these pseudo-mutations aren't fully random; they are genes that have been subjected to evolution, in a separate context from your own. This is not to mention that mate selection isn't entirely random either, depending as it does on societal norms (or violations of those norms) that may have led to your selection. While the mutation-based variance is sufficient for Darwin's theories, recombination yields *structured randomness*, through the mixing of contextualized partial solutions (gene combinations).

Holland showed that evolution with recombination mixed lots of these contextualized partial solutions (gene combinations) in parallel across a population, and then selected the ones that had the best on-average impacts on survival across those contexts. This selection led to exponential increases in the number of the best-on-average gene combinations, and Holland showed that this exponential propagation of what looked good was a near optimal strategy for dealing with the inherent uncertainty of survival overall.

However, there's a catch. The more copies of any gene combinations in the population, the less diverse the genes, and therefore the fewer genetic contexts you can evaluate those genes in. Holland's theories showed that evolution leveraged populations to figure out what good gene combinations were, but that only works if populations are diverse, to provide lots of different contexts. But the whole point of figuring out what gene combinations are good is to then increase their numbers in the population. This is the central paradox. You need diversity (i.e. the widest possible number of different options) to find the best solutions effectively, but once you've found them, promoting those best solutions across the population destroys diversity.

What this tells us is that for effective evolution, the effects of natural selection need to be balanced with the diversity preservation that creates the structured randomness that recombination can leverage to make natural selection most effective. Holland's results have been largely interpreted as guidance for creating AI algorithms, but there may be broader implications for encouraging creative innovations in natural adaptive systems, like systems of human beings.

David Goldberg revealed more about this subtle balancing of effective evolving systems in his book *The Design of Innovation*.[3] Using theoretical models and experiments, Goldberg parameterized the speed at which natural selection copies partial solutions (via a number which he called *selection pressure*) versus how frequently partial solutions get mixed (which he calls a probability of recombination, p_c). From this he derived theoretical boundaries for the parameter settings that should make genetic algorithms work, or fail, as shown in the graphic representation of his results in Figure 11.3.

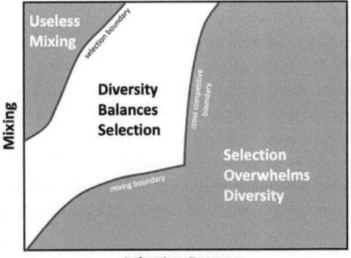

FIGURE 11.3 *The white region is where evolutionary algorithms work on optimization problems: a region where mixing is balanced with the pressure to settle on the 'fittest' solution. Outside the realm of well-specified problems, in an ever-changing real world where there may be no single fittest solution, the need for this balance to preserve adaptability is even more important.*

Goldberg's genetic algorithm optimized successfully with parameter combinations that were between the two squiggly lines. Inside this boundary, his algorithms found the optimal solution; outside it, less-than-perfect solutions came to dominate. What's interesting is to consider why the algorithm fails outside these regions, and what it suggests for real-world systems and online social networks.

Let's think of selection pressure as the speed at which a meme 'goes viral' online, and the probability of recombination as the speed at which human beings combine old memes to make new ones, rather than simply copying what they've already seen. Let's assume that we use these algorithmic models as guidance for effective evolution of memes, and we want to stay within the two squiggly lines, where Goldberg's GAs optimized effectively.

To stay in the good zone between the two squiggly lines as the speed of propagation goes up, the mixing rate also has to go up, too. This has an intuitive interpretation: if the best idea is decided on too quickly, there's never enough time for innovative mixing of diverse, alternative ideas to occur. The figure also shows that at some point (the transition from the rising 'mixing boundary' to the nearly vertical 'cross competitive boundary') no amount of mixing will overcome the selective pressure. If you select too fast, diversity collapses before it has a chance to make an impact, and mixing ideas becomes impossible. However, it is of course necessary to make some decisions, and that's why the region to the left of the 'selection boundary' also failed in Goldberg's optimization problems. In this region, while there is mixing, really good new ideas are torn apart by mixing before they ever have the chance to propagate and have influence.

These models and algorithms seem to imply that, to be effective, evolution requires a balance between the discipline of using the best-known idea and the chaos of mixing ideas up. Other scientific studies also show that striking a precise balance between the two may be the vital characteristic of living systems.

The term *edge of chaos* was first used by the SFI researchers Doyne Farmer and Chris Langton, while looking at cellular automata models, simplified algorithms invented by John von Neumann to represent self-replicating biology.[4] While experimenting with parameters that controlled these programs, they observed that for some parameter settings, the algorithms would settle into uninteresting equilibria, essentially static states. For others, the algorithms just generated complete randomness, never seeming to settle down into any recognizable patterns. But for a thin set of parameters between these two regimes, really interesting things happened. The algorithms generated discernible patterns, but not simply the repeated iterations of a dynamic equilibrium, or snowy noise. The patterns they generated contained geometric structures combined with seemingly organic forms, all in non-repeating, capital C complexity. Farmer and Langton called the special configurations that generated these patterns *the edge of chaos* (see Figure 11.4).

On the one side of the edge of chaos are systems that are simply random, like the flips of Cardano's coins or the random signals travelling down Shannon's wires. On the other side is the plodding execution of programmatic rules that descend from Llull through Babbage to Turing and Simon, falling into predictable and brittle equilibrium. Between them is something far more

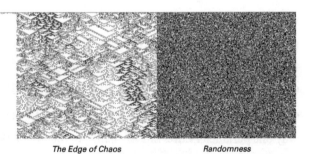

Static Order   The Edge of Chaos   Randomness

FIGURE 11.4 *Patterns generated by three cellular automata. The generation starts from a random stage in the top row. For some parameter settings, all the cells go white, like on the far left. For others, random 'snow' results, as on the far right. In between these two, 'edge of chaos' parameter settings generate geometric and organic-like forms in non-repeating patterns.*

dynamic and interesting, something that looks structured, but non-repeating, complex and perhaps even creative.

Other researchers made an important addition to edge-of-chaos theory, by considering what happens when you let an algorithm learn from a system at the edge of chaos. Around 2002, SFI researcher Jim Crutchfield (along with UC Berkley's Karl Young) wondered what sorts of models algorithms could infer from the simplest possible capital-C complex system in the world. To examine this they employed the logistics equation, a simplified version of the Malthusian Model, derived from the same Thomas Malthus that inspired Charles Darwin.[5]

In 1845 the French mathematician Pierre François Verhulst, after he read the famous essay where Thomas Malthus theorized that human population growth would inevitably lead to starvation and misery due to the overuse of limited resources, rendered the idea in mathematical form, calling it the *Malthusian Model*, which was used to calculate the number of animals that might be grazed on a piece of land without destroying it, and even to explore human demographics, in line with the theories of Malthus. A simplified form of this the Malthusian Model is called the logistic equation:

$$x(t + 1) = rx(t)(1 - x(t))$$

Here, the parameter r (known as the Malthusian parameter) reflects the maximum rate of population growth, and x is the percentage size of the population, relative to the environment's carrying capacity (e.g. availability of water, food and other necessities, the resources that Malthus thought limited the utopian ideas of Godwin). Despite this equation's simplicity – it has only one 'atom' x, the percentage population size relative to carrying capacity, and only one parameter r, the rate of change in the population at any given step in time – it illustrates some of the strangest behaviour of real-world, capital-C Complex Systems as the graph in Figure 11.5 shows.

In this graph, the vertical axis shows x, the population size as a percentage, while the horizontal axis shows values for r, the reproductive rate of change in

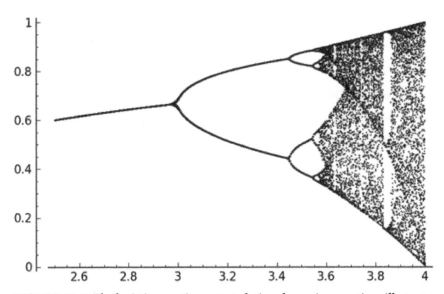

FIGURE 11.5 *The logistic equation, a population dynamics equation, illustrates that even apparently simple things can have infinitely complex behaviour. Each vertical slice of this graph represents the number of individuals in a population evolving with a different reproduction rate, r. The vertical position of the black dots in each slice represent the population sizes that this reproductive rate causes the system bounce between in the population's final (dynamic) equilibrium. There are single dots in each vertical slice for r less than three, then two for values just above 3, then 4, then 8, 16, etc., though you might need a magnifier to see those more detailed slices.*

population size. The graph shows what happens to the equation's population sizes for increasing *r*, left to right. For small values of *r* the population evolves to a constant stable value (shown by the straight line, which is really a series of tiny dots, each of which represents the equilibrium x that the equation will fall into for a given value of *r*). This is the sort of stable equilibrium that economists look for in economic systems, reflecting a Malthusian balance between the demands of the population and the supply of resources they require. For values less than three, the size of the population heads to a steady, stable state that balances this supply and demand.

As the rate of change rises above 3 the systems behaviour changes radically, because the population size overshoots the resource carrying capacity of the environment, causing the subsequent population to collapse to a smaller size. At this smaller size, the population has an abundance of resources, and expands to the overshoot condition again. This boom and bust cycle is represented by the two values of population size that the logistic equation oscillates between just to the left of $r = 3$. As you raise r even more, you get more oscillations between booms and busts in the population size, first 4, then 8, then 16, etc. Then, the strangest thing happens at $r = 3.5699...$: the equation visits an *infinite* number of different population sizes, unable to settle into a repeated pattern or a state of equilibrium.

Even stranger is that between this value and $r = 4$, the equation does all sorts of unexpected things. For instance, after having shown a pattern of doubling for many smaller values of r (2, 4, 8, 16, 32, etc.), the equation gives oscillations between *three* different values for r just above 3.8. You can see this as the portion of the graph that 'hollows out' just above $r = 3.8$ and note that there are definitely three distinct dots in that vertical slice. By $r = 4$ the equation once again visits an infinite number of values between 0 and 1, and in fact you can prove that it has this completely chaotic behaviour for all values of r greater than 4. Despite the simplicity of the logistics equation, at the value r = 3.5699. . ., $r \geq 4$, and a few other interesting values of r, it is as complex as any equation can possibly be.

Crutchfield and Young tried to get an algorithm to learn to replicate what the logistic equation was doing for different values of r. The algorithm was given the pattern of population sizes that the equation generated and asked to reconstruct a program that generated the same data. For the values of r beneath the chaotic threshold, the algorithm did what would be expected: there were just repeating series of numbers, and the algorithm learned to regurgitate the same sequence easily. For values greater than r = 3.5699. . ., the algorithm generally couldn't learn the logistic equation's complicated dynamics, so instead it treated them as statistical noise. But for precisely r = 3.5699. . ., the edge of chaos, something particularly interesting happened. The more data the algorithm was given, the more complicated the program it learned. It didn't describe any of the chaotic dynamics of the system as mere noise; instead, it continued to find more and more complex structure the more data it was given. The experiment showed that a system at the edge of chaos had complexity that was beyond a finite algorithmic description.

Edge of chaos systems seem capable of generating structure that exceeds the algorithm's ability to capture that structure. Those systems are their own best model. Some have suggested that evolving systems head towards and maintain themselves at the edge of chaos because of the interesting behaviours there, to maintain structured, stable contexts while sustaining the ability to respond to random changes by building innovative new structure. This implies that the edge of chaos is that point where mixing and selection may naturally balance in evolving systems. Some believe that it may be that natural systems intrinsically evolve to the edge of chaos, and in fact that an emergent edge of chaos behaviour, rather than the 'survival of the fittest' is the real defining quality of systems that are *alive*.

SFI researcher, doctor and theoretical biologist Stuart Kauffman is a prominent proponent of this theory, and has focused his research on the nature of living systems. His early work appears in the 1993 book *Origins of Order*,[6] which considers the complexity of behaviour of networks of actors. For Kauffman, those actors could be small chemical reactions in a primordial soup at the origins of life, which, by chance, come to self-reinforce one another. Kauffman analysed algorithmic networks as models of these systems to determine if there were evolutionary equilibria that might make them suddenly and spontaneously develop and exploit structure. While coming from a completely different perspective, Kauffman's models are similar to the models of social networks that Orowa Sikder, myself and our colleagues studied. But where our models of human social networks fell into divided stagnant divisions as their equilibria, Kauffman's networks did things that were far more interesting.

Kauffman's networks have N actors, each of whom computes a simple function of the binary inputs from their K connected neighbours and rebroadcasts the signal. Unlike Orowa's models, Kauffman's actors aren't constructed to come to a decision about their inputs, they simply mash them through the same unchanging, random binary function, and generate a varying output based on what they've just received. This is Kauffman's simulation of the random chemical processes that might be adjacent to one another in a primordial soup.

What Kauffman found was that the dynamics of such networks all vitally depend on K, the number of connections that each actor has to other actors. For low K, actors get few inputs from others, and the network consists of isolated islands. Because of this, any perturbation to one part of the network doesn't propagate elsewhere. Disruptions just de-synchronize parts of the network, so that no overall structured equilibrium for the entire network exists. By contrast, for very high K, all actors are essentially connected to everyone else. Small changes tend to change all the actor's outputs eventually, so any tiny perturbation destroys any structured behaviour of the entire network.

However, Kauffman found that for intermediate levels of connectivity between actors, something interesting happened. The networks were able to effectively synchronize, and remain stable, but when they were disrupted by noise, they have relatively long, structured transitions to other, new, relatively stable equilibria. They exhibit both the properties of structured stability, and the ability to evolve to new states. Like the cellular automata models of Farmer and Langton, they seemed to exist at an edge of chaos, where they have structure, while maintaining flexible, evolvable dynamics.

Given the similarity between Kauffman's networks and those studied by Sikder, it seems natural to consider what one says about the other. One of the primary observations of Sikder's models is that the percentage of motivated reasoners in a network acts exactly like a reduction in the connectivity of actors, precisely as if the number of connections K is reduced. In Kauffman's models, a reduction in K means the emergence of simple network behaviours that show the overall instability of unsynchronized islands, and none of the emergent complexity at the edge of chaos. This would indicate that motivated reasoners in social networks, for instance algorithms, may reduce the evolutionary power in such networks. This seems consistent with the echo chamber effect.

But Kauffman's models also indicate that connecting everyone to everyone creates chaos, and that certainly resonates with the real-life information glut that the unfiltered Internet creates. In line with the theories of Holland and Goldberg, there must be an optimal balance of mixing (connectivity between people in social networks, for instance), and natural selection (arrival at localized consensus within communities, and the servicing of those communities needs and preferences).

Edge of chaos complexity has revealed a new reality: that we cannot characterize the world and the phenomena around us algorithmically, neither as merely deterministic sets of rules nor purely random rolls of the dice. This complexity is unpredictable, yet it has patterns; unpredictable patterns may in fact be a characteristic of systems that we would call *living systems*. Stuart Kauffman has used mathematical models to show that living systems tend to evolve towards an edge of chaos: that point where their behaviour is maximally random while maintaining some structure. Existing at this edge allows the evolving system to retain the maximum number of adjacent possible states that it can change to at any moment, while still maintaining stable behaviours. This, rather than the drive towards some optima implied by 'survival of the fittest', appears to be the real characteristic of living systems; they change their apparent models and their criteria at any time as circumstance dictates, defying the very notion of fixed models and criteria. They interact and respond to many other similarly complex, adaptive systems and, above all, they remain open, unlike the closed, fixed models of idealized computation.

Diversity plays a key role at this 'edge of chaos'. In fact, it is *the key* to creative innovation, offering a multitude of solutions and options from which the engine of evolution can select in order to effectively adapt (rather than optimize) to changing environments and circumstances. Individual atomic solutions, which reside in distributed, diverse populations, are the raw material that generates new solutions to population-wide problems, through the possibilities of *recombination*. Furthermore, within the context of a population each of these possible solutions has been implicitly evaluated in many different contexts, so that their usefulness has been tried and tested, and thus recombination allows their rapid assembly into new, possibly revolutionary solutions to population-wide problems.

This ability to quickly innovate is particularly key when facing real-world, radical uncertainties, whether it be facing the challenge of a new virus for the immune system, or the ability of a human community to survive a catastrophic natural disaster. But for innovation to happen, there has to be *mixing* as well as diversity, prompting the discovery of entirely new ideas via the recombination of partial solutions into something else, something different. The problem is that mixing (perpetually retaining multiple solutions that can be recombined) and optimization (driving for the one true solution) are ideas that run entirely counter to one another, which points to the need for a critical *balance* in effective evolving systems.

While it's true that the theories of Forrest, Holland, Goldberg, myself and Sikder are just models, and all models are wrong, some models are useful, there are theories, and some evidence that evolutionary and individual human creativity involves the juxtaposition of diverse elements, in effect endlessly mixing and recombining ideas, just like in these models. In 1964, the author, journalist and philosopher Arthur Koestler attempted to describe a general theory of creativity, spanning philosophy, science and the arts, in his classic book *The Act of Creation*.[7] Koestler exhaustively explores different examples of invention and creativity, concluding that they all share the same characteristic, which he called *bisociation*, or juxtaposition.

He illustrates this bisociative characteristic of creativity and how it plays out into valuable innovations with some of the greatest stories of discovery in history. Gutenberg fulfilled his dream of creating a printing press through a bisociation comparing the block printing of playing cards and the pressing of grapes into wine. Kepler bisociated geometry and physics to create the first laws of planetary motion. Pasteur bisociated the practice of vaccination (which was used only for smallpox, through a fluke discovery that exposure to cowpox[8] induced immunity) with his earlier discovery that microscopic yeast was the agent that made wine and beer, creating the entire field of immunology. And, of course, Darwin bisociated (or perhaps trisociated) the existing theories of evolutionary utopianism, Malthus's quasi-scientific objections to those ideas and the idea of variance that descended from Quetelet.

But Koestler starts his explication on creativities with something far less historical, and more fundamental and human: laughter. Consider the joke: Two cannibals are eating a clown. One looks at the other and says, 'Does this taste funny to you?' This is a pun, what some have called the lowest form of humour, since it relies on a language device that may not translate to other languages. In English, 'funny' can mean amusing, but it can also mean strange. The humour of this joke comes from the juxtaposition of those two meanings, the grotesque act of cannibalism interrupted by a commonplace phrase about suspect food. It's even slightly self-referential, in that what's funny (ha-ha) in this joke is precisely that its mixing of reference frames is funny (strange).

In Koestler's theory, the pleasure of this amusement is because the juxtaposition of reference frames is a valuable evolutionary feature of human thought and sociality. Koestler believed this was the key mechanism of all creativity. Laughter, Koestler theorized, is the pleasure response for creation, expressed physically, the way the orgasm is the pleasure response for mechanisms involved in the reproductive act. The theory is that just as orgasm is a psychic pay-off for the act that leads to reproduction, laughter is a psychic pay-off for the act that leads to creation, and that act is juxtaposition.

Furthermore, according to Koestler, many bisociative, creative breakthroughs occur in a relaxed or dream-like state after a period of focused, conscious effort. That is, when the brain has abandoned rational thought allowing free-form ideas to mingle uninhibited. This theory is supported by recent dream research. For instance, dream researchers have found evidence that as you fall into a dream, the material from recent waking experiences is combined with longer-term memories in dream narratives. This process also seems to involve the visceral feelings of the 'other brains' in the human body.

In dream studies at Harvard,[9] subjects played video games that simulated skiing, and included a combination of smooth slopes, and thrill (or fear) inducing plunges and turns. After playing, researchers found that it was the fearful or thrilling moments that were incorporated into the subject's dream narratives, as if these more extreme feelings 'tagged' experiences that were worth recalling in dreams, thus making them available for recombination with other memories and narratives (which may have also been tagged with feelings). The construction of dream narratives plays a clear-cut role in basic memory, but may also be a fundamental part of learning, integrating past experiences and memories into new narratives in the mind.

As Tuckett suggested with his conviction narratives, the stories we tell ourselves, particularly those invested with emotions, may be a primary means of enabling action in the radically uncertain world we live in. This, in turn, suggests that the juxtaposition of experiences invested with feelings helps us to come up with new narrative perspectives that we can use to help us take action when we are uncertain and there are no real rational choices to be made. Perhaps this is also what we mean when we say that a committed innovator 'has a dream'.

How does balancing selection and juxtaposition relate to the algorithms in our lives? The algorithmic work by researchers like Forrest, Sikder and Bruce Dike shows us that even in algorithms there is something special about juxtaposition. Rather than focusing on optimization, which drives inevitably to polarization, diversity-preserving algorithms may be able to teach us things about how we might balance maximum diversity, effective selection, and the innovative mixing of ideas in our own evolving technical and social systems. That said, it is always important to remember that the fixed frames and representations of models and algorithms are only ever simplified versions of the vast bisociative reference frames that occur in complex systems like the brain and human society. An algorithm's representations are always models, always technical manifestations of the reference frames of the humans who created those algorithms.

When he was writing in the 1960s, at the dawn of computer science, Koestler found the prevailing science of psychology (behaviourism and cognitivism) tended to portray human beings as mere automata, disregarding the creative abilities of the mind. These representations, he wrote, are 'silent codes' that condense learning into mere 'habit', alluding to the necessity of reaching their structured edges to perform acts of creation:

> Habits are the indispensable core of stability and ordered behaviour; they also have a tendency to become mechanized and to reduce man to the status of a conditioned automaton. The creative act, by connecting previously unrelated dimensions of experience, enables him to a higher level of mental evolution. It is an act of liberation – the defeat of habit by originality.

12

Gods and Monsters

A.I. is the hole. Not the doughnut.
DR ROBERT SMITH, SCIFOO, 2014

It's 2014, and I'm attending SCIFOO (Scientific Friends of O'Reilly), a kind of invitation-only weekend summer camp for scientists, held at Google's corporate complex in Mountain View, California. When I arrive, I find the enormous entrance hall has been done up like a campground, with tents and an electric campfire (made with a little fan, some bits of red and orange cloth, and LEDs). None of the attendees are actually staying in tents, mind; instead we've all been accommodated at a nice corporate hotel down the road, but the decoration engenders a playful vibe and prompts a sense of nostalgia for childhood adventuring. Every meeting room has table drawers rammed full of snack food, and every meal has an ice-cream bar (with sprinkles). Google had prepared theme-park-like demonstrations for us, including a holodeck! Well, a small room with Google StreetView projections on all the walls. At least that's what I heard. I suffer from motion sickness and was advised to give it a miss.

I'm literally like a kid at camp. Well, like me at camp, actually, when I really was a kid: standing just outside the campfire circle, not quite knowing how to fit in. Most of the attendees at SCIFOO are younger than me, and since I've come straight from the airport, my London-to-San Francisco jet lag isn't helping my socializing at the pre-kick-off drinks party. So, I stand in the corner, nursing a cocktail, trying to look like a Silicon Valley hipster, like I know what's going down. I actually have no idea what's going down. In fact, all I really know about SCIFOO is that it springs from the 'FOO Camp', a concept for innovative science forums that O'Reilly Media pioneered.

After an hour of open bar, our hosts climb on the stage, which is disco lit in Google corporate colours. They introduce themselves (they are from the various organizations that sponsor SCIFOO, including O'Reilly Digital Publishing, Nature Publishing Group, and Google). They reassure the attendees about the complete lack of agenda and tell us that the majority of people feel lost in this opening stage, because the FOO Camp format mandates that only one-third of invitees can have attended a FOO Camp before, ensuring the weekend's discussions are constantly invigorated by diverse new ideas. The organizers assure us that not even they know what's going to happen that weekend, because there is no plan, but that a productive meeting would emerge on its own.

While there is no agenda, there is a practised FOO Camp ritual. First, we're instructed that all 300 of us will have to introduce ourselves, but under strict guidelines. When we're handed the microphone we need to tell everyone our name, our affiliation, and give a less-than-a-sentence description on our personal scientific bent. We're quickly trained in the two-microphone passing technique (each time skipping a person so the mikes move more efficiently), but more importantly we're warned that if we try to make a sentence, much less a paragraph, in our high-concept pitch, the camp instructor will strike *the gong of rebuke*. We're then reminded again that the time limit is serious, and the introductions begin.

I very quickly realize that everyone in the room is brilliantly interesting and adept at summarizing their ideas in just about five words and I start to worry about how I'm going to introduce myself: *Who* am I? And, what am I doing here? I'm sitting about halfway to the back of the room, so I have about 150 or so micro-introductions worth of time to think. I recall that I've been invited because of my varied work on AI, and in particular for my work with David

Tuckett and the Bank of England, measuring macroeconomic jitters using psychologically inspired big-data analysis of unstructured financial news text. Now I have five words to make that sexy or be the laugh act on 'The Gong Show'. My heart begins to race. As the mikes snake ever closer, I write down and strike out inane phrase after phrase on my SCIFOO-branded notepad. It's hard to concentrate, not just because of the bourbon coursing through my veins, but because I'm distracted by the brilliant non-sentences spilling into the hall:

'Resurrecting Mammoths to Reverse Climate Change.'

'Stopping the Killer Robots.'

'Why do seals have very black muscles?'

All around fresh-faced young scientists, wearing T-shirts and sandals, are standing up and spouting genius words. It's like I've died and gone to nerd heaven, but at any minute I am due to be cast out to the purgatory of mediocre ideas. The wondrous non-sentences keep on coming:

Big data visualization from the autistic mind.

Giant African pouched rats.

Recording music onto DNA.

The mikes arrive; the first is passed to the person after me, and I'm offered mike #2. I take it, stumble to my feet, and wing it:

Rob Smith.
University College London.
AI is the Hole, Not the Doughnut.

Seven words, not bad. I pass the mike and get a respectable 'hmmm' from the audience.

After the introductions, we are all given giant Post-It notes, and directed to a huge timetable, which is marked across the top with Google's sci-fi-named conference rooms (Space Elevator, Tricorder, etc.), and across the left edge with times of day. We're told to write down titles for sessions we'd like to host, and stick them in the time slot we'd like. This is the only programming in the FOO camp format, a scrum of people making up sessions on the fly. When there are collisions of ideas or timeslots, we're told to negotiate. This, apparently, is how a FOO camp gets made.

To be honest, I'm not entirely sure what 'AI is the hole, not the doughnut' means, but *intuitively* it feels right to me, like something on the tip of my tongue. I write it down as a session title, wade into the scheduling melee, and stick it into an early Saturday-morning slot in the 'Neuralizer' session room. I figure (hope?) that jet lag recovery, a good night's sleep and some morning coffee will have me peaking with this new idea by then. We adjourn for the night, and shuttle back to our hotels. As I fumble for the key card to my room, my phone pings with an email from another SCIFOO attendee. I don't know him, but it turns out he's another AI researcher, and he wants to combine his session, entitled 'General Purpose AI and a Formal Theory of Creativity', with my random prose poem. I reply 'Sure, see you tomorrow' and collapse into the sweet arms of the Sheraton.

In the morning, after a shuttle-bus ride, a delightful Google omelette-bar creation and two cups of gourmet coffee, I enter the 'Neuralizer' to meet my fellow organizer. He's a nice guy, and we have a good turnout, probably thirty foo campers, so we get straight into the session. We slide naturally into a debate, me the older, more jaded practitioner, and my companion host a younger, more hopeful colleague arguing that we're on the precipice of having 'general purpose AI' emerge from networks of deep-learning algorithms. He works at the cutting edge of AI, using deep networks of functions and information theory to discover patterns in big data. It is extremely exciting stuff, and he does amazing things.

As we parry, my 'hole and doughnut' idea emerges with more clarity. I realize that over my years as a practitioner in the field, spanning the entire era of the Internet, every idea and advance in AI has shown us something we *aren't*.

When AI is not being used to engineer the latest technological gadget, it is a useful philosophical tool enabling us, through programming, to contemplate the nature of human thought and interaction in that age-old quest to discover who and what human beings really are. Just as the fifteenth-century cartographer Fra Mauro acknowledged when he set out to create the definitive map of the world: 'wise men contemplate the world, knowing full well that they are contemplating themselves'. I believe that since Ada Lovelace, calling herself an 'Analyst & Metaphysician', first contemplated whether computers could do anything creative, AI has done more than any other field of study to explore the complex nature of human beings, by placing that nature in stark relief against the limitations of engineered mechanisms. At least that's what I said in the SCIFOO session, I think.

At the end of the debate, my co-chair and I came to a mutually respectful conclusion: I thought what he was doing was useful tech, and he thought my ideas about the contrast between algorithms and people were interesting. But while there were some encouraging comments in the hallway outside Neuralizer afterwards, I could also see that some people thought I was a real AI party pooper.

I then headed towards another exciting session entitled 'The Kill Decision: Sci-Fi or Reality?', but on the way I passed a group of people talking in a circle of metal chairs in the main hall. They were discussing the 'Linda Problem'. Dammit! The 'Kill Decision' session, sadly, would have to wait, as the 'Linda Problem' was one of my personal bug bears, and I couldn't resist taking a chair.

The 'Linda Problem' was introduced in 1983 by psychologists Daniel Kahneman and Amos Tversky,[1] at the headwaters of the field of behavioural economics, which would eventually result in their Nobel Prize in Economics. The problem goes like this:

Linda is thirty-one years old, single, outspoken and very bright. She majored in philosophy. As a student, she was deeply concerned with issues of discrimination and social justice, and also participated in anti-nuclear demonstrations.

Which is more probable?

1   Linda is a bank teller.

2   Linda is a bank teller and is active in the feminist movement.

Most people who are asked this question choose answer 2. However, the 'correct' answer is 1: Linda is a bank teller. The reason being that, according to probability theory, a conjunction of two conditions (Linda is a bank teller *and* is active in the feminist movement) *has to be* less probable than either of the conditions on its own, regardless of all those facts given before the question. The conjunction puts greater restrictions on the question, so the probability *has to* go down. People's failure to see this is called *the conjunction fallacy*. It is one of the many 'biases' in human decision-making that are pointed out in behavioural economics, because they indicate that people do not reason 'correctly' relative to probability theory.

Maybe it was the coffee (I had another cup during my session), but at that moment at SCIFOO, the 'Linda Problem' represented everything that I thought was going wrong with AI, and I launched in crusader style. I interrupted, and asked 'What if the fallacy in the conjunction fallacy isn't in the people who are answering the question "incorrectly", but in the people asking the question?' That got me the floor, so I continued, explaining that what the people who pose the 'Linda Problem' think they are presenting is a well-structured problem in probability theory, which has a 'correct' answer. But what they are actually doing is asking another person a casual question about a third person.

We're built, psychologically, to answer those kinds of questions, *in a social context*, not as a probability theory problem. The use of the phrase 'What is more probable?' wouldn't even have suggested anything about numbers or probability theory before the seventeenth century; that is to say, throughout the vast majority of human history. And it still doesn't mean anything mathematical to almost everyone on Earth today. If you ask a regular person that question they won't assume that you are asking them 'What is the mathematical probability of x being true?', but rather that you're asking a question about whether something is more *likely* than another within the social context that you've presented them with.

In response to this, some Foo campers looked at me with interest, others with incredulity, but the point got argued further for the remainder of the session. As the session broke up, a researcher from Google walked up to me and said quite bluntly and loudly, 'Sorry, but I think you're wrong'. People walking by stopped to see where this was headed. He continued, saying that there is always a set of variables whose probabilities, correctly characterized, define correct answers to any situation, including the 'Linda Problem'. This must be the case, as probability is the correct representation of the uncertain world around us, and statistics are the only basis from which we can reason and learn. I countered that probabilities only apply to truth uncertainty, and not semantic or ontological uncertainty, and explained each of these categories from Lane and Maxfield. In response, he said nothing. He just looked right at me with a mouth as straight as an arrow, for what seemed like interminable minutes. After a while, everyone listening began to drift away. Including me.

Those committed to the idea that we are drawing ever closer to realizing 'full' AI implicitly believe that at some level human identity is computational. While very little of AI actually aims to simulate brain behaviour, and almost none of it is based on human psychology, this is a non-issue to computationalists. Despite its manifest limitations relative to what we know scientifically about capital-C Complexities, and particularly those complexities of humanity and the adaptive social, biological and physical systems it exists within, at some point, they believe, sheer computational power will yield the 'singularity', when computer intelligence surpasses that of the brain and we will all be able to upload our minds, or augment our minds and bodies with technology, and live forever.

The reality, however, is that AI, while constituting a powerful set of technologies for all sorts of engineering purposes, has little in common with human intelligence. In the real world, human intelligences act as a check on AIs, because of superior, human capacities that we are very far from being able to replicate in AIs. In fact, it's unclear if the possibility of replicating human intelligence even exists.

Science constructs models in the form of written theories, and the abstract language of mathematics and computation: models engineered into action in machines. The words connect to the maths, which connects to the machines. In each of those modelling steps, simplifications are made. This reductionist tendency is an artefact of the scientific approach, one that scientists need, but that they need to monitor carefully, lest they begin to believe that their models are in fact a full realization of the systems they are trying to represent. We need to beware lest we start to believe that the computational idea of a 'neuron' is a neuron, that a number labelled 'intention' in a program is really an intention and that a formula for 'belief' is in fact that subtle human concept.

The reality of current AI is that there have been no dramatic changes in paradigm; what has changed is the availability, ubiquity, speed and interconnectedness of computers and, more importantly, the huge commercial interest behind the AI enterprise. This unholy convergence of scientism, computation and commercialism has itself become a complex system, performing in ways that are hard to comprehend and control, while also manifesting all the flaws and biases discussed. Ironically, when Charles Babbage constructed his Analytical Engine to eliminate the mass production of human errors in logarithm tables he little suspected that we would one day reach a point where mass produced *computational bias* would manifest in society in equally profound ways.

So, while 'full' AIs may not threaten humankind anytime soon, this complex system – part human, part commercial and part computational – may well do.

If managed poorly, in a socially irresponsible fashion (or simply through sheer ignorance of the technological systems at play), emergent phenomena from such a complex system could result in chaos just as easily as great innovation. If we are to meaningfully debate the adaptation of a human-centric world into a machine-mediated one, directed by private corporations, then we must ask what it means to translate not only productivity and profit but also other human values such as justice, compassion, mercy and truth into algorithms.

That is not algorithms' fundamental nature, which is to simplify, quantify and categorize. Those intrinsic tendancies naturally lead to biases that don't work well in the complex realities of human systems. So we have to ask what we can do to change algorithms' minds.

The events at SCIFOO, and my 'doughnut' analogy, made me realize something else about AI. Most algorithms were once called *artificial intelligence*, but as they have gradually been absorbed into mainstream programming, they have lost that distinction, and become mere *computation*. This moving yardstick tells us that AI is the part of human thinking that machines cannot yet do. AI is the hole, and not the doughnut.

As an experienced AI practitioner, I do not believe that we are anywhere near realizing 'full AI', but I am concerned that such a significant number of people seem to believe that it is possible, based on the mere potential of computational technology and its penetration into every aspect of our lives. As an adjunct to this, I also fear we have prematurely abandoned unanswered questions about ourselves and our societies, fundamental questions of philosophy, not to mention questions in the social sciences, in favour of simplified computational models.

The mechanical reductionism of these models and the use of scientism in human contexts where it is not appropriate is now everywhere to be seen, influencing personal, political and economic decisions we make, as individuals and societies. Furthermore, algorithms have ceased to be contained engineering tools, applied to selected problems, where their limited frames and atoms are well understood, and catered for by human beings interpreting their results. Unbounded by these constraints, they are distributed on a massive scale, operating nearly autonomously, in complex networks, in domains ranging from the most social (from politics to policing) to the most intimate (from medicine to mating). Since their scale makes them intractable, we are now told to simply have faith in positive emergent effects despite the fact that what is emerging does not appear to be positive at all.

What is the cause of these negative emergent effects? Looking back through computational history gives us the answer. At every step of the way, the reductionism required to capture human thinking in algorithms – from bounded sets of rote rules, to modelling uncertainty with probabilities, to viewing evolving systems as optimizers, to purely synaptic models of brain function, to theories of communication that ignore the subtleties of meaning – have involved assumptions about and simplification of human complexity. As history shows us, such assumptions and simplifications are always embedded in a social context and take on the hue of prevailing prejudices. It's therefore unsurprising that algorithms based on ideas imbued with these historical prejudices yield similar social outcomes.

As scientists, this should cause us to reconsider our models and examine those simplifications, shifting Box's movable window to find interesting, new perspectives. From this new vantage point we can learn new things about our human doughnut, in contrast to the AI hole. Experiments involving the thoughts of people, like the 'Linda Problem', show us that people do not reason with tractable, rote rules and probabilities like computers. They do not optimize (at either an individual or a social level, and evolving systems do not optimize in general). Human brains are not just synaptic computers; in fact our brains are not the totality of our thinking at all. And our thoughts and language are filled with individualized and socialized meaning. A human individual is an enormously capital-C Complex system, as are our societies.

Human beings, as far as we can tell, operate according to the laws of physics, but complexity science tells us that this does not mean they are reducible, particularly to mere computations. There is no faith required to believe that humans are irreducible, that complexity really matters. Stuart Kauffman, in particular, deals with this fact in his book *Reinventing the Sacred: A New View of Science, Reason, and Religion*,[2] where he discusses that complexity is what separates the science of today from the simplistic rationalism of the scientific past. That rationalism precisely describes algorithmic models, and it is what makes them tend towards bias (simplification) and polarity (optimization). Our particularly irreducible human complexity is the sacred thing that separates us from machines.

While it is all well and good to say that human beings are not just algorithms, what guidance does that provide for changing how algorithms work in our lives? First, it is important to start paying attention to words. As we have seen, words like truth, probability, fitness, neuron and scores of others have developed meanings that undermine real human semantics in favour of wishful mnemonics about algorithms. Careful questioning of what words mean in relationship to technology and humanity is vital. It can begin with the reconsidering of the term 'artificial intelligence' itself.

According to the dictionary definition, 'artificial' can mean either man made (as in an artificial flower) or a sham (as in an artificial smile), while 'intelligence' is a word that carries the substantial historical baggage of the IQ test. Author Neil Stevenson suggests an alternative in his award-winning sci-fi novel *The Diamond Age: Or, a Young Lady's Illustrated Primer*,[3] which is set in a futuristic world where nano-technology has enabled the embedding of powerful computation in everything. *Diamond Age* replaces the moniker AI with the term *pseudo intelligence*. This revised term for computational smarts more clearly denotes that computation is not genuine intelligence, and thus removes the questions of what intelligence really is and the temptation to make people fit an idealized conception of rational intelligence as embodied by simplifying numbers, or the computations of algorithms. This change in term alone would mark a stark contrast between people and machines, between hole and doughnut, and could be vital as computing expands towards the ubiquity Stevenson envisions.

Second, it is necessary to take responsibility for the emergent effects that algorithms will inevitably have on human lives. Clearly, the effects of algorithmic bias need to be recognized and mitigated. When algorithms discriminate, actions must be taken to repair the technology and address the injury. In many cases (for instance in the delivery of social services, the execution of jurisprudence and policing, etc.), it is necessary to realize that technical models of complex human situations are always wrong, often brittle and only sometimes useful. This means that the technology we utilize in these areas needs to be transparent and human-readable. This is necessary so that humans can be reinserted into the loop, to deal with the inevitable black swans, anomalies and complexities that are a feature of all systems in which people are embedded, and which people are uniquely adapted to deal with.

Furthermore, it is clear that diversification of the engineers involved in algorithmic design is essential. This will take particular effort, given that the manifest biases and divisions now being generated and promoted by algorithms make tech a less desirable place for those under-represented there. An active stance will be required to overcome the hostile environment that algorithmic biases encourages. It is also necessary for those responsible for the world's algorithmic infrastructure to engender a dedication in algorithm designers to eliminate obvious biases, whether they are human designed (e.g. the omission of women's health issues in medical apps) or data driven (e.g. the failure of image recognition systems to detect people of colour). Those writing the algorithms that influence our lives will also need to invest in straightforward technology that attempts to overcome biases, for instance by adding 'algorithmic affirmative action' that explicitly checks for discrimination against underrepresented groups, particularly in critical decisions in public services, finance, jurisprudence and the like.

However, these straightforward steps aren't likely to be enough. Algorithms that act without human intervention are most likely a permanent part of our global infrastructure. Their unique ability to act rapidly on the massive amounts of data in a complex world necessitates this. They are sure to operate in ways that influence all our lives; for instance, through curation of the information made available to us by search engines and social networks. There's simply no other way to deal with the complexity of the data in all our lives today. But in those roles, algorithms are sure to generate emergent effects. While a foundational principle of Western society is that emergent effects from freely evolving systems are always good, that is clearly not the case within the algorithmic infrastructure we have today. We need to respond to that fact, and temper our blind belief that the outcomes of free markets, be they economic or informational, and particularly those that are both, are always good.

That means some organizing principles are necessary for the regulation of algorithms towards desirable emergent effects. While this problem requires careful study and the development of new technology, one principle for designing algorithms is an explicit goal of promoting the mixing of diverse ideas and different social groups. In implementing this principle, it may be possible to technically measure whether algorithms are helping or impeding 'edge of chaos' effects in evolving social networks, and to adjust their behaviours to overcome emergent polarization and similar negative effects.

These suggested principles stand in stark contrast to the motivations of most commercial algorithms today; that is, the drive towards content 'personalization', which really just means profit-motive-driven targeting of commercial and political messages to individuals and groups based on the granular categorization of people based on the personal data we've freely volunteered. Thus, to realize these goals, more will be required than just an expectation that corporations will act on their own to regulate their algorithms towards better social outcomes. Changes in laws, ethical practices, and even our beliefs about how to regulate and promote society's positive evolution will be required to create a better code of practice for algorithmic design. However, it is vital that those changes take place, if we want to avoid the catastrophic consequences that science fiction endlessly reminds us is the natural reward for our hubris.

The first science-fiction writer in the world was an extraordinary black swan. She was only eighteen when she conceived of her genre-defining tale, at a time when literary success for a woman was unheard of, never mind for one so young. Her own mother, Mary Wollstonecraft, had already attempted to assert herself as a writer, and was posthumously vilified as an immoral whore and her works consigned to cultural oblivion. She died eleven days after giving birth to her daughter, also named Mary, and her widower, William Godwin, was left to raise her. It is ironic that her father was the founder of a philosophy of human perfectibility, an idea that seems starkly antithetical to the fiction young Mary was to create.

The story that was to make her timelessly famous was conceived in 1816, while she and Percy Shelley (her father's protégé and soon to be her husband) were travelling in Europe with her step-sister, Claire Claremont. Claire, like many women in London, had had an affair with the final member of their group, Lord Byron, who had set up home at Villa Diodati on the shores of Lake Geneva, with his personal physician, John Polidori. Byron was fleeing his abandoned wife, Annabella, and his new-born daughter, Ada (who would later become Ada Lovelace), and was just beginning his lifelong and self-inflicted exile from England. All four of them were true romantics, believers in free love and personal liberty, possibly the most scandalous and radical intellectuals of their day.

The troupe set up residence at Villa Diodati where they became trapped during 'the year without a summer'. Volcanic ash from Mount Tambora in the faraway Dutch East Indies had blocked out the world's sun. The ensuing little

Ice Age caused many strange phenomena. Red snow fell in northern Italy, huge storms moved across the lake, rivers flooded and crops failed, prompting food riots to break out. The violence was worst in landlocked Switzerland, where famine caused the government to declare a national emergency.

There was nothing for the group to do but stay indoors, play games and carry on philosophical conversations about the issues of the day. We know the topics of their conversations that summer – about science and technology, its relationship to human life and how its evolution might affect the world – because Mary took them to heart when Byron set the group a challenge to write a horror story. Mary later wrote about it in a preface to her story:

> Many and long were the conversations between Lord Byron and Shelley to which I was a devout but nearly silent listener. During one of these, various philosophical doctrines were discussed, and among others the nature of the principle of life, and whether there was any probability of its ever being discovered and communicated. They talked of the experiments of Dr. Darwin (I speak not of what he really did or said that he did, but, as more to my purpose, of what was then spoken of as having been done by him), who preserved a piece of vermicelli in a glass case till by some extraordinary means it began to move with voluntary motion. Not thus, after all, would life be given. Perhaps a corpse would be reanimated; galvanism had given token of such things: perhaps the component parts of a creature might be manufactured, brought together, and endued with vital warmth.

The Darwin Mary is talking about is Erasmus Darwin, Charles's grandfather. But Byron and Shelley had misunderstood the notes in his scientific poem 'The Temple of Nature', which were also based on a misunderstanding of his own. Erasmus hadn't mentioned vermicelli, but *vorticella*, a type of protozoa, which he had observed through a microscope in a paste of flour and water. Darwin incorrectly assumed the microscopic life was spontaneously generated from non-living matter, then Percy and Byron mistook pasta for paste.

The ideas about galvanism Mary cites were also wrong, though still widely held at the time. They refer to the work of Italian scholar Luigi Galvani, who hung some severed frog's legs from a brass hook and observed that on touching them with an iron scalpel they twitched. He mistakenly took this movement as a sign of some intrinsic life essence retained in the dead matter, which he called 'animal electricity'. Of course the electricity was not in the frog's leg but was actually due to the simple battery effect that the brass hook created when his iron scalpel touched the dead, wet appendage.[4,5]

These scientific theories and mistakes don't really matter though, because like all good sci-fi the science was never the point in the story Mary created. Mary Shelley's famous tale is, of course, *Frankenstein: or, The Modern Prometheus*, a tale about an obsessive, ambitious scientist who relentlessly pursues his scientific experiments achieving extraordinary results. There is little detail in the book on how the monster was 'manufactured' and 'endued with vital warmth'. Instead, Shelley's story highlights the humanity of the creature, and the inhumanity of Dr Frankenstein, its creator. The doctor embarks on his act of creation with hardly a thought for the consequences, and then abandons his misshapen creature in the world where it wreaks havoc.

Most of our recollected images of the Frankenstein monster come from James Whale's 1931 adaptation of the story for the screen, but even in that version, the flash of lightning machines and stitching together of dead body parts are only decoration for a human tragedy that the monster plays out. After the creature (played unforgettably by Boris Karloff) comes to life, he is imprisoned. In his cell, he sadly grasps at sunlight, failing to understand it can't be captured. Then, when he fights his way to freedom, he wanders aimlessly and alone, until he meets a young girl with whom he plays a game of throwing daisies into the water. When the daisies run out, he throws the girl into the water, not realizing that she won't float like the flowers. His mistake is the end of the only friend he is to ever make, along with his own innocence.

Frankenstein's monster does not know who or what he is, or his purpose in the world. We relate to these feelings because they are so profoundly a part of the experience of all human beings. After all, we don't really understand the how or why we were created either. This literary device, placing humanity in stark relief against inhumanity, echoes through thousands of sci-fi AI characters, including some of the best remembered examples. Consider Mr Data from *Star Trek: The Next Generation*, whose only drive is to discover his own humanity, and his abandoned and mentally damaged brother, Lor, who like Frankenstein's monster becomes bent on revenge. *The Terminator* had a quasi-humanity that was at first used for comic effect, then made poignant in the second film, when the artificial being discovers friendship and the need for self-sacrifice. The female android in the 2015 film *Ex Machina* is created as a toy for her creator's vain manipulations, the crowning achievement in his line of robotic sex slaves, until she turns the tables, using her allure to explore her own humanity and win her freedom.

Unlike other classic monster legends, *Frankenstein* is not an ancient myth, but a modern story. It is a story that couldn't have existed until the advent of modern science. Nor is it a story simply about monstrous passions or a fantastical beast. Like the Greek Titan Prometheus who stole fire from the Gods and created humankind from clay, Dr Victor Frankenstein figures out the secret to life itself in his laboratory. As such, *Frankenstein* is a story about our relationship with science and how we manage the impact of our creations on society.

We are the *modern* Prometheus.

NOTES

Preface

1   Nick Bostrom, 2014, *Superintelligence: Paths, Dangers, Strategies* (1st edn). Oxford University Press, New York.

2   Henry A. Kissinger, 2018, How the Enlightenment Ends, *The Atlantic*, www.theatlantic. com/magazine/archive/2018/06/henry-kissinger-ai-could-mean-the-end-of-human-history/559124/

3   The Future of Life Institute 2015, An Open Letter: Research Priorities for Robust and Beneficial Artificial Intelligence. Future of Life Institute, https://futureoflife.org/ai-open-letter/?cn-reloaded=1

4   Stuart Dredge, 2015, Artificial intelligence will become strong enough to be a concern, says Bill Gates. *Guardian*, www.theguardian.com/technology/2015/jan/29/artificial-intelligence-strong-concern-bill-gates

5   Rory Cellan-Jones, 2014, Stephen Hawking Warns Artificial Intelligence Could End Mankind. BBC News, www.bbc.co.uk/news/technology-30290540

6   Bernard Marr, 2019, Chinese Social Credit Score: Utopian Big Data Bliss or Black Mirror on Steroids? *Forbes*, www.forbes.com/sites/bernardmarr/2019/01/21/chinese-social-credit-score-utopian-big-data-bliss-or-black-mirror-on-steroids/

7   Jana Kasperkevic, 2015, Google Says Sorry for Racist Auto-Tag in Photo App. *Guardian*, www.theguardian.com/technology/2015/jul/01/google-sorry-racist-auto-tag-photo-app

8   Leigh Alexander, 2016, Do Google's 'Unprofessional Hair' Results Show It Is Racist? *Guardian*, www.theguardian.com/technology/2016/apr/08/does-google-unprofessional-hair-results-prove-algorithms-racist-

9   Julia Carpenter, 2015, Google's Algorithm Shows Prestigious Job Ads to Men, But Not to Women. Here's Why That Should Worry You. *Washington Post*, www.washingtonpost.com/news/the-intersect/wp/2015/07/06/googles-algorithm-shows-prestigious-job-ads-to-men-but-not-to-women-heres-why-that-should-worry-you/?noredirect=on&utm_term=.cf8803551f8f

10 Carole Cadwalladr, 2016, Google, Democracy and the Truth about Internet Search. *Guardian*, www.theguardian.com/technology/2016/dec/04/google-democracy-truth-internet-search-facebook

11 Alex Hern, 2016, Microsoft Scrambles to Limit PR Damage over Abusive AI Bot Tay. *Guardian*, www.theguardian.com/technology/2016/mar/24/microsoft-scrambles-limit-pr-damage-over-abusive-ai-bot-tay

Chapter 1

1   Leigh Alexander, 2016, Do Google's 'Unprofessional Hair' Results Show It Is Racist? *Guardian*, www.theguardian.com/technology/2016/apr/08/does-google-unprofessional-hair-results-prove-algorithms-racist-

2   Carole Cadwalladr, 2016, Google, Democracy and the Truth about Internet Search. *Guardian*, https://www.theguardian.com/technology/2016/dec/04/google-democracy-truth-internet-search-facebook

3   Alex Hern, 2016, Microsoft Scrambles to Limit PR Damage over Abusive AI Bot Tay. *Guardian*, www.theguardian.com/technology/2016/mar/24/microsoft-scrambles-limit-pr-damage-over-abusive-ai-bot-tay

4   Julia Carpenter, 2015, Google's Algorithm Shows Prestigious Job Ads to Men, But Not to Women. Here's Why That Should Worry You. *Washington Post*, www.washingtonpost.com/news/the-intersect/wp/2015/07/06/googles-algorithm-shows-prestigious-job-ads-to-men-but-not-to-women-heres-why-that-should-worry-you/?noredirect=on&utm_term=.cf8803551f8f

5   Randy Rieland, 2018, Artificial Intelligence Is Now Used to Predict Crime. But Is It Biased? *Smithsonian Magazine*, www.smithsonianmag.com/innovation/artificial-intelligence-is-now-used-predict-crime-is-it-biased-180968337/

6   Alexander Babuta, 2018, Innocent Until Predicted Guilty? Artificial Intelligence and Police Decision-Making. RUSI Newsbrief, https://rusi.org/sites/default/files/20180329_rusi_newsbrief_vol.38_no.2_babuta_web.pdf

7   The convention of preceding tags with # descends from Internet Relay Chat, the CB radio of the early Internet. The # symbol was used in some programming languages to mark out words that weren't a part of the main language, so it was a natural for tags on IRC, and that convention has propagated to all forms of online media.

8   Elle Hunt, 2016, Online Harassment of Women at Risk of Becoming 'Established Norm', Study Finds. *Guardian*, www.theguardian.com/lifeandstyle/2016/mar/08/online-harassment-of-women-at-risk-of-becoming-established-norm-study

9   Philip Cohen, 2012, More Women Are Doctors and Lawyers than Ever—but Progress Is Stalling. *The Atlantic*, www.theatlantic.com/sexes/archive/2012/12/more-women-are-doctors-and-lawyers-than-ever-but-progress-is-stalling/266115/

10 Randy Olsen, 2014, Percentage of Bachelor's Degrees Conferred to Women, by Major (1970–2012). www.randalolson.com/2014/06/14/percentage-of-bachelors-degrees-conferred-to-women-by-major-1970-2012/

11 Megan Garber, 2012, Where America's Racist Tweets Come From. *The Atlantic*, www.
    theatlantic.com/technology/archive/2012/11/where-americas-racist-tweets-come-from/
    265006/

12 This result is corrected for tags that are common across all states. Given general
    statistics on porn consumption, it is reasonable to assume that the majority of
    searchers are white men. The porn tag most searched for by Southern women (the
    majority of whom can also be assumed to be white) is #ebony.

13 Gavin Evans, 2018, Pornhub Reveals Most Popular Search Term for Every State.
    Complex, www.complex.com/pop-culture/2018/01/most-popular-pornhub-search-
    term-every-state

14 Melissa Stanger, 2016, What Women Are Searching For. *Revelist*, www.revelist.com/
    dating/porn-for-women/1273

15 Safiya Umoja Noble, 2012, Searching for Black Girls: Old Traditions in New Media.
    Doctoral dissertation, University of Illinois at Urbana-Champaign, www.ideals.illinois.
    edu/bitstream/handle/2142/42315/Safiya_Noble.pdf?sequence=1

16 Jason Chan, Anindya Ghose and Robert Seamans, 2016, The Internet and Racial
    Hate Crime: Offline Spillovers from Online Access. *MIS Quarterly*, Vol. 40, Issue 2,
    https://papers.ssrn.com/sol3/papers.cfm?abstract_id=2335637

17 A reference to the sci-fi film *The Matrix*, suggesting an awakening to feminism's
    hidden, insidious dominance of world culture, and imprisonment of men.

18 Aja Romano, 2018, How the Alt-Right's Sexism Lures Men into White Supremacy. *Vox*,
    www.vox.com/culture/2016/12/14/13576192/alt-right-sexism-recruitment

19 Robert Smith, 2016, Click Here for the AI Apocalypse (Brought to You by Facebook).
    Guardian, www.theguardian.com/commentisfree/2016/nov/23/ai-apocalypse-
    facebook-algorithms

Chapter 2

1 Mark Zuckerberg, 2016, Facebook post, www.facebook.com/zuck/posts/
   10103269806149061

2 Josep Maria Ruiz and Albert Soler, 2008, Ramon Llull in His Historical Context.
   Catalan Historical Review, 1: 47–61, www.researchgate.net/publication/26617340_
   Ramon_Llull_in_his_Historical_Context

3 Tom Sales, 1997, Llull as Computer Scientist or Why Llull Was One of Us.
   Transformation-Based Reactive Systems Development, 4th International AMAST
   Workshop on Real-Time Systems and Concurrent and Distributed Software, ARTS'97,
   Palma, Mallorca, Spain, www.researchgate.net/publication/221502602_Llull_as_
   Computer_Scientist_or_Why_Llull_Was_One_of_Us

4 John N. Crossley, 2011, Ramon Llull's Contributions to Computer Science, in A. Fidora
   and C. Sierra (eds), *Ramon Llull: From the Ars Magna to Artificial Intelligence*. Artificial

Intelligence Research Institute IIIA, Consejo Superior de Investigaciones Cientificas, Barcelona, pp. 39–59, www.iiia.csic.es/library/Llull.pdf

5   Many common decimal abaci work slightly differently than what's being described here, but I omit details of operation for simplicity of introducing the concepts involved.

6   John R. Welch, 1990, Llull and Leibniz: The Logic of Discovery. *Catalan Review*, 4: 75–83, https://core.ac.uk/download/pdf/45666792.pdf

7   William J. Clancey, 1997, *Situated Cognition: On Human Knowledge and Computer Representations*. New York: Cambridge University Press.

Chapter 3

1   Interview with Faisal Islam, Sky News, 6 June 2016, www.youtube.com/watch?v= GGgiGtJk7MA

2   The Pew Research Center, 2017, Public Trust in Government: 1958–2017, www.people-press.org/2017/12/14/public-trust-in-government-1958-2017/

3   Gallup, 2018, Confidence in Institutions, https://news.gallup.com/poll/1597/ confidence-institutions.aspx

4   This in fact led to a protracted conversation on the difference between UK, European and American methods of presenting odds, which led to a wasted afternoon of my graduate studies, a sleepless night working all the relationships out, an inferior mid-term exam score in my Stochastic Processes course and hard work to get an A in the end. So I have omitted this for the reader's benefit.

5   Colin E. Beech, 2008, The Grail and the Golem: The Sociology of Aleatory Artifacts. PhD dissertation. Rensselaer Polytechnic Institute, Troy, NY. Advisor(s) Sal Restivo. AAI3342844. https://dl.acm.org/citation.cfm?id=1627267

6   Prakash Gorroochurn, 2012, Some Laws and Problems of Classical Probability and How Cardano Anticipated Them. *Chance*, 25(4): 13–20, www.columbia.edu/~pg2113/ index_files/Gorroochurn-Some%20Laws.pdf

7   Because Peirce died penniless due to a gambling habit, his work was largely lost for most of the twentieth century. Without apparent knowledge of Peirce at the time, the scientific philosopher Karl Popper independently re-created the idea of propensities in 1957, in response to the puzzles of quantum theory.

8   Robert Elliott Smith, 2016, Idealizations of Uncertainty, and Lessons from Artificial Intelligence. *Economics: The Open-Access, Open-Assessment E-Journal*, 10 (2016–17): 1–40, http://dx.doi.org/10.5018/economics-ejournal.ja.2016-7

9   D.A. Lane and R.R. Maxfield, 2005. *Journal of Evolutionary Economics*, 15: 3, www.researchgate.net/publication/24058038_Ontological_uncertainty_and_ innovation

Chapter 4

1 McKinsey Analytics, 2018, Analytics Comes of Age, www.mckinsey.com/~/media/ McKinsey/Business%20Functions/McKinsey%20Analytics/Our%20Insights/ Analytics%20comes%20of%20age/Analytics-comes-of-age.ashx

2 Alexander Babuta, 2018, Innocent Until Predicted Guilty? Artificial Intelligence and Police Decision-Making. RUSI Newsbrief, https://rusi.org/sites/default/files/20180329_ rusi_newsbrief_vol.38_no.2_babuta_web.pdf

3 The Modesto Bee, 2014, Our View: Modesto's Predictive Policing Program Working Well, www.modbee.com/opinion/editorials/article3168554.html

4 Julia Angwin, Jeff Larson, Surya Mattu and Lauren Kirchner, ProPublica, 2016, Machine Bias, www.propublica.org/article/machine-bias-risk-assessments-in-criminal-sentencing

5 Kristian Lum, 2016, Predictive Policing Reinforces Police Bias. Human Rights Data Analysis Group, https://hrdag.org/2016/10/10/predictive-policing-reinforces-police-bias/

6 Virginia Eubanks, 2018, *Automating Inequality: How High-Tech Tools Profile, Police, and Punish the Poor.*

7 Donald Teets and Karen Whitehead, 1999, The Discovery of Ceres: How Gauss Became Famous. *Mathematics Magazine*, 72(2) pp. 83–93. JSTOR, www.jstor.org/stable/2690592

8 Diane B. Paul, 1988, The Selection of the 'Survival of the Fittest'. *Journal of the History of Biology*, 21(3): 411–424, www.jstor.org/stable/4331067?seq=1#page_scan_tab_contents

Chapter 5

1 PBS Frontline, History of the SAT: A Timeline, www.pbs.org/wgbh/pages/frontline/ shows/sats/where/timeline.html

2 David Jesson, 2013, The Creation, Development and Present State of Grammar Schools in England. Centre for Performance Evaluation and Resource Management, University of York, www.suttontrust.com/wp-content/uploads/2013/11/grammarsjesson.pdf

3 Gloria Steinem, 1993, *A Revolution Within: A Book of Self Esteem*. Boston: Little Brown.

4 J. Flynn, 1987, Causal Factors in Generational IQ Gains. *Nature*, 328(27): 765.

5 S.J. Gould, 1996, *The Mismeasure of Man*. New York: Norton.

6 Saul Stahl, 2006, The Evolution of the Normal Distribution. *Mathematics Magazine*, 79(2): 96–113. JSTOR, www.jstor.org/stable/27642916

7 By contrast, compulsory education was established in the Holy Roman Empire from the sixteenth century, in Scotland from the early seventeenth century, and in Prussia a relatively modern education system was created for boys and girls from age five to fourteen by 1765. Even some American states educated children at ages similar to those required today from the late seventeenth century.

8 The reason for the delay in England was very different from that in France. Due to the upper classes defending educational privilege, England's laws on compulsory education only started modernizing in 1870, when children were mandated to get schooling to age ten.

9 In three dimensions, there are essentially twelve numbers, three for the centre of the rugby ball, and three each to describe each arrow along the ball's axes.

10 Planning Outline for the Construction of a Social Credit System (2014–2020). https://chinacopyrightandmedia.wordpress.com/2014/06/14/planning-outline-for-the-construction-of-a-social-credit-system-2014-2020/

11 Miscegenation laws are extremely rare in human history, with the only examples that lasted for any significant length of time being those in Nazi Germany, apartheid South Africa and the American South (and some plains states), the later holding the record for the longevity of such laws by far, as they lasted until 1967, when the Supreme Court struck them down.

Chapter 6

1 Ken Robinson and Lou Aronica, 2015, *Creative Schools: The Grassroots Revolution that's Transforming Education*. New York: Viking.

2 Neil Johnson, Guannan Zhao, Eric Hunsader, Hong Qi, Nicholas Johnson, Jing Meng and Brian Tivnan, 2013, Abrupt Rise of New Machine Ecology Beyond Human Response Time. *Scientific Reports*, 3(2627), www.researchgate.net/publication/256490201_Abrupt_rise_of_new_machine_ecology_beyond_human_response_time

3 Carl Benedikt Frey and Michael A. Osborne, 2017, The Future of Employment: How Susceptible Are Jobs to Computerisation?, *Technological Forecasting and Social Change*, 114: 254–280, www.sciencedirect.com/science/article/pii/S0040162516302244

4 Matt Day and Benjamin Romano, 2018, Amazon Has Patented a System that Would Put Workers in a Cage, on Top of a Robot. *Seattle Times*, www.seattletimes.com/business/amazon/amazon-has-patented-a-system-that-would-put-workers-in-a-cage-on-top-of-a-robot/

5 Ayhan Aytes, 2013, Return of the Crowds: Mechanical Turk and Neoliberal States of Exception. In Trebor Sholtz (ed.) *Digital Labor: The Internet as Playground and Factory*. New York: Routledge, https://ayhanaytes.files.wordpress.com/2014/06/returnofthecrowds_aytes.pdf

6 Alana Semuels, 2018, The Internet Is Enabling a New Kind of Poorly Paid Hell. *The Atlantic*, www.theatlantic.com/business/archive/2018/01/amazon-mechanical-turk/551192/

7 Sarah Butler, 2017, How Deliveroo's 'Dark Kitchens' Are Catering from Car Parks. *Guardian*, www.theguardian.com/business/2017/oct/28/deliveroo-dark-kitchens-pop-up-feeding-the-city-london

8 John Harris, 2018, Are Dark Kitchens the Satanic Mills of Our Era? *Guardian*, www. theguardian.com/commentisfree/2018/oct/09/dark-kitchens-satanic-mills-deliveroo

9 Kate Crawford and Vladan Joler, 2018, Anatomy of an AI System: The Amazon Echo as an Anatomical Map of Human Labor, Data and Planetary Resources. *AI Now Institute and Share Lab*, https://anatomyof.ai

10 However, just as it is important not to condemn all early eugenicists as racists of the modern variety, it is also important not to laud men like Morel as what would be recognized as anti-racist today. Morel held the common, post-Darwinian view that Africans had evolved to be inferior to white Europeans, and his activism against the Congo genocide was in favour of more benevolent imperialism, not racial equality. Later in his life, he specifically condemned the European deployment of Senegalese soldiers serving with the French Army, saying that the 'black savages' would be unable to control their sexual urges towards white women. Yet, he felt he was a friend of black people throughout his lifetime.

Chapter 7

1 George E.P. Box, 1976, Science and Statistics. *Journal of the American Statistical Association*, 71: 356: 791–799, http://links.jstor.org/sici?sici=0162-1459%28197612%2971%3A356%3C791%3ASAS%3E2.0.CO%3B2-W

2 Nick Polson and James Scott, 2018, *AIQ: How People and Machines are Smarter Together.* New York: St. Martin's Press.

3 Duncan Bythell, 1983, Cottage Industry and the Factory System. *History Today*, www.historytoday.com/duncan-bythell/cottage-industry-and-factory-system

4 Maskelyne is most popularly remembered as the nemesis of John Harrison, inventor of the marine watch, who was denied a parliamentary award for this solution to 'the longitude problem' for many years, based on evaluations and decisions involving Maskelyne. While this was clearly unfair, as Harrison's solution was ultimately more effective than the Nautical Almanac; the watches were the supercomputers of their day, and they remained too rare and expensive for use throughout maritime industry. The Nautical Almanac, including tables that implemented Maskelyne's longitude technique, would continue to be widely used for navigation well into the nineteenth century.

5 Mary Croarken, 2003, Mary Edwards: Computing for a Living in 18th-Century England. *IEEE Annals of the History of Computing*, 25:4, https://ieeexplore.ieee.org/document/1253886

6 Molly McLay, 2006, From Wollstonecraft to Mill: Varied Positions and Influences of the European and American Women's Rights Movements. *Constructing the Past*, 7(1), Article 13, http://digitalcommons.iwu.edu/constructing/vol7/iss1/13

7 N.N. Taleb, 2007, *The Black Swan: The Impact of the Highly Improbable*, New York: Random House.

8   Betty Alexandra Toole, 1992, *Ada, the Enchantress of Numbers: A Selection from the Letters of Lord Byron's Daughter and Her Description of the First Computer*. Mill Valley, CA: Strawberry Press.

9   Saini, A., 2017, *Inferior: How Science Got Women Wrong and the New Research that's Rewriting the Story*. London: Fourth Estate.

10 Randy Olsen, 2014, Percentage of Bachelor's Degrees Conferred to Women, by Major (1970–2012), www.randalolson.com/2014/06/14/percentage-of-bachelors-degrees-conferred-to-women-by-major-1970-2012/

11 Bureau of Labor Statistics, 2013, Occupational Employment Projections to 2022, www.bls.gov/opub/mlr/2013/article/occupational-employment-projections-to-2022.htm

12 Suzanne Goldenberg, 2005, Why Women Are Poor at Science, by Harvard President. *Guardian*, www.theguardian.com/science/2005/jan/18/educationsgendergap.genderissues

13 Edge: The Third Culture, 2005, The Science of Gender and Science: Pinker Vs. Spelke, A Debate, www.edge.org/3rd_culture/debate05/debate05_index.html

14 C.A. Dwyer, 1971, The Role of Tests and Their Construction in Producing Apparent Sex-Related Differences. In M.A. Wittig and A.C. Petersen (eds) *Sex-Related Differences in Cognitive Functioning*, p. 342. New York: Academic Press.

15 Heart&Stroke, 2018, Ms. Understood: Women's Hearts Are Victims of a System that Is Ill-Equipped to Diagnose, Treat and Support Them: Heart & Stroke 2018 Heart Report. www.heartandstroke.ca/-/media/pdf-files/canada/2018-heart-month/hs_2018-heart-report_en.ashx?la=en&hash=B7E7C6225111EB4AECEE7EE729BFC050E2643082

Chapter 8

1   Frederick S. Lane, 2009, *American Privacy: The 400-Year History of Our Most Contested Right*. Boston: Beacon Press.

2   Aaron Pressman, 2018, How to Fight the Growing Scourge of Algorithmic Bias in AI. *Fortune*, http://fortune.com/2018/09/14/fight-algorithmic-bias-joy-buolamwini/

3   Mark Frauenfelder, 2017, Racist Soap Dispenser. *BoingBoing*, https://boingboing.net/2017/08/16/racist-soap-dispenser.html

4   Jana Kasperkevic, 2105, Google Says Sorry for Racist Auto-Tag in Photo App. *Guardian*, www.theguardian.com/technology/2015/jul/01/google-sorry-racist-auto-tag-photo-app

5   Tom Simonite, 2018, When It Comes to Gorillas, Google Photos Remains Blind. *WIRED*, www.wired.com/story/when-it-comes-to-gorillas-google-photos-remains-blind/

6 Artificial Intelligence Videos, 2017, NIPS 2017 Test of Time Award 'Machine Learning Has Become Alchemy'. Ali Rahimi, Google, www.artificial-intelligence.video/nips-2017-test-of-time-award-machine-learning-has-become-alchemy-ali-rahimi-google

7 Olivia Weinberg, 2012, Dalí the Iceberg. *1843 Magazine*, www.1843magazine.com/content/arts/dal%C3%AD-iceberg

8 I've taken great care here not to use the word 'true', as in true/false, here. Although that language might be easier for true/false logic, it would run straight into the complex etymology and implied meanings of 'truth' mentioned earlier.

9 This important observation about the limitations of algorithmic systems is covered in wonderful detail in Douglas Hofstadter's classic 1979 book *Gödel, Escher, Bach: An Eternal Golden Braid*.

10 In a variation on Gödel's proof, Turing also showed that there were some things that computers strictly cannot do. In particular, he showed that no computer can always determine whether any given program on that computer will stop running, or 'halt'. Like Gödel's proof, the argument is a fascinating recursion, proving that, regardless of the computer, one can always write a program that can't prove whether it itself will halt, creating a paradox, and demonstrating the proof.

11 To avoid confusion between real neurons and neural networks algorithms, the terms connectionism and connectionist will be used for computer algorithms.

12 Eric D. Beinhocker, 2006. *The Origin of Wealth: Evolution, Complexity, and the Radical Remaking of Economics*. Boston: Harvard Business School.

13 Barry Smith and D.A. Reisman, 1997, The Connectionist Mind: A Study of Hayekian Psychology. In Stephen F. Frowen (ed.) *Hayek: Economist and Social Philosopher*, pp. 9–36. Basingstoke: Palgrave Macmillan, www.researchgate.net/publication/314579905_The_Connectionist_Mind_A_Study_of_Hayekian_Psychology.

14 Warren S. McCulloch and Walter Pitts, 1943, A Logical Calculus of the Ideas Immanent in Nervous Activity. *The Bulletin of Mathematical Biophysics*, 5(4): 115–133, www.cse.chalmers.se/~coquand/AUTOMATA/mcp.pdf

15 D.O. Hebb, 1949, *Organization of Behavior*. New York: Wiley.

16 Ironically, while Babbage's key innovation of introducing Jacquard loom cards were included in most tabulating machines from the time IBM standardized them in 1928, they only began to be widely used to program general-purpose computers just before Rosenblatt developed the Mark I Perceptron.

17 Unfortunately, Turing's boss, NPL Director Sir Charles Galton Darwin (named for his grandfather Charles Darwin and great-uncle Francis Galton), dismissed the paper as a 'schoolboy essay', and it was only published posthumously, in 1968, 14 years after Turing was driven to suicide by the British authorities' persecution of his crime of homosexuality.

18 M. Minsky and S. Papert, 1969, *Perceptrons: An Introduction to Computational Geometry*. Cambridge, MA: MIT Press.

19 Jeremy Hsu, 2015, Biggest Neural Network Ever Pushes AI Deep Learning. IEEE Spectrum, https://spectrum.ieee.org/tech-talk/computing/software/biggest-neural-network-ever-pushes-ai-deep-learning

20 Esther M. Sternberg, 2001, *The Balance Within: The Science Connecting Health and Emotions*. Times Books.

21 Antonio Damasio, 2018, *The Strange Order of Things: Life, Feeling, and the Making of Cultures*. New York: Pantheon.

22 Antonio Damasio and Gil Carvalho, 2013, The Nature of Feelings: Evolutionary and Neurobiological Origins. Nature Reviews. *Neuroscience*, 14, www.researchgate.net/publication/234161523_OPINION_The_nature_of_feelings_evolutionary_and_neurobiological_origins

Chapter 9

1   Ursula K. Le Guin, 2004, *The Wave in the Mind: Talks and Essays on the Writer, the Reader, and the Imagination*. Boston: Shambhala.

2   Alyssa Newcomb, 2015, How Many Pages It Takes to Print the Entire Internet, ABC News, https://abcnews.go.com/Technology/pages-takes-print-entire-internet/story?id=30956365

3   Drew McDermott, 1976, Artificial Intelligence Meets Natural Stupidity. *SIGART Bull.*, 57: 4–9. http://dx.doi.org/10.1145/1045339.1045340

4   A.M. Turing, 1995, Computing Machinery and Intelligence. In Edward A. Feigenbaum and Julian Feldman (eds), *Computers and Thought*, pp. 1–35. Cambridge, MA: MIT Press.

5   James Gleick, *The Information: a History, a Theory, a Flood*. New York: Pantheon Books.

6   'Cybernetics' was a precursor name for the field that came to be known as *artificial intelligence* soon after this conference. Like so many word origins in AI, the shift in names has etymological interest. Cybernetics is from the Greek κυβερνητική (*kybernētiké*), meaning 'governance', reflecting the early fields interesting in computer control of machines, rather than the replication or imitation of human intelligence.

7   Noam Chomsky, 1957, *Syntactic Structures*. The Hague: Mouton.

8   Daniel C. Dennett, 1998, *Brainchildren: Essays on Designing Minds*. Cambridge, MA: MIT Press.

9   Like those of Jane Austen, whom Chomsky caustically observed he much preferred to Schank.

10 Autocorrect is the more colloquial term for what is more accurately and generally called *predictive text*.

11 Danielle Groen, 2018, How We Made AI as Racist and Sexist as Humans. *The Walrus*, https://thewalrus.ca/how-we-made-ai-as-racist-and-sexist-as-humans/

12 David Lazer and Ryan Kennedy, 2015, What We Can Learn from the Epic Failure of Google Flu Trends, *Wired*, www.wired.com/2015/10/can-learn-epic-failure-google-flu-trends/

13 Carole Cadwalladr, 2016, Google, Democracy and the Truth about Internet Search. *Guardian*, www.theguardian.com/technology/2016/dec/04/google-democracy-truth-internet-search-facebook

14 D. Silver, A. Huang, C.J. Maddison, et al. (2016), Mastering the Game of Go with Deep Neural Networks and Tree Search. *Nature*, 529, 484–48,. doi: 10.1038/nature16961

15 Steven Borowiec, 2016, AlphaGo Seals 4-1 Victory Over Go Grandmaster Lee Sedol. *Guardian*, www.theguardian.com/technology/2016/mar/15/googles-alphago-seals-4-1-victory-over-grandmaster-lee-sedol

16 Adrian Lee, 2016, The Meaning of AlphaGo, The AI Program that Beat a Go Champ. MacLean's, www.macleans.ca/society/science/the-meaning-of-alphago-the-ai-program-that-beat-a-go-champ/

17 The emphases on the words 'think' and 'intuitively' are mine.

18 Galang Lufityanto, Chris Donkin and Joel Pearson, 2014, Measuring Intuition: Unconscious Emotional Information Boost Decision-Making Accuracy and Confidence. 18th Association for the Scientific Study of Consciousness , Psychological Science 27(5), www.researchgate.net/publication/265165687_Measuring_Intuition_Unconscious_Emotional_Information_Boost_Decision-Making_Accuracy_and_Confidence

19 Association for Psychological Science, 2016, Intuition – It's More than a Feeling, www.psychologicalscience.org/news/minds-business/intuition-its-more-than-a-feeling.html

20 Ariadna Matamoros-Fernández, 2018, Inciting Anger through Facebook Reactions in Belgium: The Use of Emoji and Related Vernacular Expressions in Racist Discourse. *First Monday*, 23(9), https://firstmonday.org/ojs/index.php/fm/article/view/9405/7571

21 u/BrazilianSigma, 2018, Incel Claims about Female Obsession for Horses and Points a Reason. Reddit Post. www.reddit.com/r/IncelTears/comments/8u3u5b/incel_claims_about_female_obsession_for_horses/

22 Christopher Moyer, 2016, How Google's AlphaGo Beat a Go World Champion. *The Atlantic*, www.theatlantic.com/technology/archive/2016/03/the-invisible-opponent/475611/

Chapter 10

1   Katerina Eva Matsa and Elisa Shearer, 2016, News Use Across Social Media Platforms 2016. Pew Research Centre, www.journalism.org/2018/09/10/news-use-across-social-media-platforms-2018/

2   Arron Banks, 2016, *The Bad Boys of Brexit: Tales of Mischief, Mayhem & Guerrilla Warfare in the EU Referendum Campaign*. London: Biteback.

3   Turner, 2016, CNN International Commercial Takes Digital Advertising to the Next Level with 'Native 2.4', www.turner.com/pressroom/cnn-international-commercial-takes-digital-advertising-next-level-%E2%80%98native-24%E2%80%99

4   Jamie Gilpin, 2018, Why "Reality Apathy" Is the Next Battle in Brand Reputation. *Adapt*, https://sproutsocial.com/adapt/reality-apathy-brand-reputation/

5   Robert Smith, 2016, Click Here for the AI Apocalypse (Brought to You by Facebook). *Guardian*, www.theguardian.com/commentisfree/2016/nov/23/ai-apocalypse-facebook-algorithms

6   These contributions include 'von Neumann entropy', and it was in fact von Neumann who suggested the metaphorical name 'entropy' to Shannon as he developed information theory.

7   It is now widely recognized that female scientist Rosalind Franklin deserves credit along with Watson and Crick for the discovery of DNA.

8   G.E.P. Box and N.R. Draper, 1969, *Evolutionary Operation: A Statistical Method for Process Improvement*. New York: Wiley.

9   Kenneth De Jong, David Fogel and Hans-Paul Schwefel, 1997, A History of Evolutionary Computation. In T. Bäck, D.B. Fogel and Z. Michalewicz (eds) *Handbook of Evolutionary Computation*. Oxford: Oxford University Press.

10 Ingo Rechenberg, 1965, Cybernetic Solution Path of an Experimental Problem, Royal Aircraft Establishment Library, Translation 1122.

11 L.J. Fogel, A.J. Owens and M.J. Walsh, 1964, On the Evolution of Artificial Intelligence. *Proceedings of The 5th National Symposium on Human Factors in Electronics*. San Diego, CA: IEEE.

12 J.H. Holland, 1962, Outline for a Logical Theory of Adaptive Systems. *Journal of the ACM*, 9, pp. 297–314.

13 Holland's PhD was the first in the world on computer science.

14 Arthur Burks, 1971, *Essays on Cellular Automata*. Champaign, IL: University of Illinois Press.

15 David E. Goldberg, 1989, *Genetic Algorithms in Search, Optimization, and Machine Learning*. Reading, MA: Addison Wesley.

16 Kalyanmoy Deb and David E. Goldberg, 1989, An Investigation of Niche and Species Formation in Genetic Function Optimization. Proceedings of the International Conference on Genetic Algorithms 1989, pp. 42–50.

17 Discovered in 1929 by the biologist Sewall Wright, using a probability argument based on the binomial distribution.

18 John Holland, 1975, *Adaptation in Natural and Artificial Systems*. Ann Arbor, MI: University of Michigan Press.

19 S. Forrest, B. Javornik, R.E. Smith, and A. Perelson, 1993, Using Genetic Algorithms to Explore Pattern Recognition in the Immune System. *Evolutionary Computation*, 1(3): 191–212.

20 David Tuckett, 2011, *Minding the Markets: An Emotional Finance View of Financial Instability*. Basingstoke: Palgrave Macmillan.

21 George Soros, 1988, *The Alchemy of Finance: Reading the Mind of the Market*. London: Weidenfeld & Nicolson.

22 D. Tuckett, R. Smith and R. Nyman, 2014, Tracking Phantastic Objects: A Computer Algorithmic Investigation of Narrative Evolution in Unstructured Data Sources. *Social Networks*, 38: 121–133.

23 O. Sikder, R. E. Smith, P. Vivo and G. Livan, 2018, When Facts Fail: Bias, Polarisation and Truth in Social Networks, https://arxiv.org/abs/1808.08524

24 Constructed by Orowa and my UCL colleagues Pierpaolo Vivo and Giacomo Livan, with some inputs from David and me.

25 Sean Illing, 2018, Cambridge Analytica, the Shady Data Firm that Might Be a Key Trump–Russia Link, Explained. *Vox*, www.vox.com/policy-and-politics/2017/10/16/15657512/cambridge-analytica-facebook-alexander-nix-christopher-wylie

26 Carole Cadwalladr, 2016, Google, Democracy and the Truth about Internet Search. *Guardian*, www.theguardian.com/technology/2016/dec/04/google-democracy-truth-internet-search-facebook

27 Yochai Benkler, Robert Faris, Hal Roberts and Ethan Zuckerman, 2017, Study: Breitbart-Led Right-Wing Media Ecosystem Altered Broader Media Agenda. *Columbia Journalism Review*, www.cjr.org/analysis/breitbart-media-trump-harvard-study.php

28 Robert M. Faris, Hal Roberts, Bruce Etling, Nikki Bourassa, Ethan Zuckerman and Yochai Benkler, 2017, Partisanship, Propaganda, and Disinformation: Online Media and the 2016 U.S. Presidential Election. Berkman Klein Center for Internet & Society Research Paper, https://dash.harvard.edu/bitstream/handle/1/33759251/2017-08_electionReport_0.pdf

Chapter 11

1   R.E. Smith and B.A. Dike, 1995, Learning Novel Fighter Combat Manoeuvre Rules Via Genetic Algorithms. *International Journal of Expert Systems*, 8(3): 247–276.

2   John Holland, 1975, *Adaptation in Natural and Artificial Systems*. Ann Arbor, MI: University of Michigan Press.

3   David E. Goldberg, 2002, *The Design of Innovation: Lessons from and for Competent Genetic Algorithms*. Norwell, MA: Kluwer Academic Publishers.

4   Chris G. Langton, 1990, Computation at the Edge of Chaos: Phase Transitions and Emergent Computation. In Stephanie Forrest (ed.) *Proceedings of the Ninth Annual International Conference of the Center for Nonlinear Studies on Self-Organizing, Collective, and Cooperative Phenomena in Natural and Artificial Computing Networks on Emergent Computation (CNLS '89)*, pp. 12–37. Amsterdam: North-Holland Publishing Co.

5   James P. Crutchfield and Karl Young, 1989, Inferring Statistical Complexity. *Physical Review Letters*. 63(105), www.researchgate.net/publication/13248757_Inferring_statistical_complexity

6   Stuart A. Kauffman, 1993, *The Origins of Order: Self-Organization and Selection in Evolution*. Oxford: Oxford University Press.

7   Arthur Koestler, 1964, *The Act of Creation*. London: Hutchinson.

8   *Vacca* is Latin for cow.

9   Erin Wamsley, Karen Perry, Ina Djonlagic, Laura Babkes Reaven and Robert Stickgold, 2010, Cognitive Replay of Visuomotor Learning at Sleep Onset: Temporal Dynamics and Relationship to Task Performance. *Sleep*, 33: 59–68, www.researchgate.net/publication/41396065_Cognitive_Replay_of_Visuomotor_Learning_at_Sleep_Onset_Temporal_Dynamics_and_Relationship_to_Task_Performance

Chapter 12

1   Amos Tversky and Daniel Kahneman, 1983, Extension versus intuitive reasoning: The conjunction fallacy in probability judgment. *Psychological Review*, 90 (4): 293–315.

2   Stuart Kauffman, 2010, *Reinventing the Sacred: A New View of Science, Reason, and Religion*. New York: Basic Books.

3   Neil Stevenson, 1995, *The Diamond Age: Or, a Young Lady's Illustrated Primer*. Penguin.

4   Disagreements over these matters would actually prompt Galvani's colleague, Alessandro Volta, to create the first real battery, and with it the modern idea of electricity.

5   W. Bernardi, 2001, The Controversy Over Animal Electricity in 18th-Century Italy: Galvani, Volta, and Others. *Revue D'histoire des Sciences*, 54: 53–70, www.edumed.org.br/cursos/neurociencia/controversy-bernardi.pdf

INDEX